SOUTHWEST
Foraging

SOUTHWEST
Foraging

117 wild and flavorful
edibles from barrel cactus
to wild oregano

JOHN SLATTERY

TIMBER PRESS
Portland, Oregon

Frontispiece: Manzanita berries are among the Southwest's favorite foraged edibles.

Photo credits appear on page 309.

The information in this book is true and complete to the best of our knowledge. All recommendations are made without guarantee on the part of the author or Timber Press. The author and publisher disclaim any liability in connection with the use of this information. In particular, eating wild plants is inherently risky. Plants can be easily mistaken and individuals vary in their physiological reactions to plants that are touched or consumed.

The Haseltine Building
133 S.W. Second Avenue, Suite 450
Portland, Oregon 97204-3527
timberpress.com

Printed in China
Text and cover design by Benjamin Shaykin

Library of Congress Cataloging-in-Publication Data

Names: Slattery, John, 1974- author.
Title: Southwest foraging: 117 wild and flavorful edibles from barrel cactus to wild oregano / John
    Slattery.
Description: Portland, Oregon: Timber Press, 2016. | Includes bibliographical references and index.
Identifiers: LCCN 2015047857 | ISBN 9781604696509 (pbk.: alk. paper)
Subjects: LCSH: Wild plants, Edible—Southwestern States.
Classification: LCC QK98.5.U6 S53 2016 | DDC 581.6/320979—dc23 LC record available at
    http://lccn.loc.gov/2015047857

To all the indigenous peoples of the land we now call the Southwest,
and their legacy of plant knowledge which has carried on.

Contents

Land of Abundant Beauty

Firethorn, resplendent with fruit.

A spiral of barrel cactus buds emerge in the midsummer heat.

Early spring harvest: cholla buds, graythorn berries, and blue palo verde blossoms.

Whortleberry's sweet-tart fruit is a foraging favorit

My path to wild plant foods is perhaps different than most. The idea of there being desirable, useful, or easy-to-find wild plant foods was not part of my upbringing. However, I strongly gravitated toward the use of local plants as medicine while traveling for a year throughout Central and South America. Meeting with indigenous healers and herbalists throughout this journey, I began to appreciate the concept of developing relationships with plants—not just herbs as a capsule, tincture, or other product to be purchased off the shelf.

This was one experience among many that opened my eyes and heart to what was available. Although my interest in wild plant foods and wild plant medicines occurred simultaneously, foraging initially took a backseat to botanical medicine. At first, I saw the pursuit of wild foods as a survival technique, a way to live as people once lived long ago. With limited opportunities to explore this style of living, I wasn't implementing many wild foods into my diet other than major foods such as mesquite meal, cholla buds, saguaro fruit, prickly pear fruit, and palo verde beans—certainly more exotic ingredients than the average person employs, but I wanted these foods to become an even bigger part of my life. I began adding them to my diet in novel and unconventional ways, parting with the traditions I had learned, and fueling my passion for wild foods with my creative impulse to cook—an impulse I've had since childhood. New creations were popping into my mind as they once did with cultivated foods. I was grinding barrel cactus seeds for flour to make bread or cooking its fruit into a chutney; combining flowering stems of wild plants to make sauerkraut; frying mesquite-breaded New Mexico locust blossoms with cinnamon in butter, topped with saguaro syrup. My perspective had shifted!

I was not alone in this new viewpoint. It seems there has been an increased interest in this direction for a certain segment of our population, and the enthusiasm continues to grow. Of course, it's far from accurate to characterize this trend as new. Mesquite pods, prickly pear pads and fruit, chia seeds, amaranth greens, and other superfoods have all been part of the local cuisine in the southwestern United States for thousands of years. The region, with its tremendously varied terrain, flora, and fauna, and its rich cultural tradition of interaction with the land, has the longest continual history of agriculture within our nation—4000 years in Tucson, Arizona. And wild plant foods, prized for their dense nutrition and rich dietary attributes (not to mention their unique and delicious flavors) have long been widely known across the globe, cherished by foragers, and often cultivated wherever they have taken root. The people here gathering wild foods to complement their daily diets are both new converts and the most recent generation of a long ancestral chain.

If you have not foraged for your food, you have not yet fully lived on this Earth. Becoming fully engaged with one's senses, engaging with other life-forms as one walks across the land for the purpose of sustenance, for satiating a taste, could quite possibly encapsulate what it means to be human. Foraging is our birthright, if not our responsibility, in a sense. How else can we better take account of our home, and our surroundings, as we engage with the life around us?

To those who have yet to become acquainted with our beautiful region, I invite you to discover the culinary riches that abound in the deserts, plains, forests, and mountains of the Southwest. To those who live within this area of abundant beauty, I urge you to explore more deeply—to join me on this natural path, to delight in gathering the wild foods that await.

Foraging in the Southwest:
A Wild Path of Discovery

Blooming ocotillo and cacti of many shapes and sizes are familiar Southwest sights.

This guide focuses on the wild plants that foragers may encounter throughout the Southwest region. It encompasses the states of Arizona, New Mexico, Oklahoma, Texas, and southern Utah and Nevada. Although this region can be collectively referred to as the Southwest, there is a great diversity of habitats therein. Plant communities are differentiated by a host of conditions, including sun exposure, soil type, latitude, elevation, rainfall, and other defining influences. In the Southwest, these plant communities overlap frequently, thus making new, unique localized communities, or ecozones, enriching the local habitat and making for greater diversity among all life-forms present. Although one will find a greater density of vegetation in other regions of the country, the biodiversity of the Southwest is in many ways unrivaled on this continent. This presents tremendous possibilities as one explores the terrain, observing the plants as they change from season to season. Each step of a foraging adventure offers an opportunity to deepen our relationship with place, to hone our awareness of self. Our lives are interwoven with all living things on Earth.

As we descend into the Southwest terrain, it makes sense to explore some of the major habitats. Developing a familiarity with the local landscape and the plants of this book will help the habitats take shape, as the senses drink in the colors and textures of the landscape.

Desert

Desert habitat covers a wide swath of Southwest terrain and encompasses a great many plants featured in this book. This ecozone possesses the greatest floral diversity of all of the Southwest habitats, converging succinctly in southeastern Arizona. The desert habitat can be broken down further into cactus forests, desert grasslands, and desert riparian areas.

Cactus forests occur primarily at the western edge of the region. Although cacti are part of our entire region's flora, they are nowhere else as dominant or as diverse as in the U.S. portion of the Sonoran Desert. This habitat is characterized by desert mountains and *bajadas*: long, gradually sloped hillsides resulting from eons of erosion. These forests occur from approximately 3500 feet in elevation to

Fog layers are sometimes slow to burn off in the Sonoran Desert.

sea level, and are often punctuated by saguaro cactus. The average rainfall ranges from about 2 to 12 inches annually, with two significant rainy seasons: summer and winter. Shrubs such as jojoba, wolfberry, and desert hackberry are found in this habitat.

Interspersed throughout the region are **desert riparian** zones. One can be standing in a desert grassland talking to a friend 15 feet away who's standing in a desert riparian zone. These riparian zones are like ribbons streaming through the desert. Rainwater runoff flows through these seasonally dry drainages, bringing substantial moisture to the plants making their home here, such as ironwood, mesquite, and blue palo verde.

The overall appearance of **desert grasslands** can change considerably as one travels through our region, but a notable feature is the distinct variety of grasses.

Oftentimes, these grasses are overlooked for the mesquite trees or various cacti. The elevation of a desert grassland can range from 2500 feet to over 5000 feet. It is true that this landscape has been altered considerably over the last 100 to 150 years due to cattle grazing. This habitat can be found in every state of our region but disappears as you head east into Central Texas and Oklahoma. A few plants you are likely to encounter here are barrel cactus, mariposa lily, sotol, and cholla.

Oak woodlands

These temperate forests are found interspersed throughout the Southwest. The habitat is often thoroughly mixed with grasslands, with wetlands below and conifer forests above. A great variety of oaks can be found here in canyons, on hills, and across rolling plains. The elevation is generally above 4000 feet in the western half

Mesquite is common to desert riparian zones. Here, seedpods are starting to mature.

of our Southwest region, but lower elevations prevail from Central Texas eastward. As drought lengthens and heavy groundwater pumping continues throughout the Southwest, this habitat is greatly threatened. Along with finding acorns in oak woodlands, one might forage for blue dicks, pamita, juniper, or henbit.

River valleys and canyons

These exceptionally fertile zones run their courses all across our region, and interact with nearly all other habitats. At their most defined, they are called riparian zones; this refers to the watercourse itself and the vegetation immediately adjacent. Reaching up from the river, the riparian habitat extends into drier forests, which can include a variety of life-forms depending upon the elevation, soil type, and annual rainfall. Here we find ample stands of pecans, mesquite, hackberry, mulberry, and American bulrush.

Conifer forests

Often comprised of dense trees, conifer forests largely occupy the higher elevations (above 7000 feet) of our region; the low-elevation pine forests of East Texas are an exception. The ground is often frozen several months at higher elevations, with limited foraging opportunities. Water is most abundant in this habitat of the Southwest. Upon summer's arrival, the terrain offers substantial rewards for the enthusiastic forager. Among many other plants, you will find wild strawberry, wild raspberry, wild oregano, nettle, and elderberry.

Banks of creeks and rivers are often fertile foraging spots.

Where the high plains and canyon country meet, you'll find piñon pine nuts, juniper berries, Indian tea, and much more.

Hardwood forests

As the eastern forest extends into East Texas and Oklahoma, we encounter hardwood forests with a dramatically different terrain and floral community. These lands experience much higher annual rainfall, possess significantly different soil compositions, and provide unique foraging opportunities. Hickory, farkleberry, beautyberry, and greenbrier are some of the more common examples.

Swamps and bogs

The eastern portion of our range is characterized by higher bedrock formations and greater rainfall, and encounters with swamps and bogs are much more likely. Although present throughout our region to some degree, they are far more common in the far eastern section. The soils are often heavily acidic, as plant matter decomposes as part of a stagnant soup in natural depressions. There is a great deal of shade here, with trees reaching up high around the swamps and bogs, and smaller aquatic plants residing within or at the very edges of the water, or where sunlight reaches.

Look for cattail, duckweed, red bay, watercress, and monkeyflower here.

High plains

The high plains are found from eastern New Mexico into the panhandles of Oklahoma and Texas. This area provides minimal floral diversity compared to most of our region. Where the high plains meets hill country marks the transition from prairie to forest.

Texas Hill Country

This region is specific to Texas and is centered around Austin and San Antonio and its adjacent areas. Characterized by rolling limestone hills and dense live oak groves, this area is a forager's dream in the late summer, when wild foods such as acorns, prickly pear fruit, pecans, walnuts, mesquite pods, persimmons, and many other tasty wild foods are at various stages of ripeness.

Gulf Coast

This unique, relatively flat habitat extends southward from Port Arthur, Texas, all the way to Mexico along the Texas coast. This area is very sandy and is subject to extremely high winds. Many plants adapt to the heavy salinity of the air and the groundwater. The northern section receives considerably more rainfall. Extensive oak groves are often found along this coastal region. Annual rainfall ranges from 22 inches in the south to 60 inches in the north.

Where Do I Begin?

Start where you live. How well do you know the plants around your home? Those that are a five-minute walk from your home, or in your neighborhood? Take walks on a regular basis and practice observing the plants in your area. You'll begin to see how they change with the seasons, and you'll develop a greater sensitivity to their subtle characteristics, which will aid in your identification of all plants. Appreciate their features and unique beauty. Once you've developed your identification skills, the places to harvest may become more apparent. Avoid areas where any chemicals are used. Avoid foraging close to the ground in areas that pets or other animals frequent. Some locations become more favorable for gathering immediately after rains.

Stewardship in foraging: sustainability

As we forage for our food, we enter into a relationship with the land. Our actions, however small, can have widespread ramifications. Entering willingly and consciously into this relationship breeds a sense of care for our home, and a deeper awareness of the beauty which surrounds us. As we have grown apart from this

The Gulf Coast terrain and flora vary greatly from other areas of the Southwest; foraging is different here, too.

intrinsic connection, and the sense of mutualism it instills, we have lost touch with a profound connection to a sense of humility, gratitude, and well-being. Sailing the world in search of new lands to conquer, ancient colonial superpowers often found illustrious gardens upon their arrival. Oftentimes, these gardens were semi-wild woodlands, floating gardens in a network of aqueducts, or desert *bajadas* managed by fire and rich with nutritious, seasonal greens. These indigenous peoples were true stewards, participating in a mutually beneficial relationship with their natural surroundings. They were caretaking for generations of the future. We as a culture are reawakening to these principles and perspectives, even as our available resources are severely declining and our food systems are lacking in the nutritional density they once had. Our return to foraging is both a logical and heartfelt element of this reconnection. We must hold the perspective of being stewards as we interact with our local, natural environment as foragers.

In the field

There is basic information one compiles when beginning to harvest wild plants for food; it informs future harvests and helps convey necessary information to others seeking to learn—you will find this key information covered in this guide. We are all governed by time, so we first note the harvest seasons. Several plants can be found at various times of year (most true in milder climates). Simply knowing

Practicing sustainability helps maintain wild foods for the next generation of foragers.

the season will often narrow possibilities when identifying a plant. Note the type of habitat in which the plant is growing. What plants are growing nearby? There are no absolutes, and exceptions always exist, but gathering this information is essential. Now bring your focus down to the level of the plant. What are its characteristics, including its size and shape? Does it have a smell? What colors are present? Is it flowering? How does it feel to the touch? Are there any visible seeds or fruits? Of course, you also need to know what part of the plant you intend to use. All these factors and more are involved in identifying a plant in the field—aka field botany.

ABCs of botany

The science of botany is dedicated to identifying plants through the description and classification of their reproductive parts. Although we can get to know a plant as foragers regardless of its reproductive parts (it may be too late to harvest, or too early), that is what botany covers. The terminology of botany is foreign to most. However, a few basic concepts and a rudimentary vocabulary can open a door to a whole new world of discovery and discussion regarding our beloved plants, whether we are foragers or admirers. This book utilizes some botanical nomenclature in order to synthesize meaning and convey identifying terms in a specific way—for example, terms referring to reproductive cycle, size of plant, leaf arrangement, shape of leaf, or growth habit. A plant's reproductive cycle refers to how long it takes to produce a seed. Annual plants do that within one year; biennials within two years. Perennials do it annually (most years); herbaceous perennials die back to the ground each year and have no woody parts. Some plants flower only once in their lifetime. The size of the plant may refer to it being a low-growing annual, or a shrub (generally less than 10 feet), a vine, or a tree. Getting more specific, we define leaf arrangement and flower anatomy in a variety of ways. See the accompanying sidebar on botanical terms.

A Basic Glossary of Botanical Terms

Leaf terminology

Alternate Leaves emerge at each node, staggered along the stem

Basal Leaves all emerge at the base of the plant

Cauline Leaves are borne along the stem

Entire Leaves have a continuous margin or edge; no notches or teeth present

Opposite Leaves emerge across from one another at the same node

Petiole A leaf stalk

Pinnate Leaves resemble feathers, with leaflets arranged opposite each other

Serrate Leaves with sawtooth margins

Whorl Clusters of three or more emerging from the stem and generally arranged in a circular pattern

Flower terminology

Axillary Positioned or arising where the leaf meets the stem (axil)

Bract A reduced leaf, or leaflike structure, at the base of an inflorescence

Calyx Collective term for all the sepals of a flower; the outer perianth whorl

Compound With two or more like parts in one organ

Corolla Collective term for all the petals of a flower; the inner perianth whorl

Fruit A ripened ovary and any other structures which are attached and ripened with it

Inflorescence The flowering part of a plant; the flower cluster

Interrupted spikes Not a continuous inflorescence; with bare space in between

Ovary The expanded basal portion of the pistil which contains the ovule(s)

Perianth The floral structure comprised of the calyx and corolla, especially when the two whorls are fused

Petal An individual segment of a corolla

Pistil The female reproductive organ of a flower, usually consisting of a stigma, style, and ovary

Wild oregano is an herbaceous perennial which resprouts each spring. With ample moisture, it often puts out fresh growth toward the end of summer.

Raceme An unbranched, elongated inflorescence maturing from the bottom upward

Sepal A segment of the calyx

Stamen The male reproductive organ of a flower, usually consisting of an anther and filament

Terminal Occurring at the tip or apex

Foraging essentials: equipment to have on hand

Drinking water is the forager's best friend in the relatively hot and dry desert Southwest. In higher elevations this may be less of a concern, but sudden elevation changes also require enhanced hydration. Each person discovers their favorite foraging tools and vessels. Some may embrace this aspect with great zeal; others simply relish the time outdoors and grab whatever implement or collecting vessel is handy. However, several types of tools will be useful if not essential during the gathering and processing of food plants in the Southwest. My list of foraging tools varies, but often includes:

> backpack
> water bottle or hydration pack
> leather work gloves
> canvas or paper bags
> buckets (1- to 5-gallon)
> sharpened knife
> sharpened pruners
> folding saw
> hori-hori
> folding shovel
> short pickax
> pick mattox

I may also have a flora (a book to help identify plants) and a 10× loupe for close-up detail in identifying plants when I'm in a new area. There are several other helpful foraging tools which are more unique to our region, such as a *kuiput* (a pole for harvesting made from a saguaro rib), or tongs for gathering cactus fruits and buds. After my water bottle and hydration pack are full (I bring 1 quart for every hour I plan to be gone, plus an extra 2 quarts), I make sure my tools are sharp. I use sharpening stones to keep my pruners and general purpose knife up to the task. I prefer bypass pruners (one sharp blade) with a simple latch to hold the blade closed. If I don't have a holster, I'll wrap the pruners in a bandana to keep them clean and safe in my bag. I prefer to use a fixed-blade knife kept within a sheath; folding knives can open accidentally and cause injury, or fold while being used. I prefer canvas bags for durability—they can last for many years and allow some breathability for harvested plant material. For heavier harvests (such as bellotas [acorns], pine nuts, or saya roots), I use paper bags if I don't have plastic food-grade buckets or large baskets available; they are easy to find and break down into a backpack (or can be stored in a vehicle for impromptu foraging opportunities). I have even gathered large amounts of fleshy fruits (such as elderberries or prickly pear) when all I could muster were paper bags.

These essentials will prepare you for a great many gathering opportunities. When I'm preparing for harvesting something below ground, I pack my trusty folding shovel and a small pickax, which break down to fit in my backpack. If I'm really serious, I'll bring the pick mattock as well.

Two pick mattocks (large and small), a folding shovel, a hori-hori (yellow handle), and leather gloves. All but the large pick mattock can be stored in a daypack for a quick foraging hike. Thistle roots, for instance, can be dug quickly with the larger pick mattock.

The folding shovel has a fold-out pick, but due to its short length I find it of limited use. The spade end of the shovel, however, will dig you into plenty of good eating (especially when the soil is moist). For those who enjoy a walking stick, I suggest making a digging stick from a local hardwood. Fire-hardening employs heat to rapidly desiccate and toughen a green piece of wood, but it produces nothing harder than a similar piece of aged, dry wood. Explore your local species to see which you like best.

From top to bottom, folding cross-cut saw, full tang knife, knife sheath, and bypass pruners. All easily fit into a backpack for a foraging walk, or the knife and pruners can be worn on the belt for easy access.

Foraging Safety

There is an element of danger inherent in all of life. But there's no reason to put oneself in harm's way unnecessarily. Please, take your time getting to know the plants if you're new to this. Don't rush it. Go out with a friend, even if they don't know plants. Having a second pair of eyes, a second mind, along for the journey can help you see things you might otherwise miss. Make earnest attempts to confirm your plant identifications with more experienced botanists or foragers. Go to your local herbarium if you have one, or take a class in person, in the field, with someone who is experienced. Please don't rely exclusively on information gathered from internet groups or posted photos online.

That can be sketchy at best. Also keep in mind that salmonella alone causes 1.2 million illnesses and four hundred fifty deaths per year (according to the Centers for Disease Control) in the United States, and that's from produce sanctioned by the U.S. Food and Drug Administration. When foraging for your own food, you take control out of the hands of big agribusiness and put it back into your own hands. Take this responsibility to heart, and your foraged food may actually be *safer*.

The consumption of anything may pose an acute risk to anyone at any time. Essentially, one person out of a large population may respond negatively to a given food, for any number of reasons. If you or someone in your family is particularly sensitive, keep that in mind. Test unusual foods with a tiny taste (or even a small amount rubbed onto the skin for those inclined to conditions such as eczema, asthma, or allergies) and wait at least thirty minutes to check for any unusual reactions. If a reaction occurs, decrease your intake of this food to slight amounts, or stop consuming it altogether. Overt cautions have been noted throughout this book in regard to particular wild plant foods. Additionally, unusual but recorded, potentially adverse reactions have been listed in order to inform the reader who seeks validation for their perhaps unusual reaction. Observe, take time with the plants, listen, proceed with a caution matching your experience level, and safely enjoy what these abundantly nutritious wild plant foods have to offer.

Plant Storage and Preparation

Processing, preparing, and storing wild plant foods includes a wide world of possibilities. Simply having the raw material in hand can be fertile ground for inspiration. However, the beginning forager may come up with countless questions about the hows and whats of this whole process. Don't despair. You will make mistakes and you will learn from them, and you will have stories to tell for years to come. Experience breeds real knowledge. The following are general guidelines to supplement the specific details included with plant profiles later in this book.

Process your plants as soon as you can; leaving them untended can cause molding, spoilage, unwanted fermentation, and

Cooked cholla buds are traditionally dried in the sun for preservation.

general waste. This pertains in particular to plants that are best consumed fresh with little or no further processing. In our relatively dry Southwest environment, this is often a limited concern.

Fresh foods such as fruit can be stored whole in sealable freezer bags or containers made of glass or plastic. They can also be sun dried. Foods such as bellotas (acorns) may require sun drying to prepare them for further processing. Spread out plants to dry on clean sheets or screens, or loosely bundle them in paper or cloth bags. Greens may be blanched, cooled, then stored in plastic bags in the freezer. Fermenting fresh plant foods (adding salt, for instance) may extend their shelf life, while creating unique flavors as well as adding nutrients through microbe activity. Cooking food may prolong its shelf life, such as with canning, reducing (jams, jellies, syrups), or boiling then dehydrating in the sun (good for cholla buds).

Although freezing can be the easiest method and often preserves food in a similar state as fresh, it takes substantial room to store frozen items and is comparatively expensive. Dehydration may take longer, but preserves nutrients, makes it easy to store foods on the shelf, and is essentially free (especially if you use the sun to dehydrate). Canning offers some long-term storage options, but it can also

A midspring harvest of manzanita berries from the oak and juniper belt.

be costly (jars and pressure canner, if necessary). Canning also requires an intensive process.

Today's forager has numerous storage and preservation options that were unavailable to our ancestors. Proceed wisely and you will have ample time to explore your creativity with wild plant food processing and storage.

Harvesting with the Seasons

Nothing engages us in the changing of seasons quite like foraging for our food. As we pursue our sustenance, a great sense of wholeness can emerge. The delight of harvesting one's own deliciously sweet cactus fruit in the heat of summer is addictive. Gathering piñon nuts or acorns among pine, juniper, and oak trees in autumn is walking the path of our ancestors, preparing for winter, and taking in the nourishment the land has to offer.

When a forager harmonizes with the environment through frequent visits, the plants tell their stories to those with keen insight. The optimal times for picking berries become apparent, the moment to collect nuts is at hand, greens are recognized to be in their most robust form, roots are seen as mature and ready for harvest. With each season, the abundance of a plant's cycle ebbs and flows.

The following is a breakdown of the four major seasons and the plant foods to gather during these times in our region. Each season is further divided into habitats, informing foragers where to look for a desired food, or what foods one may encounter in a particular terrain in a given season. The lists have been collated to fit the region as a whole. As a result, some foods are noted as available in a given season but may only be available in certain locales. They are, however, available in other locales in the preceding or following season.

Spring

In the desert, the renewal of life and fruits of early spring appear at lower elevations in late winter. Some cactus fruits—barrel cactus and cholla fruits, among others—have lingered throughout the winter. Various leafy greens present themselves. As moisture wanes at low elevations, seeds ripen, while at higher altitudes, nutrient-rich starchy roots become available. The concentrated sweetness of mescál's tall, flowering stalk marks the apex of warm, verdant spring, as the desert begins to dry, conserve energy, and prepare for the anticipated arrival of the summer rains.

Prickly pear flower in spring.

Spring Harvest by Habitat

Deserts and Desert Grasslands

algerita berries

banana yucca budding flower stalks, flowers, immature fruit, and leaf base

barrel cactus fruit*

biscuit root leaves, stems, and roots

black nightshade berries and greens

blue dicks

capita

chia seeds

cholla fruit and sap

desert willow flowers

dock flower stalks

elder flowers

epazote greens

evening primrose leaves and roots

filaree leaves

fragrant flatsedge rhizomes

graythorn berries

henbit

horseweed leaf tips

lamb's quarters leaf tops

London rocket seeds

manzanita berries

mariposa lily

mescál flowers, flower stalks, hearts, and leaf base

mesquite beans and sap*

Mormon tea seeds

miner's lettuce

monkeyflower leaves

mulberries

ocotillo flowers and seeds

oreganillo

pamita seeds

pellitory

peppergrass

pincushion cactus fruit

prickly pear flowers and pads

sotol flower stalks and root crown

thistle flower stalks and roots

wild grape leaves

wild onion

wolfberries*

wood sorrel leaves

Disturbed Areas, Gardens, Trail Sides, Clearings (covers a wide elevation range)

black nightshade berries*

chickweed*

dandelion flowers and roots

dock leaves

epazote greens*

evening primrose leaves and roots

filaree leaves

fragrant flatsedge rhizomes

greenbrier rhizomes and shoots

henbit

horseweed leaf tips*

lamb's quarters leaf tops*

London rocket leaves and seeds*

mallow leaves, roots, and seeds

melonette

mesquite beans and sap*

mulberries

nettle leaves

pamita seeds

peppergrass

pony's foot

prickly pear flowers and pads

salsify roots, shoots, and young leaves

sheep sorrel

Siberian elm inner bark, young leaves, and young samaras

sow thistle flowers, leaves, roots, and stalks

thistle flower stalks and roots

Turk's cap flowers and young leaves

wood sorrel leaves

Gulf Coast

alligator weed

cattail immature inflorescence, pollen, rhizomes, shoots, and stem base

dock leaves

epazote greens

fragrant flatsedge rhizomes

horseweed leaf tips

pennywort

melonette

nettle leaves

peppergrass

pony's foot

prickly pear flowers and pads

red bay leaves

smartweed tops

Turk's cap flowers and young leaves

violet leaves

wolfberries

wood sorrel leaves

Hardwood Forests and Piney Woods, Swamps and Bogs, East Texas and Oklahoma

alligator weed

banana yucca budding flower stalks, flowers, immature fruit, and leaf base

elder inner bark, sap, and young leaves

bracken fern rhizomes and shoots

cattail immature inflorescence, pollen, rhizomes, shoots, and stem base

chickweed

dandelion flowers and roots

dock leaves

elder flowers

epazote greens

evening primrose leaves and roots

fragrant flatsedge rhizomes

greenbrier rhizomes and shoots

henbit

horseweed leaf tips

lamb's quarters tops

mallow leaves, roots, and seeds

melonette

mulberries

peppergrass

pony's foot

red bay leaves

sheep sorrel

Siberian elm inner bark, young leaves, and young samaras

thistle flower stalks and roots

Turk's cap flowers and young leaves

violet leaves

wild onion

wood sorrel leaves

High Desert

algerita berries

banana yucca budding flower stalks, flowers, immature fruit, and leaf base

biscuit root leaf, stem, and roots*

blue dicks

cattail immature inflorescence, pollen, rhizomes, shoots, and stem base

cholla fruit and sap

desert willow flowers

dock leaves

evening primrose leaves and roots

filaree leaves

fragrant flatsedge rhizomes

horseweed leaf tips

lamb's quarters leaf tops

mariposa lily

monkeyflower

pamita flowers and leaves

peppergrass

pine inner bark and pollen*

prickly pear flowers and pads

Rocky Mountain bee plant young greens

salsify roots, shoots, and young leaves

Siberian elm inner bark, young leaves, and young samaras

thistle flower stalks and roots

wild rose petals

wolfberries

wood sorrel leaves

* indicates primary area of occurrence

High Elevations and Conifer Forests

banana yucca budding flower
stalks, flowers, immature
fruit, and leaf base

biscuit root leaves, stems,
and roots

elder inner bark, sap, and
young leaves

bracken fern rhizomes and
shoots

cattail immature inflorescence, pollen, rhizomes,
shoots, and stem base

chickweed

dandelion flowers and roots

evening primrose leaves and
roots

filaree leaves

fragrant flatsedge rhizomes

horseweed leaf tips

lamb's quarters leaf tops*

mallow leaves and roots

mescál flowers, flower stalks,
hearts, and leaf base

monkeyflower leaves

mountain parsley greens

nettle leaves

pine inner bark and pollen

salsify roots, shoots, and
young leaves*

sheep sorrel

smartweed tender leaf and
stem tops

Solomon's plume shoots

thistle flower stalks and roots

violet leaves

watercress

wild grape leaves

wild onion

wild rose petals

wood sorrel leaves

High Plains

algerita berries

banana yucca budding flower
stalks, flowers, immature
fruit, and leaf base

biscuit root leaves, stems,
and roots

black nightshade berries

cattail immature inflorescence, pollen, rhizomes,
shoots, and stem base

dock leaves

fragrant flatsedge rhizomes

horseweed leaf tips

London rocket leaves

pamita flowers, leaves, and
seeds

prickly pear flowers and pads

Rocky Mountain bee plant
young greens

salsify roots, shoots, and
young leaves

thistle flower stalks and roots

wood sorrel leaves

Oak Woodlands

algerita berries

banana yucca budding flower
stalks, flowers, immature
fruit, and leaf base

barrel cactus fruit

cholla fruit and sap

dandelion flowers and roots

filaree leaves

fragrant flatsedge rhizomes

henbit

horseweed leaf tips

lamb's quarters leaf tops

manzanita berries

mescál flowers, flower stalks,
hearts, and leaf base

miner's lettuce

monkeyflower leaves

mountain parsley greens

nettle leaves

pamita seeds

peppergrass

pincushion cactus fruit

pine inner bark

prickly pear flowers and pads

sotol flower stalks and root
crown

thistle flower stalks and roots

violet leaves

watercress

wild grape leaves*

wild oregano

wild onion

wild rose petals

wood sorrel leaves

Rivers and Canyons

alligator weed

American bulrush pollen, shoots, stem base, and rhizomes

barrel cactus fruit

black nightshade berries

elder inner bark, sap, young leaves, and flowers*

box elder inner bark, sap, young leaves, and flowers*

capita

cattail immature inflorescence, pollen, rhizomes, shoots, and stem base*

dandelion flowers and roots

desert willow flowers

dock flower stalks and leaves

filaree leaves

fragrant flatsedge rhizomes

graythorn berries

henbit

horseweed tips

lamb's quarters tops

London rocket leaves

mescál flowers, flower stalks, hearts, and leaf base

mesquite sap*

monkeyflower leaves*

mulberries

nettle leaves*

oreganillo

pamita seeds

pellitory

pincushion cactus fruit

Rocky Mountain bee plant young greens

smartweed tender leaf and stem tops

thistle flower stalks and roots

Turk's cap flowers and young leaves

watercress

wild grape leaves*

wild oregano*

wild rose petals

South Texas Plains

algerita berries

cattail immature inflorescence, pollen, rhizomes, shoots, and stem base

fragrant flatsedge rhizomes

graythorn berries

horseweed leaf tips

lamb's quarters leaf tops

London rocket leaves

mescál flowers, flower stalks, hearts, and leaf base

mesquite beans, sap

nettle leaves

peppergrass

pincushion cactus fruit

prickly pear flowers and pads

thistle flower stalks and roots

wild onion

Texas Hill Country

algerita berries

banana yucca budding flower stalks, flowers, immature fruit, and leaf base

cattail immature inflorescence, pollen, rhizomes, shoots, and stem base

dock leaves

elder flowers

fragrant flatsedge rhizomes

henbit

horseweed leaf tips

lamb's quarters leaf tops

London rocket leaves

nettle leaves

pamita seeds

peppergrass

pincushion cactus fruit

prickly pear flowers and pads

thistle flower stalks and roots

Texas persimmon fruit

Turk's cap flowers and young leaves

violet leaves

wild onion

wood sorrel leaves

* indicates primary area of occurrence

Summer

In the Southwest there are two distinct summers: dry summer, followed by wet summer. A forager will find unique foods to harvest within each of these distinct periods. The delectable saguaro cactus fruits ripen during the hottest, driest days, as do the pods of our abundant desert legumes. However, prickly pear fruits ripen in the heart of the monsoons—in fact, without ample moisture their production will be deeply curtailed. Dry summer is a time of tremendous growth, flowering, and fruiting, and there is a sense of robust bounty. Peak times for greens, flowers, fruits, nuts, and seeds overlap, and the forager is left scrambling to decide which food to gather next. As summer heats up, most of our edible greens disappear, but the nutritious greens of pigweed (*Amaranthus* species) can be tremendously prolific. When heavy downpours drench the parched soil, the impressive varieties of resilient plants are finally revived. Summer fruits ripen to a supreme sweetness under the sun's baking warmth.

New Mexico locust blossoms can brighten summer salads.

Summary Harvest by Habitat

Desert and Desert Grasslands

algerita berries

banana yucca fruit

barrel cactus flower buds*

biscuit root seeds

black nightshade berries

bull nettle seeds

capita

cholla fruit and sap

desert hackberries

desert willow flowers

devil's claw immature fruit

elder flowers and fruit

epazote greens

evening primrose flowers and
    leaves

filaree leaves

fragrant flatsedge rhizomes

hackberries

henbit

horseweed leaf tips

Indian tea

ironwood flowers and seeds

jewel flower leaves, flowers,
    and fruit

jojoba nuts

juniper berries

lamb's quarters leaf tops

lemonade berries

mescál heart and leaf base

mesquite beans and sap*

milkvine flowers and
    immature fruit

oreganillo

palo verde seeds*

pápalo quelite

pellitory

peppergrass

pigweed greens

prickly pear fruit

purslane

saguaro fruit

saya fruit, leaves, and roots

sotol root crown

thistle stalks

walnuts

whitestem blazing star seeds

wild grapes and leaves

wild onion

wolfberries*

wood sorrel leaves and
    tubers

Disturbed Areas, Gardens, Trail Sides, Clearings (this zone covers a wide elevation range)

apple

beautyberries

black nightshade berries*

chickweed*

dandelion flowers

dayflower

devil's claw immature fruit

dock leaves

epazote greens*

evening primrose flowers and
    leaves

filaree leaves

fragrant flatsedge rhizomes

greenbrier rhizomes and
    tender leaves

hackberries

henbit

Himalayan blackberries

horseweed leaf tips*

Indian tea

lamb's quarters leaf tops*

mallow leaves, roots, and
    seeds

melonette

mesquite beans and sap*

milkvine flowers and

immature fruit

nettle seeds

New Mexico locust blossoms*

palo verde seeds

pellitory

peppergrass

pigweed greens

pony's foot

prickly pear fruit

purslane*

red dates

red raspberries

salsify flower buds and young

* indicates primary area of occurrence

Disturbed Areas, Gardens, Trail Sides, Clearings *(continued)*

leaves

sheep sorrel

Siberian elm inner bark and
seeds

thistle stalks

Turk's cap flowers, fruit, and
leaves

wood sorrel leaves and
tubers

Gulf Coast

alligator weed

cattail immature inflorescence, pollen, rhizomes,
shoots, and stem base

dayflower

dock leaves

epazote greens

fragrant flatsedge rhizomes

horseweed leaf tips

pennywort

melonette

nettle seeds

peppergrass

pigweed greens

pony's foot

prickly pear fruit

red bay leaves

smartweed tender leaf and
stem tops

Turk's cap flowers, fruit, and
leaves

violet leaves

wild grapes and leaves

wolfberries

wood sorrel leaves and
tubers

Hardwood Forests and Piney Woods, Swamps and Bogs, East Texas and Oklahoma

alligator weed

banana yucca fruit

beautyberries

bull nettle seeds

cattail immature inflorescence, pollen, rhizomes,
shoots, and stem base

chickweed

chokecherries

dandelion flowers

dayflower

devil's claw immature fruit

dock leaves

elder flowers and fruit

epazote greens

evening primrose flowers and
leaves

fragrant flatsedge rhizomes

greenbrier rhizomes and
tender leaves

henbit

horseweed leaf tips

juniper berries

lamb's quarters leaf tops

mallow leaves, roots, and
seeds

melonette

peppergrass

pony's foot

red bay leaves

serviceberries

sheep sorrel

Siberian elm inner bark and
seeds

thistle stalks

Turk's cap flowers, fruit, and
leaves

violet leaves

walnuts

wild grapes and leaves*

wild onion

wild plum

wild strawberries

wood sorrel leaves and
tubers

High Desert

algerita berries

banana yucca fruit

biscuit root seeds*

cattail immature inflorescence, pollen, rhizomes,
shoots, and stem base

cholla fruit and sap

dayflower

desert willow flowers

dock leaves

evening primrose flowers and leaves

filaree leaves

fragrant flatsedge rhizomes

horseweed leaf tips

Indian tea

juniper berries

lamb's quarters leaf tops

lemonade berries

mesquite beans and sap

pamita seeds

peppergrass

pigweed greens

pine inner bark*

prickly pear fruit

purslane

Rocky Mountain bee plant young greens

salsify flower buds and young leaves

Siberian elm inner bark and seeds

thistle stalks

wax currants

whitestem blazing star seeds

wild grapes, leaves

wolfberries

wood sorrel leaves and tubers

High Elevations and Conifer Forests

apple

banana yucca fruit

biscuit root seeds

cattail immature inflorescence, pollen, rhizomes, shoots, and stem base

chickweed

chokecherries

dandelion flowers

dayflower

elder flowers and fruit

evening primrose flowers and leaves

filaree leaves

fragrant flatsedge rhizomes

gooseberries

harebell flowers and leaves

horseweed leaf tips

juniper berries

lamb's quarters*

mallow leaves, roots, and seeds

mescál heart and leaf base

mountain parsley greens

nettle seeds

New Mexico locust blossoms

peppergrass

pigweed greens

red raspberries

salsify flower buds and young leaves*

serviceberries

sheep sorrel

smartweed tender leaf and stem tops

thimbleberries

thistle stalks

violet leaves

walnuts

watercress

wax currants

whortleberries

wild grapes and leaves

wild oregano

wild onion

wild strawberry

wood sorrel leaves and tubers

High Plains

algerita berries

biscuit root seeds

black nightshade berries

cattail immature inflorescence, pollen, rhizomes, shoots, and stem base

dayflower

devil's claw immature fruit

dock leaves

fragrant flatsedge rhizomes

horseweed leaf tips

mesquite beans, sap

pigweed greens

prickly pear fruit

Rocky Mountain bee plant young greens

salsify flower buds and young leaves

thistle stalks

wild grapes and leaves

wild plum

wood sorrel leaves and tubers

* indicates primary area of occurrence

Oak Woodlands

algerita berries

banana yucca fruit

barrel cactus flower buds

bellotas (acorns) *

chokecherries

cholla fruit and sap

dandelion flowers

dewberries

filaree leaves

fragrant flatsedge rhizomes

henbit

Himalayan blackberries

horseweed leaf tips

juniper berries

lamb's quarters leaf tops

lemonade berries

mescál heart and leaf base

mesquite beans and sap

monkeyflower leaves

mountain parsley greens

nettle seeds

peppergrass

pine inner bark

prickly pear fruit

purslane

sotol root crown

thistle stalks

violet leaves

walnuts

watercress

wild grapes and leaves*

wild oregano

wild onion

wood sorrel leaves and
tubers

Rivers and Canyons

alligator weed

American bulrush rhizomes

barrel cactus flower buds

bellotas (acorns)

black nightshade berries

capita

cattail immature inflorescence, pollen, rhizomes,
shoots, and stem base*

chokecherries

dandelion flowers

desert willow flowers

devil's claw immature fruit

dewberries

dock leaves

elder flowers and fruit

filaree leaves

fragrant flatsedge rhizomes

gooseberries

hackberries

henbit

Himalayan blackberries

horseweed leaf tips

lamb's quarters leaf tops

mescál heart and leaf base

mesquite beans and sap*

milkvine flowers and
immature fruit

monkeyflower leaves*

nettle seeds*

New Mexico locust blossoms

oreganillo

palo verde seeds

pellitory

pigweed greens

Rocky Mountain bee plant
young greens

serviceberries

smartweed tender leaf and
stem tops

thimbleberries

thistle stalks

Turk's cap flowers, fruit, and
leaves

walnuts*

watercress

whitestem blazing star seeds

wild grapes and leaves*

wild oregano*

South Texas Plains

algerita berries

cattail immature inflorescence, pollen, rhizomes,
shoots, and stem base

desert hackberries

devil's claw immature fruit

fragrant flatsedge rhizomes

horseweed leaf tips

lamb's quarters leaf tops

mescál heart and leaf base

mesquite beans and sap

nettle seeds

pápalo quelite

peppergrass

pigweed greens

prickly pear fruit

saya fruit, leaves, and roots

thistle stalks

wild onion

Texas Hill Country

algerita berries

bellotas (acorns)

bull nettle seeds

cattail immature inflorescence, pollen, rhizomes, shoots, and stem base

dayflower

devil's claw immature fruit

dewberries

dock leaves

elder flowers and fruit

fragrant flatsedge rhizomes

hackberries

henbit

horseweed leaf tips

juniper berries

lamb's quarters leaf tops

lemonade berries

mesquite beans and sap

nettle seeds

peppergrass

pigweed greens

prickly pear fruit

purslane

thistle stalks

Turk's cap flowers, fruit, and leaves

violet leaves

walnuts

wild grapes and leaves

wild onion

wild plum

wood sorrel leaves and tubers

* indicates primary area of occurrence

Autumn

Cool, crisp nights followed by warm, dry days: this is the backdrop for autumn in the Southwest. The remaining nuts, seeds, and fruits are coming to prime ripeness—some awaiting our first freeze to completely ripen (such as rose hips). Root vegetables are at their fullest until the spring to follow. Winter annuals become available as microgreens, and many trees begin to go dormant, sending their sap into the roots. Shorter days inspire the eager forager to get out early in the cold mornings and forgo the afternoon nap of those long summer days.

Acorns of southern live oak are found throughout southeastern Texas, and in landscapes of southern Arizona.

Autumn Harvest by Habitat

Deserts and Desert Grasslands

barrel cactus fruit*

black nightshade berries

bull nettle seeds

cholla fruit and sap

desert hackberries

devil's claw seeds

epazote greens

evening primrose roots

fragrant flatsedge rhizomes

ground cherries

hackberries

henbit

horseweed leaf tips

lamb's quarters leaf seeds

mescál heart and leaf base

milkvine immature fruit

oreganillo

pecan (cultivated)

pigweed seeds

prickly pear fruit

snakewood fruit

thistle roots

whitestem blazing star seeds

wild sunflower seeds

wolfberries*

wood sorrel bulbs and leaves

Disturbed Areas, Gardens, Trail Sides, Clearings

apple

beautyberries

black nightshade berries*

chiltepín

cocklebur seeds

dandelion roots*

dayflower tubers

devil's claw seeds

dock seeds*

epazote greens*

evening primrose roots

firethorn fruit

fragrant flatsedge rhizomes

ground cherries

hackberries

henbit

horseweed leaf tips

lamb's quarters seeds

mallow leaves, roots, and seed

melonette

milkvine immature fruit

nettle seeds

pigweed seeds

pony's foot

prickly pear fruit

salsify roots

sow thistle

thistle roots

Turk's cap flowers, fruit, and leaves

wild rose hips

wild sunflower seeds

wood sorrel bulbs and leaves

Gulf Coast

alligator weed

cattail rhizome

dayflower tubers

dock seeds

epazote greens

fragrant flatsedge rhizomes

ground cherries

hackberries

horseweed leaf tips

pennywort

melonette

nettle seeds

pigweed seeds

pony's foot

prickly pear fruit

red bay leaves

Turk's cap flowers, fruit, and leaves

violet leaves

wild rose hips

wild sunflower seeds

wolfberries

wood sorrel leaf and tuber

* indicates primary area of occurrence

Hardwood Forests and Piney Woods, Swamps and Bogs, East Texas and Oklahoma

alligator weed
beautyberries
box elder inner bark
elder inner bark
bracken fern rhizomes
bull nettle seeds
cattail rhizomes
dandelion roots
dayflower tubers
dock seeds
epazote greens
evening primrose roots

farkleberries
fragrant flatsedge rhizomes
greenbrier rhizomes and
    tender leaves
ground cherries
hackberries
henbit
horseweed leaf tips
juniper berries
lamb's quarters seeds

mallow leaves, roots, and seeds
melonette
pony's foot
red bay leaves
thistle roots
Turk's cap flowers, fruit, and
    leaves
violet leaves
wild rose hips
wild sunflower seeds
wood sorrel bulbs and leaves

High Desert

biscuit root*
cattail rhizomes
cholla fruit and sap
dayflower tubers
devil's claw seeds
dock seeds*
evening primrose roots
fragrant flatsedge rhizomes

ground cherries
horseweed leaf tips
juniper berries*
lamb's quarters seeds
pigweed seeds
pine nuts*
prickly pear fruit
salsify roots

thistle roots
wax currants
whitestem blazing star seeds
wild rose hips
wild sunflower seeds
wolfberries
wood sorrel bulbs and leaves

High Elevations and Conifer Forests

apple*
bellotas (acorns)
biscuit root
elder bark
bracken fern rhizomes*
cattail rhizomes
dandelion roots*
dayflower tubers
evening primrose roots

fragrant flatsedge rhizomes
horseweed leaf tips
juniper berries
lamb's quarters seeds*
mallow leaves, roots, and
    seeds
mescál heart and leaf base
nettle seeds
pigweed seeds

salsify roots*
thistle roots
violet leaves
watercress
wax currants
wild rose hips
wood sorrel bulbs and leaves

High Plains

biscuit root
black nightshade berries
cattail rhizomes
cholla fruit and sap
dayflower tubers
devil's claw seeds

dock seeds
fragrant flatsedge rhizomes
ground cherries
henbit
horseweed leaf tips
pigweed seeds

prickly pear fruit
salsify roots
thistle roots
wild rose hips
wild sunflower seeds
wood sorrel bulbs and leaves

Oak Woodlands

barrel cactus fruit
bellotas (acorns) *
chiltepín
cholla fruit and sap
dandelion roots
fragrant flatsedge rhizomes
ground cherries
henbit

horseweed leaf tips
juniper berries
lamb's quarters seeds
mescál heart and leaf base
monkeyflower leaves
nettle seeds
pine nuts
prickly pear fruit

Texas persimmon fruit
thistle roots
violet leaves
watercress
wild rose hips
wild sunflower seeds
wood sorrel bulbs and leaves

Rivers and Canyons

alligator weed
American bulrush rhizomes
barrel cactus fruit
bellotas (acorns)
black nightshade berries
box elder inner bark*
elder inner bark*
cattail rhizomes*
cocklebur seeds
dandelion roots
devil's claw seeds
dock seeds

fragrant flatsedge rhizomes
ground cherries
hackberries
henbit
horseweed leaf tips
juniper berries
lamb's quarters seeds
mescál heart and leaf base
milkvine immature fruit
monkeyflower leaves*
nettle seeds*
oreganillo

pecans*
pigweed seeds
thistle roots
Texas persimmon fruit
Turk's cap flowers, fruit, and
   leaves
watercress
whitestem blazing star seeds
wild rose hips
wild sunflower seeds

South Texas Plains

chiltepín*
desert hackberries
devil's claw seeds
fragrant flatsedge rhizomes
ground cherries
hackberries

henbit
horseweed leaf tips
lamb's quarters seeds
mescál heart and leaf base
nettle seeds
pigweed seeds

prickly pear fruit
snakewood fruit
thistle roots
wild sunflower seeds
wolfberries
wood sorrel bulbs and leaves

* indicates primary area of occurrence

Texas Hill Country

bellotas (acorns)
bull nettle seeds
cattail rhizomes
chiltepín
dayflower tubers
dock seeds
fragrant flatsedge rhizomes
ground cherries
hackberries

henbit
horseweed leaf tips
juniper berries
lamb's quarters seeds
nettle seeds
pecans
pigweed seeds
prickly pear fruit
thistle roots

Turk's cap flowers, fruit, and
  leaves
violet leaves
wild rose hips
wild sunflower seeds
wood sorrel bulbs and leaves

* indicates primary area of occurrence

Winter

The sun descends on the horizon, and most plant life turns inward during this season of short days and cold, or at least cooler, nights. However, certain areas of the Southwest experience a relatively mild winter. Foragers can remain engaged with the plant life in their midst throughout the winter (no, there's no rest for dedicated foragers in much of the Southwest). Wild greens are plentiful in such locations as Houston, Phoenix, El Paso, and Tucson. Barrel cactus fruit ripens just as winter sets in, and hackberries reside on the trees through winter—sustenance for winged and human foragers alike.

While they mature in the fall, juniper berries can sometimes be found on trees throughout the winter, if the fruits are in plentiful supply.

Winter Harvest by Habitat

Deserts and Desert Grasslands

banana yucca leaf base
barrel cactus fruit*
biscuit root
black nightshade berries and
  greens
cholla fruit and sap
dock leaves
epazote greens
evening primrose roots

filaree
fragrant flatsedge rhizomes
hackberries
henbit
London rocket leaves
mescál heart and leaf base
miner's lettuce
monkeyflower
oreganillo

pamita flowers and leaves
pellitory leaves
peppergrass
pincushion cactus fruit
sotol root crown
thistle leaf base and roots
wild onion
wood sorrel leaves

Disturbed Areas, Gardens, Trail Sides, Clearings
(this zone covers a wide elevation range)

black nightshade berries*
chickweed*
dandelion flowers and roots
epazote greens*
evening primrose roots
filaree
fragrant flatsedge rhizomes
greenbrier leaves, rhizomes,
  shoots, and stems

henbit
London rocket leaves*
mallow leaves and roots
nettle leaves and seeds
pamita flowers and leaves
pellitory leaves
peppergrass
pony's foot

sow thistle flowers, leaves,
  and roots
thistle leaf base and roots
Turk's cap flowers and young
  leaves
wood sorrel leaves

Gulf Coast

alligator weed
cattail rhizomes and shoots
curly dock leaves
epazote greens
fragrant flatsedge rhizomes

melonette
nettle leaves and seeds
peppergrass
pony's foot
red bay

smartweed
Turk's cap flowers and young
  leaves
violet leaves
wood sorrel leaves

Hardwood Forests and Piney Woods, Swamps and Bogs,
East Texas and Oklahoma

alligator weed
box elder inner bark
elder inner bark
cattail rhizomes and shoots
chickweed

curly dock leaves
dandelion flowers and roots
epazote greens
evening primrose roots
fragrant flatsedge rhizomes

greenbrier leaves, rhizomes,
  shoots, and stems
hackberries
henbit
mallow leaves and roots

melonette
pellitory leaves
peppergrass
pony's foot

red bay
sow thistle flowers and
   leavesthistle leaf base and
   roots

Turk's cap flowers and young
   leaves
wild onion
wood sorrel leaves

High Desert

banana yucca leaf base
biscuit root*
cattail rhizomes and shoots
cholla fruit and sap

evening primrose roots
filaree
fragrant flatsedge rhizomes
monkeyflower

pine inner bark*
thistle leaf base and roots

High Elevations and Conifer Forests

biscuit root
box elder inner bark
elder inner bark
cattail rhizomes and shoots
chickweed
dandelion flowers and roots

evening primrose roots
filaree
fragrant flatsedge rhizomes
mallow leaves and roots
mescál heart and leaf base
monkeyflower

nettle leaves and seeds
pine inner bark
thistle leaf base and roots
watercress

High Plains

banana yucca leaf base
biscuit root
black nightshade berries

cattail rhizomes and shoots
fragrant flatsedge rhizomes
London rocket leaves

thistle leaf base and roots
wood sorrel leaves

Oak Woodlands

banana yucca leaf base
barrel cactus fruit
cholla fruit and sap
dandelion flowers and roots
filaree
fragrant flatsedge rhizomes

henbit
mescál heart and leaf base
miner's lettuce
monkeyflower
pamita leaves and flowers
pine inner bark

sotol root crown
thistle leaf base and roots
watercress
wild onion
wood sorrel leaves

Rivers and Canyons

alligator weed
American bulrush rhizomes
barrel cactus fruit
black nightshade berries
box elder inner bark*

elder inner bark*
cattail rhizome and shoots*
dandelion flowers and roots
dock leaves
filaree

fragrant flatsedge rhizomes
hackberries
henbit
London rocket leaves
mescál heart and leaf base

* indicates primary area of occurrence

Rivers and Canyons (*continued*)

monkeyflower*
nettle leaves*
oreganillo

pamita flowers and leaves
pellitory
smartweed

thistle leaf base and roots
watercress

South Texas Plains

cattail rhizome and shoots
curly dock leaves
fragrant flatsedge rhizomes
London rocket leaves
mescál heart and leaf base

nettle leaves
pamita flowers and leaves
pellitory leaves
peppergrass

sow thistle flowers and
    leaves
thistle leaf base and roots
wild onion

Texas Hill Country

banana yucca leaf base
cattail rhizomes and shoots
curly dock leaves
fragrant flatsedge rhizomes
henbit
London rocket leaves

mallow flowers and leaves
pamita flowers and leaves
pellitory leaves
nettle leaves
sow thistle flowers and
    leaves

thistle leaf base and roots
wild onion
wood sorrel leaves

* indicates primary area of occurrence

Foraging by Plant Part

Leaves, Stems, and Shoots

alligator weed (*Alternanthera philoxeroides*)

biscuit root (*Lomatium species*)

black nightshade (*Solanum americanum*)

bracken fern (*Pteridium aquilinum*)

capita (*Atriplex wrightii*)

cattail (*Typha dominguensis*)

chickweed (*Stellaria media*)

dandelion (*Taraxacum officinale*)

dayflower (*Commelina species*)

dock (*Rumex species*)

elder (*Sambucus species*)

epazote (*Dysphania ambrosioides*)

evening primrose (*Oenothera elata*)

filaree (*Erodium cicutarium*)

greenbrier (*Smilax species*)

henbit (*Lamium amplexicaule*)

horseweed (*Conyza canadensis*)

Indian tea (*Thelesperma megapotamicum*)

lamb's quarters (*Chenopodium species*)

London rocket (*Sisymbrium irio*)

mallow (*Malva neglecta*)

miner's lettuce (*Claytonia perfoliata*)

monkeyflower (*Mimulus guttatus*)

mountain parsley (*Pseudocymopterus montanus*)

nettle (*Urtica species*)

oreganillo (*Aloysia wrightii*)

pápalo quelite (*Porophyllum ruderale*)

pellitory (*Parietaria species*)

pennywort (*Hydrocotyle species*)

peppergrass (*Lepidium species*)

pigweed (*Amaranthus palmeri*)

pony's foot (*Dichondra species*)

purslane (*Portulaca oleracea*)

red bay (*Persea borbonia*)

Rocky Mountain bee plant (*Peritoma serrulata*)

sheep sorrel (*Rumex acetosella*)

smartweed (*Polygonum species*)

sow thistle (*Sonchus oleraceus*)

thistle (*Cirsium species*)

Turk's cap (*Malvaviscus arboreus*)

violet (*Viola species*)

watercress (*Nasturtium officinale*)

wild oregano (*Monarda species*)

wild onion (*Allium species*)

wood sorrel (*Oxalis species*)

Roots and Bulbs

American bulrush (*Schoenoplectus americanus*)

biscuit root (*Lomatium species*)

blue dicks (*Dichelostemma capitatum*)

cattail (*Typha dominguensis*)

dandelion (*Taraxacum officinale*)

evening primrose (*Oenothera elata*)

fragrant flatsedge (*Cyperus odoratus*)

mescál (*Agave species*)

salsify (*Tragopogon dubius*)

saya (*Amourexia palmatifida*)

sotol (*Dasilyrion species*)

thistle (*Cirsium species*)

wild onion (*Allium species*)

wood sorrel (*Oxalis species*)

Buds and Flowers

banana yucca (*Yucca baccata*)

barrel cactus (*Ferocactus wislizenii*)

cattail (*Typha dominguensis*)

cholla (*Cylindropuntia* species)

dandelion (*Taraxacum officinale*)

desert willow (*Chilopsis linearis*)

Indian tea (*Thelesperma megapotamicum*)

ironwood (*Olneya tesota*)

mountain parsley (*Pseudocymopterus montanus*)

New Mexico locust (*Robinia neomexicanum*)

palo verde (*Parkinsonia microphylla*)

peppergrass (*Lepidium* species)

salsify (*Tragopogon* species)

sotol (*Dasilyrion* species)

Turk's cap (*Malvaviscus arboreus*)

violet (*Viola* species)

wild onion (*Allium* species)

Fruit

algerita (*Mahonia* species)

apple (*Malus pumila*)

banana yucca (*Yucca baccata*)

barrel cactus (*Ferocactus wislizenii*)

beautyberry (*Callicarpa americana*)

black nightshade (*Solanum americanum*)

chiltepín (*Capsicum annuum* var. *glabriusculum*)

chokecherry (*Prunus virginiana*)

cholla (*Cylindropuntia* species)

desert hackberry (*Celtis pallida*)

dewberry (*Rubus arizonensis*)

devil's claw (*Proboscidea parviflora*)

farkleberry (*Vaccinium arboreum*)

gooseberry (*Ribes pinetorum*)

graythorn (*Ziziphus obtusifolius*)

greenbrier (*Smilax* species)

ground cherry (*Physalis* species)

hackberry (*Celtis laevigata*)

Himalayan blackberry (*Rubus armeniacus*)

juniper (*Juniperus* species)

lemonade berry (*Rhus aromatica*)

manzanita (*Arctostaphylos* species)

melonette (*Melothria pendula*)

mesquite (*Prosopis* species)

prickly pear (*Opuntia* species)

raspberry (*Rubus idaeus*)

red date (*Ziziphus zizyphus*)

saguaro (*Carnegiea gigantea*)

serviceberry (*Amelanchier alnifolia*)

thimbleberry (*Rubus parviflorus*)

Turk's cap (*Malvaviscus arboreus*)

walnut (*Juglans major*)

wax currant (*Ribes cereum*)

whortleberry (*Vaccinium myrtillus*)

wild grape (*Vitis* species)

wild plum (*Prunus mexicana*)

wild rose (*Rosa* species)

wild strawberry (*Fragaria* species)

wolfberry (*Lycium* species)

Nuts and Seeds

barrel cactus (*Ferocactus wislizenii*)

bellota (acorn) (*Quercus emoryi*)

bull nettle (*Cnidoscolus angustidens*)

chia (*Salvia columbariae*)

cocklebur (*Xanthium strumarium*)

devil's claw (*Proboscidea parviflora*)

dock (*Rumex* species)

elder *(Sambucus* species)

fragrant flatsedge (*Cyperus odoratus*)

ironwood (*Olneya tesota*)

jojoba (*Simmondsia chinensis*)

Mexican palo verde (*Parkinsonia aculeata*)

Mormon tea (*Ephedra* species)

pamita (*Descurainia* species)

pecan (*Carya illinoiensis*)

pigweed (*Amaranthus* species)

pine (*Pinus* species)

red bay (*Persea borbonia*)

Rocky Mountain bee plant (*Peritoma serrulata*)

Siberian elm (*Ulmus pumila*)

smartweed (*Polygonum* species)

sotol (*Dasilyrion* species)

Turk's cap (*Malvaviscus arboreus*)

walnut (*Juglans major*)

whitestem blazing star (*Mentzelia albicaulis*)

wild sunflower (*Helianthus* species)

Inner Bark

elder (*Sambucus* species)

lemonade berry (*Rhus aromatica*)

pine (*Pinus* species)

Siberian elm (*Ulmus pumila*)

Wild Edible Plants
of the Southwest

The Sonoran Desert landscape becomes lush with the arrival of summer rains.

algerita

Mahonia species

barberry, hollygrape, agarita, palo amarillo

`EDIBLE` berries, flowers

A tart berry with roots in ancient Persian cuisine, algerita can take your foraged meals to new heights.

How to Identify

The common name algerita can be used to refer to a number of *Mahonia* species. *Mahonia trifoliolata* is a woody evergreen shrub ranging in height from 3 to 12 feet when mature. The smooth stem bark is gray with purple tones. The divided, rigid leaves possess sharp spines along the margins, but spines are absent from the rest of the plant. The clusters of brilliant yellow flowers appear in the late winter and early spring, calling attention to large stands, which may have gone unnoticed previously. The round, juicy berries may be red or purple, depending on the species. *Mahonia repens* is a non-shrubby, low-growing, creeping perennial, and *M. wilcoxii* (Wilcox hollygrape) can become shrubby, or it may occur in individual stems rising 1 to 15 feet off the ground. All species possess dark blue fruits.

Where and When to Gather

Algerita is found in desert grassland and piñon-juniper habitat, on hillsides, in canyons, and woodlands throughout our region. *Mahonia haematocarpa* and *M. fremontii* often occupy piñon-juniper woodlands and desert grasslands. Wilcox hollygrape is found in moist, mid-elevation canyons in southeast Arizona. *Mahonia repens* grows at high elevation amid aspen and conifers throughout the western half of our region. *Mahonia swaseyi* (Texas barberry) is found on limestone ridges in Texas Hill Country and is known to have sweet fruit. All these species possess edible fruit. The various fruits ripen from midsummer into the autumn season.

How to Gather

Clusters of berries can be harvested at once, by hand.

Ripe berry of Wilcox hollygrape (*Mahonia wilcoxii*).

Opening flower buds of Wilcox hollygrape.

How to Use

The rather tart berries can be consumed raw, but are commonly made into jelly by the addition of sugar and water. Further, the resultant tea can be fermented into wine with the addition of wine yeast. Traditionally, the berries were sometimes roasted before they were eaten. The fruit of our native *Mahonia* species can also be used similarly to those of European barberry, a classic component of Persian cuisine that is a close relative of our *M. trifoliolata*. Sauté fruits in butter and use to flavor rice, or add to ground meats. Add the fresh flowers to salads or vegetable ferments, or prepare them as a refreshing tea.

Future Harvests

Only gather what you plan to use, and refrain from gathering in areas when fruit production is particularly low (usually following prolonged drought).

alligator weed

Alternanthera philoxeroides

`EDIBLE` leaves, shoots, stems

An abundant, nutrient-rich aquatic plant, alligator weed makes an excellent salad green.

How to Identify

Alligator weed forms large mats, falling over itself as it grows up to 15 feet long. It has long, pointed, opposite leaves with contrasting lightly colored midveins. It generally grows in staid water and it can even tolerate some brackish water. The pearly flower is relatively inconspicuous and reminiscent of other Amaranth family plants.

The tender growth tip of alligator weed pulled fresh from a bog.

Where and When to Gather

This plant grows along streams, ditches, ponds, bogs, and bayous at the southeastern edge of our region—perhaps not surprisingly, anyplace alligators are found. The food part is available for harvest about nine months of the year; only unavailable during winter.

How to Gather

Use scissors or pruners, or simply pinch off the new growth tips with your fingers. The upper several inches of leaf growth will be quite tender and flexible.

How to Use

Alligator weed can be enjoyed raw in salads, but be sure to wash well to remove any bacteria acquired from its wet locale. Blanch and sauté, boil in soups and stews, or freeze for later use (once blanched). The tender young leaf and stem have nice texture and don't require much cooking. Enhance your meals with alligator weed's exceptional nutrition.

Future Harvests

Not much to worry about here. This plant is considered an invasive species—all the more reason to reap the bounty and enjoy its nutritional value.

Cautions

Be sure that any water from the harvest area is not contaminated with heavy metals or other toxins, as this mineral-rich plant may accumulate and concentrate what's available nearby. Cooking will diminish the plant's oxalic acid content, if that's a concern.

Alligator weed is said to not produce seed in North America.

American bulrush

Schoenoplectus americanus
club rush, three-square bulrush

EDIBLE fruit, pollen, rhizomes, shoots, stem base

American bulrush offers sweet starch, tender vegetables, and nutritious pollen.

American bulrush can grow abundantly in marshy areas.

How to Identify

The location of American bulrush (near, or in water) will be the first clue. Next, look at the leaf shape: there are three equidistant ribs with a curved (occasionally flat) space in between, running the length of each leaf. The flowers, in small clusters, will be found near the tips of the leaves, appearing as if glued on. They look like tiny, thin pine cones with yellow pollen at the end.

Where and When to Gather

American bulrush is found along the Gulf Coast and scattered throughout our region, in wet, marshy areas, or alongside running water. In the warmest zones, the rhizomes are available year-round. The pollen, shoots, and stem bases are available throughout the spring. The fruit, or seeds, appear in the late spring to early summer.

How to Gather

Gather the delectable stem bases by pulling back the green, fibrous leaf blades to arrive at the pure white, tender central core. A shoot may be found near the leaf bases or slightly below ground. Simply break it off with your fingers, or cut across the base of the shoot with a sharp knife. The rhizomes are dug, or pulled, from the muck in which they grow. The outer portion can be removed to get at the starchy white center cord, or dried whole and ground and sifted later to process into flour. The pollen is collected in a way similar to that of cattail, by shaking the loose pollen into a bag or open container. The small seeds can be stripped by hand.

How to Use

Use the shoots and stem bases of American bulrush like many other vegetables, diced raw, steamed, or sautéed. These delicate parts require very little cooking. The rhizomes can be processed into a starchy flour for making breads and cakes (see accompanying sidebar). The dry method creates a more fibrous flour; the wet method results in a more refined starch. The pollen and the ground seeds are also used as flour for breads and cakes. Try adding the shoots and stem bases to vegetable ferments such as kimchi and sauerkraut.

Future Harvests

This plant occupies a rarefied niche in the dry Southwest desert, as a resident of riparian and wetland habitats. Harvest wisely after observing the entire population for a time. Keep in mind that the area of Scottsdale, Arizona, was originally named for this plant, but it has now nearly disappeared from there.

Processing Rhizomes or Dried Inner Bark

The simplest method of extracting nutrients from starchy rhizomes or inner bark is to dry the material entirely, grind to a fine powder or flour, then sift to remove any remaining fiber. This flour can now be used in your favorite recipes or experimentations. Alternatively, fresh rhizomes or inner bark can be pounded thoroughly while soaking in water. Allow the flour (or starches) to settle to the bottom of the vessel. Pour off the water, being careful not to discard your flour. Continue filtering through a cloth, if necessary. Use wet, or spread out with proper airflow to dry for storage.

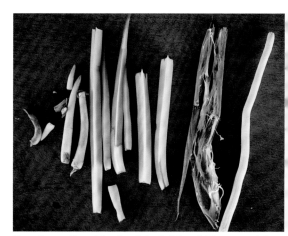

The various portions of American bulrush: (left to right) new growth, inner tender blades (both edible), outer skin of rhizome (not edible), inner starchy rhizome (edible).

apple

Malus pumila

wild apple, domestic apple, manzana

`EDIBLE` fruit

Tart, crisp, and bountiful, apples grow wild throughout the Southwest, remnants of old homesteading attempts.

How to Identify

One can easily identify an apple tree when the fruit is in season. However, there are a few characteristics to look for when apple is not in fruit. As a member of the rose family it has numerous white to pink, five-petaled, fragrant flowers which appear in the spring. The often-smooth bark is a gray-brown with purple tones. It may be thoroughly pockmarked from woodpecker activity. The branches and their tips possess flower buds with a soft, fuzzy coating present throughout the winter. Apple has alternating leaves. Ripe apples are generally available in the late summer in our region.

An apple tree pockmarked by fastidious woodpeckers.

Where and When to Gather

Look to cooler, moist habitats such as riparian areas, coniferous forests, canyons, and sandstone cliffs, generally occurring above 4000 feet. However, in the far eastern part of our region the elevation may be much lower. Apples are ripe and ready to gather in mid- to late summer.

How to Gather

Too easily overlooked, apples can be an abundant, easy-to-harvest wild food source. When heading out to gather, you have a few options: (1) pick fallen apples from the ground if they're not thoroughly bruised, (2) shake the tree and hope the fallen apples don't bruise too badly, (3) bring a ladder, a cloth shoulder bag, and a partner to stabilize the ladder or catch apples (this can be the safest, surest method), or (4) climb the tree and toss them down to a catcher on the ground, or if you are alone, gather them in a shoulder bag (this requires the most strength and agility). Hard, crisp apples can be stored fresh for many months where temperatures are moderately cool.

How to Use

Once you've had the fun of gathering more than your weight in apples in a relatively short period of time, you can begin processing them. A peeler and a corer can be good investments. Peeling is not necessary if drying apples, but coring is. When baking or canning apples, or making applesauce or apple butter, it is your choice whether or not to core and peel the fruit, though keep in mind that consuming an excess of apple seeds is not healthy (see Cautions). If your harvest is bountiful, I suggest procuring a press in order to make cider; freeze any excess or begin fermenting and bottling your own. Many possibilities for flavoring and sweetening are possible. Enjoy using apples in breads, pies, cakes, crisps, pancakes, jelly, and other creations.

Future Harvests

All cultivated apples come from a clone. You don't know what you'll get from a seed. If you find one you really like, graft it onto a root stock from a local nursery or apple orchard.

Cautions

Apple seeds contain amygdalin, which can create a toxic effect when a high quantity of seeds are ground or chewed and consumed. To be on the safe side, if you are consuming uncored apples, eat no more than one per day.

Although fruits begin to form in early summer, apples may take several months to reach full maturity.

banana yucca

Yucca baccata

Spanish dagger, palmilla, dátil

EDIBLE budding flower stalk, flowers, fruit, leaf base

Banana yucca was one of the sweetest foods available to Southwest foragers before the arrival of honeybees and their honey.

How to Identify

Banana yucca is identified by its long, dagger-like, blue-green leaves ending in a sharp spike. The leaf makes a U shape in cross section, and its margins are often covered in thin, curling white fibers. The inflorescence of banana yucca just barely extends beyond the leaves or may be contained within the rosettes. The cream-colored (sometimes tinged with pink or purple) flowers droop down languidly. They have a thick, moist texture, a beautiful aroma, and a soapy, acrid taste when fresh. The green, fleshy fruits can be quite large and hang downward in large clusters along the upright central stem. The black seeds are compressed together in circumferential rows throughout the length of the fruit.

The leaf margins of *Yucca baccata* shed strands of its white fibers, and the flowering stalk does not rise much above the leaf tips.

Where and When to Gather

Banana yucca can be found throughout the western half of our region, including southwest Texas. All broad-leaf *Yucca* species possess edible fruits. The fruits of narrow-leaf *Yucca* species are too fibrous to be edible. All *Yucca* species have edible parts and can be found in desert grasslands, chaparral, oak woodlands, and the piney woods of East Texas. The budding flower stalks and flowers are gathered in the spring, immature fruits in the early summer, and the sweet, mature fruits in the late summer to early autumn.

Yucca madrensis, a related species, can produce numerous large fruits in the late summer in Arizona and southwest New Mexico.

How to Gather

The flower petals of banana yucca may be gathered by hand, fresh off the stalk. The dried petals can also be removed easily from the stalk. I recommend gathering only dried flower petals in years of minimal flowering, to allow for fertilization of the fruits and sufficient seed maturation and dispersal. For this reason, one may also avoid gathering flowering stalks unless they are in great supply. When harvesting, cut the stalk before it has begun to open (it will resemble asparagus). The immature fruits can be gathered in the mid- to late spring, once they have grown to full size but still contain soft, white seeds. Mature fruits are gathered once a thick amber sap has begun to form on the fruits' exterior.

How to Use

Various parts of *Yucca* species within our region have been used for food—the flower stalk, flower buds, flower petals, unripe and ripe fruits, and the leaf base. I enjoy the unripe fruits of banana yucca sliced, diced, and sautéed with chopped bacon and mushrooms, or simmered with stew meat and red chiles. The mature fruits of banana yucca can ripen to the texture and sweetness of fresh custard when the conditions are right. Traditionally, they were baked, then the skins, seeds, and fiber were removed and the sweet pulp was formed into cakes to dry for storage. This substance formed the primary sweetener, or sweet food, for many indigenous peoples of the Southwest prior to the arrival of the colonialists. These dry cakes can be reconstituted in water and drunk as a sweet, nourishing beverage, or added to a variety of foods such as *atoles* (a kind of southwest porridge), squash, meat, and bean stews. The whole or ground dried flowers can be cooked into soup or mixed into acorn burgers. The unopened flowering stem was traditionally pit baked in a way similar to sotol or mescál. The thicker leaf bases can be baked over hot coals as well, similarly to mescál. The seeds of Y. *brevifolia* and Y. *faxoniana* were eaten, but otherwise avoided in other species.

Future Harvests

Harvesting fruits in years of bounty is an ancient and sustainable practice. However, whenever gathering reproductive parts, be sure that a sizable population will be available for reseeding in the future.

The fresh flowers of banana yucca are edible, but often taste acrid and soapy. They are best cooked.

barrel cactus

Ferocactus wislizenii

biznaga, compass barrel, fishhook barrel cactus

EDIBLE flower buds, fruit, inner pulp, seeds

The sour fruit of barrel cactus contains delicious, nutty seeds great for grinding and baking into bread.

How to Identify

Barrel cactus approaches being a columnar cactus as it grows to over 7 feet tall under certain circumstances, yet is unbranched (except after injury). The spines along the edge of the deep vertical pleats encircling the cactus are a rosy sunrise pink. The central spine in each areole is curved like a fishhook. Flowers atop the cylindrical cactus are yellow to red, and the waxy fruits are bright yellow with a dry, scruffy peduncle (dried flower) still attached.

Where and When to Gather

Ferocactus species exist throughout the western half of our region, down into the southern plains of Texas. Barrel cactus likes expansive flat areas and hill country,

Ripe barrel cactus fruit ready for picking. Notice that the fruit is entirely yellow.

Freshly cut barrel cactus fruit halves drying in the winter solstice sun. The mucilaginous (highly moistening) seeds can be removed easily once dry.

and is occasionally found in canyons. It can also be plentiful in urban areas as a landscape plant. Barrel cactus can be a source of food year-round. Flower buds can be gathered June through September. The fruits begin to ripen in November and can remain on the cactus through the end of spring; they are ready to gather once they are easily dislodged with a slight wiggle and pull.

How to Gather

The buds are not easily removed and I only harvest in areas of great abundance (dozens of cactus plants with ample buds). Tools of the trade include pliers, a flat-head screwdriver, and wide, flat tongs. Do what you must to dislodge the stout, persistent buds. The fruit can be gathered by pinching the persistent peduncle and pulling slightly as you twist. You may find a party of ants beneath the fruit. Don't worry, the insects are attracted by the extra floral nectaries, which produce tasty morsels.

How to Use

Brined or pickled barrel cactus buds make a true delicacy, especially when combined with your favorite seasonal spices. The sour, mucilaginous fruits can be candied, chopped and added to baked goods, made into chutney, or dried for later use. Chopped and soaked in water, they make a nice hair conditioner. The reddish-black, fatty seeds within are the true treasure. They are edible raw although somewhat bland. Toast them to bring out more flavor, or grind raw seeds and add the flour to baked goods, soups, and *atoles*. This flour combines beautifully with ground saguaro seed, a cornmeal-mesquite meal, and other wild seed meals. Indigenous peoples of our area have used the curved spines for fish hooks and the straight spines for tattooing. They have also relied upon the flesh of the cactus during times of drought (year-round in some locations) as a source of moisture—however, this is not recommended, as it kills the cactus. Early desert travelers knew the plant as compass barrel because of its tendency to lean toward the southern horizon.

A bowl of toasted barrel cactus seed flour.

Barrel cactus flower buds at various stages of growth.

Future Harvests

Barrel cactus grows slowly, so harvesting of the flesh is not encouraged. Great expanses of the plant were depleted in the early to mid-twentieth century when they were harvested for their flesh to produce "cactus candy." Always leave at least one-third of the fruit you find unharvested, and scatter seeds in areas you believe they may grow after a good summer rain. Also, look to rescue barrel cactus plants from planned construction sites.

beautyberry

Callicarpa americana
American beautyberry, French mulberry
`EDIBLE` fruit

Showy ripe berries call attention to this understory shrub at the margins of East Texas forests. Beautyberries possess a unique sweetness.

How to Identify

Beautyberry frequently grows in the shade. Leafless during the winter season, the shrub's drooping, opposite leaves begin to appear in the spring. Leaves emerge from woody stems which all rise from the base of the plant. White flowers appear at the leaf axils (where the leaf attaches to the main stem). Bright purple-magenta fruits make this plant easy to identify late summer through autumn.

Where and When to Gather

From East Texas up into Oklahoma, beautyberry is ubiquitous in some areas. It is often found as an element of landscaping along roadsides and in the clearings and edges of forests. A pioneer plant, it grows profusely after burns. In late summer, you may easily stumble upon tremendous amounts of ripe berries (and have very little doubt as to what you've found). Gathering continues through autumn.

How to Gather

Simply pull or garble berries from the bush and collect them in a bucket. Garbling means gently or vigorously massaging the clusters of berries over a collection vessel to urge the berries loose from their stem.

Ripe clusters of beautyberry fruit growing under canopy cover.

How to Use

Berries can be eaten raw. Prepare the fruit as a unique-tasting jelly, straining out seeds and skin during processing; use pectin to ensure jelling. Beautyberry leaves have also been used successfully in mosquito repellant preparations—a noteworthy fact in its native habitat! The stems can be used for friction fire spindles.

Future Harvests

Beautyberry comes by its name honestly— it's a lovely plant to use in landscaping. Simply leave ample amounts of berries for birds and other wildlife to disperse. Decades of suppressed fire in eastern pine forests have limited its range.

Shade-loving beautyberry thrives in dappled sunlight.

bellota

Quercus emoryi
Emory oak
Quercus virginiana
southern live oak

EDIBLE bellota (acorn)

The mother of all wild plant foods, bellotas have arguably sustained human life more than any other food.

The stately Emory oak stands tall throughout canyons and grasslands of the Southwest.

The ripening nut of southern live oak (*Quercus virginiana*), an excellent low-tannin bellota.

How to Identify

Emory oak possesses dark green, generally pointed leaves with serrated margins. It grows upright with a single trunk covered in dark gray bark. The undersides of the leaves are a lighter gray and largely free of hairs. Emory oak flowers in early April and its acorns ripen near the end of June—just before the arrival of summer rains. The male (staminate) flowers occur near the branch ends and appear yellow-orange to rusty red. The female (pistillate) flowers are along the branch, and that's where you'll later find acorns, or bellotas, as they're widely called in the Southwest. Emory oak bellotas are yellow (high in beta-carotene), and the inside of the shells possesses a soft white fuzz. Bellotas are produced annually. Southern live oak (*Quercus virginiana*) similarly produces relatively sweet, low-tannin acorns annually, and it also possesses leathery, dark green leaves with small, pointed teeth.

Processing Bellotas

Historically, bellotas have played a significant role in the diet and survival of humans. Very few people eat acorns today, though, and that is unfortunate. In fact, many have come to believe they are poisonous. It is true that many acorns are high in tannin, a type of acid. However, the bellotas of the Emory oak (*Quercus emoryi*) and southern live oak (*Quercus virginiana*)—both bountiful throughout our region—contain very low levels of tannin. Indeed, they are still gathered and eaten raw by the indigenous peoples of the greater Southwest United States and northern Mexico. For individuals who may be especially sensitive to tannin, a simple process can easily remove most or all of the substance.

The leaching method described here involves exposing the shelled bellotas to cool water. There are various tannin-leaching methods known and practiced; the process described here involves exposing the shelled acorns to cool water. It can be applied to the acorns of both the Emory oak and the southern live oak, and seems to work efficiently and effectively in a modern kitchen, providing an excellent acorn flour for a variety of applications.

Grinding southern live oak acorns.

Materials

gathered bellotas (acorns)
half-gallon jar
clean water
muslin cloth
wide-mouthed jar or food-grade plastic
    bucket large enough to hold produced
    flour

Instructions

1. Grind the fully dry bellotas into a coarse or fine flour (whatever your preference). This helps expose more surface area to water than leaving the bellotas whole.

2. Add 1 cup of the flour to a half-gallon jar, and fill with clean water. Shake well and then let the flour settle.

3. Once settled, shake the jar again to expose the flour to unsaturated water again. Repeat three or four times.

4. Cover the wide-mouthed jar or plastic bucket with the muslin cloth and attach it to the container's rim.

A half-gallon jar of bellota flour in water.

5. Once the mix has fully settled, decant the water from the jar until small amounts of fine flour begin to pour out.

6. Continue pouring the entire contents through the cloth strainer.

7. Pulling together the ends of the cloth (or closing the cloth bag), slowly squeeze out the remaining moisture. Continue squeezing until the flour is only damp and not dripping wet.

Now you have moist flour ready to add to a recipe. Flour can also be dried in a dehydrator, in the sun on sheet pans, or by any method you prefer.

I suggest limiting the flour's exposure to heat, in order to preserve the flour quality in baking applications. Stir frequently to help the flour avoid molding in moist climates. You may find that one full jar of water is not sufficient to entirely leach the bitterness out of your bellota flour. Simply repeat the steps with more clean water in order to continue leaching. Store your dry, leached flour in glass containers in the refrigerator or freezer.

A bellota burger with marinated Mexican palo verde beans and fries with oreganillo.

Southern live oak shells, however, are smooth, not fuzzy. Its bark is thick and dark.

Where and When to Gather

Find Emory oak on mountainsides, amid rolling hills in desert grasslands and oak savannahs, and throughout canyons and rugged basins. It can be found throughout the southwestern portion of our region, below the Mogollon Rim and down into Southwest Texas. Southern live oak produces substantial annual acorn masts midautumn, and is found from Central Texas to the Gulf Coast.

How to Gather

Gathering bellotas requires timing. Each year the harvest is different, with good mast years occurring every several years or so. Many animals count on these nuts for survival, so in years of low production, gathering by humans should be limited. In good mast years, make haste to arrive before the rains to avoid the quick putrification of the sweet, oily acorns. In other words, get 'em while they're dry. Then fully sun dry before shelling or storing.

Shelled acorns from a southern live oak.

How to Use

The people of the Sonoran and Chihuahuan desert areas still eat the bellotas of
Emory oak without any processing. The
unprocessed nuts contain bitter and
astringent tannin, but in very low quantities compared to most acorns. However,
the presence of any tannin at all may cause
some irritation in the throat when eaten in
excess. You can leach out the tannin with
water to make a sweeter acorn flour. Use
the flour to make breads, cakes, cookies,
pancakes, pizza, pie, biscuits, or other
baked goods. Roasted acorns bring a nice
flavor to coffee or spiced chai. Combine
savory spices and eggs with acorn flour to
make a veggie burger. I ferment acorn
pancake batter for a day or two, which
makes the batter a bit lighter. The acorns
of Southern live oak can be used identi-
cally to those of Emory oak; in fact,
Southern live bellotas are the preferred
acorn by some.

Future Harvests

I have been inspired by the tale of a man
who reforested a vast area by planting
acorns throughout his adult life. Considering the amount of food produced by one
tree in its lifetime, his was a worthy
endeavor.

Bellota-mesquite biscuits.

biscuit root

Lomatium species
chimaja, wild parsley

EDIBLE leaves, roots, stems, seeds

Biscuit root is a pungent, aromatic plant useful as a spice, condiment, or a wild source of starch.

How to Identify

Biscuit root is an herbaceous perennial related to wild carrot, wild parsley, and many other wild and cultivated edible and medicinal plants in the celery family. The shapes of the leaves, flowers, seeds, and roots can differ considerably between species. Although the flowers range from yellow to white to even maroon or purple, the shape of the fruits is distinctive among the celery family. The fruits are relatively flat across the top with a thin wing covering the sides. Thin, vertical lines (colored red-brown) can be viewed in the fruits as they are maturing. The leaves of biscuit root are reminiscent of cilantro, parsley, and celery in that they're mostly basal and dissected. In some species, however, the leaves may be long, thin, and wispy.

Where and When to Gather

Biscuit root inhabits the dry woodlands and mountains of the desert Southwest. Look to piñon-juniper or oak woodlands, coniferous forests, sagebrush flats, and brushy slopes. Desert parsley (*Lomatium simplex*, *L. bicolor*) can be found in the

The edible young leaves of biscuit root emerge as the spring warms.

northwest quadrant of our region, and northern biscuit root (*L. orientale*) can be found scattered throughout the western Southwest and over into the panhandles of Texas and Oklahoma. Its root is not spicy. Biscuit root is available year-round (where the ground is not frozen over), but is best gathered in spring and autumn. The leaves are collected in the spring before flowering, and the seeds during the summer.

How to Gather

The leaves, stems, and seeds can all be broken off by hand. The roots are easily dug up (when the soil is moist) with a hand trowel, small spade shovel, or hori-hori (Japanese digging tool and knife).

How to Use

The seeds, shoots, and fresh leaves of biscuit root have all been consumed fresh in a variety of ways. However, the acrid pungency of some species necessitates using the seeds sparingly. The leaves can be added to salads, briefly steamed or sautéed, or chopped and added to soups for a few minutes before serving. Think of biscuit root as a relative of parsley, celery, and cilantro—not kale, spinach, or chard. The roots of various species have traditionally been eaten raw, baked, or dried and ground into flour before consuming. Indigenous peoples have roasted, mashed, and formed cakes with biscuit roots to dry in the sun for later use. Briefly baking freshly mashed roots (combined with a bit of moisture) before consuming may serve to mellow the pungent flavor. It is best to peel the root before consuming.

The fruits of biscuit root are winged on the side.

Future harvests

Be aware of the local biscuit root populations before gathering roots. Some areas have significantly more plants than others. Leaves and stems can handle more gathering. Only small amounts of seeds are needed, but the roots can potentially be overharvested. *Lomatium dissectum*, for example, which is used widely for respiratory viruses, is considered at risk in much of its habitat, and I encourage foragers to not harvest the roots of this particular species. Press mature seeds into the soil in the appropriate habitat to help grow the population.

black nightshade

Solanum americanum

purple nightshade, chichiquelite

`EDIBLE` ripe fruit, young leaves

A berry with unique flavor and a degree of mystique, too. Wow your friends with a pie made from superbly delicious and nutritious black nightshade berries.

How to Identify

The characteristics of black nightshade can change considerably depending on local conditions. It can be an annual or perennial. Its alternate leaves can be coarsely toothed or smooth at the edges, and often appear wavy along the margins. The flowers, which are quick to appear and present in clusters, resemble potato flowers, with white petals and a yellow center. The flowers point out or downward. The alternate stems possess a striking characteristic of appearing in a V shape. Clusters of black nightshade berries ripen from green to shiny black-purple on green stems, which are about as long as the fruit. The plants can grow 3 to 5 feet tall.

Where and When to Gather

These plants inhabit waste places, agricultural and riparian areas, and gardens—in other words, areas where the soil is regularly disturbed. Ripe berries may be available from March through December (or longer in our warmest areas). The young leaves are available in the spring and summer.

How to Gather

Unfortunately, I haven't come up with a better technique of picking berries than by hand. One can thumb several berries from a cluster at once if they are all ripe, but this method can lead to a mixture of ripe and unripe berries, which is not recommended (unripe berries should not be consumed). Young leaf tips may be plucked from the plant (which encourages more to grow); do not harvest leaves after the plant has gone into flowering.

The ripened berries of black nightshade appear nearly black and are sweet and juicy.

How to Use

In all varieties I have encountered, the ripe berries are delicious eaten fresh. They also cook up nicely to create pies, syrups, and jellies. Add the berries to breads, muffins, or a curry dish; use them to flavor oatmeal or make a syrup. The tender young leaves are a delicacy—lightly sauté them in butter or olive oil for several minutes, with or without garlic. These makes a nice addition to meat or bean dishes.

Future Harvests

The Arabian proverb, "If the camel once gets his nose in the tent, his body will follow" certainly applies to this plant's growth habit. Cultivate at your own risk. Black nightshade proliferates under the right conditions.

Cautions

Black nightshade has had a resurgence of popularity in recent years, despite having been written off as toxic by many. The toxic rap is not true, however, if you want to be ultra-cautious, gather only ripe berries and cook them before eating, and avoid consuming the greens.

The young leaves of black nightshade make a wonderful sautéed green.

blue dicks

Dichelostemma capitatum

covena

EDIBLE bulbs, flowers, stems

The sweet, moist bulb makes a refreshing snack on the trail, and was once harvested in great numbers by indigenous peoples of the Southwest.

The bulbs, flowers, and leaves of blue dicks are all edible.

How to Identify

Look for the reddish-pink flowering stems emerging in early spring. They possess clusters of flowers which can be pink, light purple, or blue, emerging from a translucent, papery white envelope. The petals are in multiples of threes. The bulb is covered in thin, rusty brown—fibrous remnants of previous years' leaves.

Where and When to Gather

Found throughout the western half of our region, blue dick was likely a welcome sight to early foragers in the spring as food supplies dwindled. Look to rocky hillsides, mesas, open woodlands, coniferous forests, and prairies for the emerging spring flowers. Blue dicks can grow in clay soils, which makes for difficult digging of the bulb in dry soil—wait until after a good rain for easier access. It is likely that indigenous peoples reaped great harvests after intentional fires were set to chosen grasslands.

How to Gather

Bring a shovel, digging stick, and pickax. You will be prepared for whatever conditions you encounter. You may want to switch to the digging stick when you're getting close to the bulb. Keep in mind that these moist bulbs exist year-round in a very dry desert environment, so you will have to trace the thin underground stem for up to 12 inches to arrive at the moist, sweet bulb. It works well to dig up a good chunk of preferably moist soil about 1 in. adjacent to the bulb, then dig out the bulb from the side with one's hands.

How to Use

Although this may seem like a good deal of work for a tiny morsel, I understand blue dick was cherished by traditional foragers. Bulbs were consumed fresh, roasted in earthen ovens, boiled or dried for later use, then reconstituted or ground into powder before cooking. Another interesting use was lining woven baskets with smashed, fresh bulbs in order to harvest small seeds. The leaves and flowers are a nice snack and can be added to salads for color.

Future Harvests

Take a long walk around the area before you harvest in any quantity. Make sure you are gathering a sustainable amount (no more than 10 percent of the known population) so you can return to abundance in the future. Rotate among different harvesting locations, giving areas a break every year or two. Gather seeds when mature, then spread them in the fall in an area known to produce blue dicks. Once germinated, these will be ready for harvest within several years.

Cautions

As a monocot (having a single, grasslike seed leaf), blue dicks can be confused with other toxic plants, such as death camas (*Zigadenus* species). Waiting until the plant flowers is a fail-safe method to ensure you have the correct plant, as death camas flowers look nothing like blue dicks. Death camas blooms are cream colored, yellow, and green and have an entirely different form.

The flowers of blue dicks range from light pink to lavender.

box elder

Acer negundo

three-leaf maple, fresno de guajuco

`EDIBLE` inner bark, sap, young leaves

The bitter, spicy young leaves of box elder make a wonderful spring green by themselves or mixed with other greens in salads, soups, and stir-fries.

The opposing leaves of box elder, in three parts. Notice the young leaf growth with a reddish tinge.

How to Identify

Box elders are shrubby trees in wet locations in the Southwest found growing in large clusters, often with branches hugging close to the ground. But they can also rise up to 30 to 50 feet in height under ideal conditions. Like the closely related maple, box elder has opposite stems and leaves, the difference being that box elder leaves are compound and in three-part groups. The leaves emerge just after the dangling flower clusters (male and female flowers are on separate plants) and can be tinged a brick red when very young. They possess winged fruit, or samaras, which appear in pairs quite similar to those of maples (*Acer* species). Maple leaves are entire and palm-shaped.

Where and When to Gather

Look for box elders in shady riparian areas. They often grow as an understory, within the western half of our region, beneath trees such as cottonwood, sycamore, alder, or walnut. They prefer to grow within some shade. If you're in an area that experiences freezing temperatures at night and warm days in the late winter and early spring, you may be able to tap the tree for sap at this time. Gather the young leaves shortly after the flowers emerge in early spring. The bark is best harvested in the fall or early spring. Maples are found at higher elevations so their seasons are a bit shorter.

How to Gather

The young leaves can be broken off in clusters by hand from the ends of the opposing branches. Gather bark from younger, smooth-barked branches about 1½ to 3 inches in diameter. Strip the bark

Harvesting Inner Bark

Although most would not consider eating tree bark, it is not the bark we are after, but what lies directly beneath it. Trees consist of several distinct vertical layers of growth. For the purposes of foraging for food, we are concerned with the cambium layer, which lies just inside the hard, rough bark we see on the outside. Since mature bark can become thicker and harder (and more difficult to remove), we focus on younger branches when gathering for food.

Young branches gathered in the spring or autumn are best for harvesting inner bark.

Seasonally, inner bark is best gathered in the spring (as tree sap is rising), or secondarily in the autumn, just before the sap descends into the roots. Inner bark can also be gathered at other times of year with moderate results. A branch with a diameter of 1½ to 3 inches is generally the perfect size. We're also searching for relatively smooth bark on a straight branch (if possible), with very few or no secondary stems.

Once a preferred branch is chosen, locate the stem base. With a handsaw, you will begin cutting ½ to 1 inch up the branch from the junction. Make a starter cut into the bottom, or opposite, side of the branch. Then begin your final cut directly parallel to—and in-line with—the first cut, completing it all the way through the branch. This technique will help prevent bark from tearing farther down the tree trunk. One method of bark removal is to simply whittle away all layers of bark (down to the wood) via long strokes with a sharpened blade. Alternatively, make circumferential cuts every 8 to 12 inches along the branch and cut the bark off in strips, until the entire space is bare down to the wood. Then move on to the next section. Depending on ambient conditions, tree bark should be processed within several hours to 3 or 4 days; weather conditions will influence how quickly the bark dries on the branch. Bark can be dried on a sheet or screen, or in a basket. Keep the bark out of sunlight and near a good cross breeze, if possible. If there is no air movement underneath, be sure to move the bark around frequently. See page 54 for how to process dried inner bark.

Cut bark off in strips from the branch, then dry away from sunlight.

from the wood within three or four days to ensure freshness. This light pruning will often be beneficial for the tree when performed in the spring or fall. The sap can be harvested by drilling (with a sterile bit) an upward-angled hole 8 to 12 mm across, then inserting a food-grade plastic tube of the same diameter. This tube should then be run into a food-grade plastic bucket. When you are finished, promptly cork up the hole or block with moist earth. Be sure to process the sap within a day. The ripened seeds can be pulled from the tree by hand, or picked up from the ground if they've recently fallen.

The white inner bark of box elder is bland and slightly sweet.

Clusters of tender young box elder leaves; these are bitter and spicy when fresh.

How to Use

In the Southwest, I prefer the flavors of box elder over maple, which is more bitter and whose young leaves lack spiciness. Add the spicy young leaves of *Acer negundo* to soups, or sauté with garlic, olive oil, and fresh lemon juice for a bitter, piquant side dish to accompany grilled meat. The leaves also make a nice tea in the spring. The freshly harvested sap will need to be cooked down to concentrate the sugars; you will need about forty ounces of sap to wind up with one ounce of shelf-stable syrup. It is said that box elder can have the sweetest sap of all *Acer* species. The inner bark has been traditionally boiled down with water until the sugars concentrate. Additionally, you can dry and pound the bark, then sift the light, starchy inner bark from the fiber.

Future Harvests

When harvesting sap, be sure to rotate trees so you only tap a given tree once every two or three years. Otherwise, box elder populations are healthy where they exist. Simply regulate your harvests according to the population. If you have the right terrain at home (wet, shady riparian areas or high elevation), it's probably already there.

bracken fern

Pteridium aquilinium

fiddlehead fern, western brake fern

fiddleheads, rhizomes

With a flavor reminiscent of asparagus, fiddleheads are a tasty delicacy when in season.

Bracken fern grows in dense colonies in pine forests in the Southwest.

How to Identify

Fortunately, within our region there are no ferns to confuse with bracken fern. The rusty brown, hairy, curled-up leaf tips (aka fiddleheads) emerge midspring from the pine needle–covered forest floor. The top of the unfurled, emerging leafstalk will be tender and flexible toward the tip before opening up to three distinct stems (often likened to a hawk's talons). The pinnate leaf blades become leathery as they mature. Spores produced on the undersides of the leaves appear dark brown when present (usually midsummer). Bracken fern is generally 3 to 5 feet tall within our region, but may grow to be over 10 feet tall. The whole plant turns beige in the fall and dies back to the ground.

Where and When to Gather

Bracken fern can be found in the eastern and western halves of our region, but is absent from the drier uplands of Central Texas to eastern New Mexico. Look to conifer forests. The young, curled fronds are gathered in the spring when just emerging. The starchy rhizomes can be gathered in the early spring or fall.

How to Gather

As if you were preparing asparagus from the market, gently bend the stem below the fiddleheads until it snaps off where the tender part ends. The rhizome must be dug up. Stick a shovel into the ground near a leaf stem, and move it back and forth to loosen the soil. Identify a rhizome attached to a leaf stem and work it loose from the adjoining soil with your hands. You may need to loosen the soil further or work around tree roots or nearby rocks. The outer portion of the rhizome is too fibrous and must be removed.

How to Use

It is believed to be essential to cook bracken fern fronds in two changes of water to remove potential toxins and

Freshly gathered fiddleheads, ready for boiling.

Gather bracken fern's young, tender tips when they are still curled up.

carcinogenic substances. Once completed, they are ready to eat or serve. Sauté for a couple minutes with garlic and olive oil to enhance the flavor. Similar to asparagus, a purée can be made with the softened, boiled fronds. Place over roasted vegetables in the final minutes of baking.

Future Harvests

Not to worry. Some believe bracken fern to be the world's worst weed. Eat up.

Cautions

Bracken fern is considered to possess potent nerve toxins, as well as carcinogenic and mutagenic substances. However, following the special instructions for preparing the young fronds makes this plant safe to enjoy as a food, as it has been for millennia.

bull nettle

Cnidoscolus angustidens
mala mujer
Cnidoscolus texanus
Texas bull nettle

`EDIBLE` seeds

Don't let the spines scare you away. Bull nettle produces a sweet, oily nut with a flavor similar to cashew.

How to Identify

Bull nettle is an herbaceous perennial with large, palmate, deeply lobed leaves covered in milky white spines (a feature impossible to overlook). It grows to about 2 feet in height. When cut, all parts of the plant exude a milky sap. The plain white flowers occur above the foliage in spreading clusters, making this plant noticeable from a distance. Every part of the plant is covered in sharp, bristly hairs, except the seeds (once removed from their spiny shells) and the opened flower sepals. The unripe seed capsule is bright green, covered in milky white dots and thin, white spines. The seeds can be fully brown or mottled (similar to their close relative, the toxic castor bean).

Where and When to Gather

Bull nettle can be located amidst the grasslands, oak woodlands, and canyons of the border region of southeast Arizona. Texas bull nettle can be found throughout

Once freed from their spiny shells, grayish-brown bull nettle seeds can be eaten raw or toasted.

Only the seeds of *Cnidoscolus angustidens* are eaten.

Texas bull nettle (*Cnidoscolus texanus*) is found in Texas and Oklahoma. As with *Cnidoscolus angustidens*, we eat only the seeds of this plant.

Texas Hill Country, the South Texas Plains, and the eastern hardwood forests of Texas north into Oklahoma. The seeds of both species begin to ripen in the late summer to early autumn.

How to Gather

Using tongs or thick leather gloves, pull the nearly ripened seed capsules off the plant and place into a paper bag. Set aside for several days in a dry place, allowing the seedpods to mature and open up inside the bag.

How to Use

Bull nettle is foraged for its seeds, which may be eaten raw. Some may prefer to toast them. All proclaim them delicious. Forager and herbalist Sam Coffman likes to put the ripening seed capsules of Texas bull nettle in a paper bag, ensuring that all seeds are captured when the capsules open. Bull nettle and Texas bull nettle are of the seed-eating varieties. First- and

secondhand experience dictate that the roots of these two plants are not edible—although it is tempting, as a good deal of food could be obtained with little effort.

Future Harvests

These highly drought-tolerant plants have existed under foraging pressure from humans and animals alike over many millennia. However, to enhance the accessibility and secure the presence of bull nettle, this plant can be brought into the home and agricultural landscape.

Cautions

Approach bull nettle with caution. It is covered with sharp spines that possess a toxin known to greatly irritate the skin. The pain and irritation is of short duration for most, but infection may result if the irritated area is not cleansed promptly.

capita

Atriplex elegans
saltbush, wheelscale saltbush
Atriplex wrightii
saltbush, Wright's saltbush

EDIBLE leaves, stems

A salty addition to your soups, stews, salads, and stir-fries, capita is one of our most tender and delicious wild greens.

How to Identify

Capita species that frequent our area generally have leaves with wavy edges, although not always. Wright's saltbush leaves are light green on top and gray-green on the underside, whereas wheelscale saltbush leaves are gray-green on both sides. Both of these annuals grow to a height of 8 to 20 inches, depending on moisture. The seeds of wheelscale saltbush are shaped like wheels, appearing to have teeth like a tiny gear. This characteristic is most notable. The stem and maturing seeds of Wright's saltbush can appear reddish, especially when grown on exposed ground. As with many plants, it is best to scout harvesting locations a year in advance.

A patch of young, tender, salty capita, ready for harvest.

Where and When to Gather

Capita occurs across the southern tier of our range. Wheelscale saltbush can be found growing as an urban weed on any disturbed ground across the southwestern portion of our region. Wright's saltbush will be found along seasonal drainages or river bottoms. The gathering season can be extended with favorable weather and location, but generally occurs early April through early June, when the plants begin to toughen up and go to seed. An additional species found in coastal locales, beach orach (*Atriplex cristata*), is similarly edible. It is variable in its appearance: opposite or alternate leaves, sprawling or erect, annual or perennial, but certainly salty in taste. There are no toxic *Atriplex* species, although not all have been used for food.

How to Gather
Pluck the leaves and stem by hand.

How to Use
Capita greens are wonderful eaten fresh, cooked, or dried for later use. Combine them with scrambled eggs, add them to soups and stews, or use them as a side dish to accompany meat. I like to quickly blanch the greens, then sauté with oil and garlic. In this way capita is certainly similar to spinach. Quick blanching also allows you the option to freeze for later use. You can also shade-dry the leaves and add to soups throughout the year.

Capita can provide plentiful nutrition; many indigenous peoples have utilized the greens to get concentrated nutrients (including calcium, magnesium, manganese, iron, and vitamins A, C, and K) not found in quantity in other plant or animal foods. Although one can't consume 30 pounds of fresh capita greens at once, there are many options for preservation or storage.

Future Harvests
I have cultivated Wright's saltbush with moderate success. It is a delicious, crisp green well worth the effort. Visit your location in the late summer and early fall to gather seed. Identify a similar location with adequate moisture potential where the plant is not established, and scatter

the seeds before winter rains arrive. Likewise with wheelscale saltbush. If you don't have access to seeds via foraging, obtain them from native plant growers. Capita grows well with adequate rainfall.

Hang the fresh leaves of capita in bundles to dry for later use in soups and rubs.

Tender, new growth of Wright's saltbush can be found in the spring.

cattail

Typha domingensis
Southern cattail, tule

`EDIBLE` immature inflorescence, pollen, rhizomes, shoots, stem base

Always in season, cattail provides a wide variety of vegetable harvests from rich, golden pollen to sweet, tender shoots.

How to Identify

This grass-like plant is found growing in or very near water in most cases. Occasionally it sits on dry ground, but only when water is close to the surface. The stiff, light-green leaf blades are about ¼ to 1 inch wide and anything from 1 foot (when very young) to 14 feet tall. The leaf base is arranged in a fan shape akin to a poker player's hand, but the leaves have a rounded depth to them, and are not flat across. The hot dog–like inflorescences usually appear even with the height of the tallest leaf blades; if the inflorescences are buried within the leaves you may have *Typha angustifolia*, which is similarly edible. The top inflorescence (male, from which we gather the pollen) will appear thinner than the female, or pistillate, flower below. In *T. latifolia*, also edible, the male and female inflorescences are essentially touching each other. Cattail rhizomes, or lateral-growing rootstalks below ground, appear beige to white within, and possess a thin, central cortex, or cord, which runs the length of the rhizome (we eat what's around it). Cattail locations can be easily identified during the autumn and winter, as the female inflorescences unfurl like puffy party favors dispersing millions of seeds into the wind.

Where and When to Gather

Cattail requires wet ground so look to drainages, particularly those with perennial water flow such as riparian areas. Cattail is more of a canyon and spring seepage plant in the Southwest than the aquatic plant found in lakes across much of the rest of the country. As major floods can wash out entire populations inhabiting canyons, visit your local patches regularly to keep up on their status. Cattail rhizomes can be gathered year-round (permitting ground is not frozen), but the pollen and immature inflorescences are only found during the early spring to early summer, depending on your location. The shoots and leaf bases are most populous late winter through early summer.

How to Gather

Gathering pollen may be the most fun aspect of cattail foraging. Because it requires collecting a fine substance which is readily blown by the wind, and Southwest winds can be both unpredictable and

A thriving cattail population at an oasis marsh in the middle of the desert.

significant, I suggest inserting the male inflorescence into a bag, or an appropriate plastic container (a 2-liter soda bottle, for instance), and shaking vigorously while tilting the flower stalk downward, to contain the pollen in the collecting vessel. Next, shake the contents out into a fine strainer to remove any bugs or the flower's fiber content. The terminal flower cluster (male inflorescence) can be broken off at its base when still green. Cut back or break off the fan-shaped leaf arrangement from the base of the plant and remove all surrounding green leaves from the cluster to arrive at the tender, pure white leaf base. The rhizomes are dug by hand (in soft, muddy, or sandy soil) or with a shovel. Search with your fingers underground, near the base of the plant, to find the tender shoots emerging and break them off where they meet the rhizome.

How to Use

A great starch plant, cattail is used like many of our classic starches—in baking. Cook with the strained pollen to create pancakes, muffins, or breads, or process the fresh or dried rhizomes to produce flour. For the fresh version of flour, wash the rhizome, then grind by hand underwater and allow the starch to settle. Alternatively, dry the rhizomes in short segments, then grind and sift out the fibrous material to derive your starchy flour. The shoots and tender leaf bases can be prepared as many vegetables are: steamed, boiled, sautéed, roasted, or eaten raw. The young male inflorescences can be steamed or boiled, then nibbled off the tough central cortex, or scraped off and integrated with other food. It is good practice to wash all cattail parts (except the inflorescences) when harvesting from unknown areas.

Future Harvests

Cattail is not particularly abundant in the Southwest as it relies on sufficient groundwater near the surface. Our best hope for maintaining or developing cattail habitat is wise rainwater management (for example, catchment basins) or creating graywater catchment systems to foster growth where most appropriate.

Cautions

Because cattails are aquatic plants, pathogenic organisms, inorganic chemicals, or heavy metals can settle in the basin where they grow, concentrating in the cattail plants. So in addition to washing the lower parts of the plant, be aware of the run-off situation in the local watershed before consuming any in-ground parts of the plant. Pollen would be considered safe.

The staminate flower spike (on top) is full of yellow pollen ready for harvest.

chia

Salvia columbariae

chan

`EDIBLE` seeds

The legendary seed of the desert packs tremendous nutrition and makes an excellent gluten-free flour.

How to Identify

You may smell chia before you see it. The opposite leaves and square stem of this member of the mint family possess a pungency reminiscent of skunk. The small indigo blue flowers appear in whorls of interrupted spikes on this short annual plant, beginning in late winter and lasting until spring. The spiny, purple-green bracts of the flower clusters are soft at first, but then sharp to the touch as they dry to a light beige color.

The calyces of chia are brilliant purple.

Where and When to Gather

Chia is found throughout the western half of our region. Check the edges of seasonal desert washes, or where any tiny rivulet of rain run-off appears along the *bajadas* of desert mountains. I often find chia harvesting locations when out gathering saguaro fruit in June, although they may begin drying out and releasing their seeds as the hot, dry spring comes on in early May. You can find them into early July, but the seed content will likely be diminished. Other less common species come out following the summer rains, providing for extended harvests.

How to Gather

Bend large plants and shake them into a collecting vessel. Otherwise, break off the dry plant below the lowest seedpod and turn it over, shaking into a bag or bucket. Winnow out any extra plant debris that comes along with the seeds, then they are ready to consume. It's a labor of love.

How to Use

Chia seed is a stand-alone ingredient in any cooling summer drink. Simply add a small amount (1/4 cup per gallon) and stir

Note the whorls of dry, spiny bracts along the chia stem—these house the mature seeds in late spring.

vigorously to prevent clotting. Let it sit twenty minutes, and enjoy. It is an exceptional aid in guarding against overheating and moisture loss. Traditionally, the seeds have been parched, ground, and made into *atole*. You can grind the seeds to make a gluten-free flour substitute. The whole seeds also make a great addition or topping to granola, breads, muffins, yogurt, and fruit and nut bars. Interestingly, the plant's root is being studied for its beneficial effects on cardiovascular health.

Future Harvests

I've been happy to see *Salvia columbariae* become a regular feature in roadside re-vegetation projects. Simply gather the seeds in late spring and scatter around areas which are subject to minor flooding during the winter rainy season. They appear to do well in sandy, well-drained soils.

Gathering and Cleaning Seeds

Seed gathering may seem daunting, and like a lot of work for very little reward. Areas of concentrated supply can make for a satisfying harvest, however. Some easily foraged wild seeds within our region include chia, pigweed, whitestem blazing star, pamita, and London rocket. There's also barrel cactus, saguaro, pecan, piñon, and palo verde, but those seeds are larger and come via different delivery systems, so do not apply to the basic techniques described here.

A bowl of winnowed chia seeds ready for use, storage, or further processing.

Gathering

Knocking plants or seedpods with a stick to release seeds into a pile, a sheet, or a bowl is an age-old technique. The work is direct and energized—not fussy, stringently conservative, nor greedy. Actually, tapping plants with a hand or a stick of manageable size to force them to shed their seeds is a technique for both collection and for reseeding. You'll never catch all the seeds, and you know you're already in an appropriate area for germination. Next step is to dislodge seeds that are still enclosed in a fruit or seedpod. Mechanical crushing or rubbing will suffice.

Cleaning

What you do catch will need to be cleaned (threshed) to remove all the non-seed material. The ancient method is called winnowing. It requires a steady unidirectional breeze to be effective. Combine all of your seed material in a container such as a wide bowl. With a flick of the wrists, and a forward-upward movement from the arms (bent 90 degrees at the elbow), toss the material into the air. If the non-seed material is lighter, it should be carried away by the light breeze. However, lightweight seeds may require care so you do not discard them with the fibrous pod material. Continue this motion until the seeds are clean and clear of non-seed, fibrous material. Additionally, knocking or quickly vibrating the bowl percussively may help to move the non-seed material into one corner atop the seeds. Pick up this material carefully and discard. One more method useful for very lightweight seeds can be found in the Processing Pigweed Seeds sidebar on page 220.

chickweed

Stellaria media

chickenwort

EDIBLE flowers, leaves, seeds, stems

A weed with such delicate flesh should make it to the table of all foragers. A little salt, vinegar, and olive oil are all you need.

How to Identify

Chickweed grows as an annual (winter or summer) with a slender taproot in our region. Its opposing oval-shaped leaves come to a point. The flowers appear on long stems with five white sepals, which look like deeply cleft hearts. The sprawling herb may grow upright or fall over itself. Like other species in the genus *Stellaria*, chickweed has hairs in a single line along its stem. Related edibles, species of *Cerastium*, will have hairs encircling their entire stems.

Where and When to Gather

Chickweed exists scattered throughout our region, but is most profuse in the far eastern portions (eastern Texas and Oklahoma). Look to disturbed ground, cultivated areas, waste places, open woodlands, and woodland clearings. At lower elevations with warm winters, chickweed can be available through the winter, and at higher elevations with cold winters, it's a summer annual. Gather any time it's available.

All aboveground parts of chickweed can be eaten.

How to Gather

I like to trim chickweed with a pair of pruners or kitchen shears.

How to Use

Delicately tender, chickweed is edible raw, but many prefer it cooked. Perfect lightly sautéed, blanched, or steamed, and well suited to salads and soups. When combining with other foods, such as soups, add chickweed near the end of the cooking time.

Future Harvests

Allow a given patch to set sufficient flowers for seeding. Scatter seeds anyplace that seems an advantageous habitat (and is easy for you to access for gathering).

chiltepín

Capsicum annuum var. *glabriusculum*

chilipiquín, chilepepín, wild chile, bird pepper, chile del monte

`EDIBLE` fruit

This wildly hot, berrylike pepper graces tables across the Southwest in the form of salsa, pickled greens, and whole dried fruits.

How to Identify

When not in fruit, chiltepín disappears into the lush green of its surroundings. The leaves appear opposite each other along the stem. White, down-turned flowers arise from the centers of the stem joints at the arrival of summer rains. The fruits stand individually on upright stems just above the leaves. Chiltepín may grow from 2 to 4 feet in height. Early morning or evening light may facilitate better sighting.

Chiltepin is notable for its bright red fruit.

Where and When to Gather

As the northernmost wild species of *Capsicum* in the Americas, chiltepín will only be found wild in the southern portion of our region. In Texas, it can be found from the Edwards Plateau south. An understory plant, chiltepín exists beneath tiers of plants such as wolfberry, elder, and hackberry, primarily in riparian forests. One can begin harvesting green fruits for brining or pickling near midsummer. Toward the end of summer into early autumn, the green fruit will begin to ripen bright red, then hundreds of eager foragers will comb the forests and riparian areas for this highly prized pepper. The dry fruits can persist on plants for several months. Wispy chiltepín uses capsaicin—the substance that lights our mouths on fire—to keep vertebrates from eating its fruits. But its bright color tempts birds to spread it wherever they alight.

How to Gather

Pick the small chiltepín peppers one by one off the plant and gather them in a bucket or a small paper or cloth bag. You may wish to use gloves to protect your skin from the oils. Please do not engage in the popular practice of cutting back the entire plant or ripping off whole branches and bringing these large plant sections back home, where the fruits fall off once dry.

How to Use

Eat chiltepín fruit one at a time, as the bite of its heat slowly consumes you. For the brave of heart, or those generally fond of spicy foods, crush a dried pepper into a bowl of soup, or a few into your stir-fry or bowl of fresh salsa. Jars of the pickled green fruit commonly occupy dining tables throughout Sonora, Mexico. The accompanying vinegar from the pickled peppers is sprinkled over tacos or bowls of menudo, while the tangy-spicy fruits are eaten whole. Narrow-chambered, upright grinding vessels made of ironwood and carved into various animals, reptiles, cacti, or sea creatures are used to pound the dried fruits into powder to use in salsa or to sprinkle over food (thus avoiding finger and hand contact with the potentially irritating oils). Exo Roast Co. in Tucson, Arizona, makes a delicious cold-brewed coffee infused with wild-harvested chiltepín from Sonora, Mexico. You can use this wild pepper in any way you would use its close cousin cayenne.

Future Harvests

Follow the general rule of thumb when harvesting fruits from the wild: harvest no more than a third of what you see (and there are always more plants than you can see). Harvests of chiltepín depend upon bird dispersal. Our primary concern for future harvests of chiltepín is maintaining healthy multistory forests where chiltepín growth and dispersal occurs. This plant is highly susceptible to hard frosts. Additionally, you can scatter seeds from crushed peppers beneath chiltepín's common nurse trees.

Cautions

As with all hot peppers, reduce exposure to skin, and consume carefully. They're hot.

The down-turned flower of chiltepín is reminiscent of its close relative the tomato.

chokecherry

Prunus virginiana
chokecherry
Prunus serotina
black chokecherry
Prunus emarginata
bitter cherry

`EDIBLE` fruit

Cherished food of foragers for ages, antioxidant-rich chokecherries make amazing syrups and jellies.

The darker fruits of chokecherry are ripe, tart, and juicy.

How to Identify

Chokecherry is a deciduous tree growing up to 30 feet in height. Closely related black chokecherry grows much smaller in the western portion of the country (20 to 30 feet) than it does on the east coast (up to 100 feet). The smooth, almost bronzed bark has tiny white marks, or lenticels, appearing horizontally. Chokecherry and black chokecherry will fully leaf out (alternate and serrate) before its long racemes of white, five-petaled flowers emerge from the leaf axils along the branches. Conversely, bitter cherry will flower over bare branches, with its much shorter flower clusters emerging near the branch tips. Crush the leaves to discover the cherry-almond scent of a cyanide-producing compound. The red to black berries are about ½ inch in diameter.

Where and When to Gather

Chokecherry, black chokecherry, and bitter cherry can be found throughout the mountains of the Southwest. Look to canyons, oak woodlands, high elevation creeks, and clearings and mountainsides in coniferous forests. The berries ripen near the end of summer, just as bears are foraging and gorging for their autumn and winter sustenance—so keep an eye out!

How to Gather

Reach up or bend young, flexible branches downward to pull off the berries by hand, or climb up to pick them. Collect the fruits in a cloth bag or bucket. Once finished gathering, process the fresh berries, or set them out to dry. Similar to rose hips, the fruits are often preferred after the first frost.

How to Use

The entire genus *Prunus* has been widely used for food and medicine across the globe. Our chokecherry is no exception. Certain tribes of North America relied upon it as the primary fruit in their diet. Although the fresh fruits can be consumed, they are generally bitter-sour, although some can be juicy and sweet. Do not eat the fresh seeds, which contain a cyanide-producing compound, amygdalin. The fresh fruits can be cooked into jelly, jam, and syrup, or fermented to make a wine—all requiring the addition of sugar. Historically, the fresh fruits were often ground, formed into cakes, and sun dried by indigenous peoples. The resultant meal could be incorporated into pemmican (combined with fat, meat, or fish eggs, and dried for preservation), or cooked with other foods. Bitter cherry fruit should be cooked before consuming.

Future Harvests

Gather no more than you can use and leave plenty of fruit for wildlife. They will do the job of seed dispersal.

Cautions

Although it would require eating numerous fresh chokecherry seeds to become poisoned, it's best to avoid consuming any fresh seeds, which contain the toxin amygdalin. Seeds that have been dried and ground are fine for consumption.

Black chokecherry flowering in the spring.

cholla

Cylindropuntia species

EDIBLE flower buds, fruit, sap

Cholla buds are a nutritious food staple of the Tohono O'Odham people of the Sonoran Desert. The buds possess a slight acidic tartness and their moist consistency approaches that of okra.

Cholla buds emerge in early spring.

The yellow flowers of staghorn cholla (*Cylindropuntia versicolor*) in bloom.

or much longer and clustered tightly around the stem. Chollas do not produce leaves—like other cacti, their green stems are the source of photosynthesis. Flower colors include yellow, green, pink, purple, maroon, and carmine red. Plants hybridize readily.

How to Identify

Cholla cacti are quite diverse in size, ranging from 1½ to over 12 feet tall. The plants are very similar to prickly pear but their stems are cylindrical (hence the genus name *Cylindropuntia*). The spines can be shorter than an inch and spread out,

Where and When to Gather

Cholla can be found throughout North American deserts. The greatest populations and diversity are found in the Sonoran and Chihuahuan deserts. Some chollas provide better buds for foragers, others provide better fruit—then there's the sap. In the greater Sonoran Desert region, species that flower in the spring are

Chain-fruit cholla (*Cylindropuntia fulgida*) flowers during summer rains and produces long chains of fruit growing off the previous years' growth. These fruits are consumed throughout the winter and spring by the Seri tribe of Mexico.

Cholla buds being gathered with tongs. To brush off the spiny glochids, use a bundle of a nearby plant (burroweed here) and rub on a rough surface, such as gravelly ground.

generally better for harvesting buds, and those whose fruits persist through the autumn and winter can be gathered then. Yellow, green, red, and purple fruits are all edible. The sap can be gathered at any time.

How to Gather

This is the tricky part, but it needn't be intimidating. Although several methods exist, I have found the greatest success by simply brushing off the prickly glochids (tiny barbed hairs) with a bundle made from a nearby plant. Fresh, green creosote bush works quite well. Bend and pull off each bud with a pair of tongs. Remove the remaining glochids by brushing the buds across a semi-rough surface such as gravel. You can also wait until getting them home—boil buds thoroughly; then simply pull the spines out with your fingers.

How to Use

In order to consume or preserve cholla buds, they must be cooked first. Boiling is an effective method. Sun dry after cooking to store for later use. Cholla buds can also be cooked into pots of beans, or any soup or stew. They make a wonderful addition to fresh salsa (as would fresh cholla fruit, for a sour flavor). Dried cholla buds were once ground into flour to be added to *atoles* or corn tortillas. The fresh fruit possesses little to no glochids, but brush first to be sure. Slice off the skin before consuming. The fruits can be eaten raw, blended and stirred into summer drinks, or used to accompany tequila (for its sour and salty flavor). They are quite cool: I have seen a drink made of the mashed fruit, sugar, and salt bring an unaccustomed traveler back from the edge of heatstroke under the hot summer Sonoran sun. The sap was a favored food, used by the Seri tribe in Sonora, Mexico, to make *atole*. After toasting the dried sap over hot coals, it was ground into a powder and dissolved into water while adding wild honey.

Future Harvests

There currently seems to be no danger of losing cholla populations, but I do suggest transplanting (by a single 6-inch stem cutting) favorable specimens to your yard, neighborhood, or property. Select plants which have few glochids, or those whose buds can be easily harvested, as all specimens are not the same in this regard.

Cautions

Don't eat more than half a dozen fruits too quickly as they can promote loose stool.

Ripened cholla fruits often remain on the cactus through winter. The inner sour flesh is edible.

cocklebur

Xanthium strumarium

cadillo

`EDIBLE` seeds

Cocklebur's sweet, nutty seeds are reminiscent of its close relative, sunflower.

How to Identify

Cocklebur is perhaps easiest to identify in its fruiting stage, as it is named for its dark brown, burred seedpods (which purportedly inspired the idea for hook and loop tape, also known as Velcro®) which cling to the terminal stems. When young, the rough, triangular-shaped leaves resemble those of sunflower (a close relative), and you may find numerous red-purple blotches along the stem.

Where and When to Gather

Look to seasonal drainages, river beds, and disturbed ground. It is best to avoid cocklebur growing near large agribusinesses. Gather the seedpods when brown and fully ripened, usually late summer.

How to Gather

Use gloves. Cocklebur is prickly and can cling stubbornly to the stem of the plant. I like to pick them individually and toss them in a paper bag or bucket as I gather them. I've had good luck cutting through the pods with pruners—they are pliable and don't crack or split well.

How to Use

The seeds can be eaten as snacks like sunflower seeds. Traditionally, they were made into a meal or paste and cooked as cakes, perhaps with other seed flours. Cocklebur leaves were used among indigenous foragers of the Sonoran Desert in their process of pit-roasting or fermenting mesquite pods.

Future Harvests

Cocklebur is often plentiful where it grows and mostly overlooked, if not frowned upon. As usual, simply gather what you can use and leave the rest.

Cocklebur's burred seedpods occur all along the stem.

The stem of cocklebur is often covered in purple splotches.

dandelion

Taraxacum officinale

diente de león

`EDIBLE` leaves, stems, flower buds and flowers, roots

This vibrant green, ubiquitous, so-called weed is either overlooked or deeply appreciated, depending on which camp you're in. To foragers, dandelion is a go-to edible with myriad culinary possibilities.

One can often find flower buds, open flowers, and closed flowers on one dandelion plant.

How to Identify

The serrated leaves of this perennial forb are often apparent during our winters in the Southwest. Dandelion leaf stems can be tinged purple, and the tips often look like a blunted arrowhead. Dandelion often hugs the ground, as if afraid to grow above 4 inches in height (an inherited trait induced by lawnmowers, no doubt). The flowering stems are round and hollow, exuding a milky white latex when broken (as does any part of the plant). The bright yellow inflorescences may contain forty to over one hundred florets per head. When mature, the flowers become the blow-away feathery seed puff beloved by toddlers. Dandelion's tap root has a beige-brown skin covering the off-white root flesh.

Where and When to Gather

Look for dandelion in disturbed areas, lawns, riparian areas, coniferous forests, or just about anywhere ample moisture is found. The particular type of habitat within our range will vary a bit depending on moisture. Otherwise, dandelion is everywhere. The roots are best gathered in late autumn and winter. Harvest leaves before the plant flowers, and collect the flowers whenever they are available. The leaf stems can be picked at any time, and when blanched by the surrounding vegetation, may contain very little bitterness.

How to Gather

Most edible parts of a dandelion can easily be gathered by hand. The roots will likely require a digging device, unless they're in your garden bed. A hori-hori can make this extraction very easy.

How to Use

The variety of foods and drinks prepared from dandelion is impressive, belying its vilification by the proponents of a perfectly uniform lawn. The leaves, flowers, and roots can be used in salads, soups, syrups, beer, wine, coffee substitutes, chai, ice cream, jellies, infused honey, vinegar infusions, fritters, cakes, pancakes, breads, muffins, egg dishes, and pesto. They can also be fermented and pickled—and certainly many more options exist. Although dandelion leaves are bitter, don't let this deter you. A splash of vinegar or slightly pickling them in a sweet vinegar solution can gently ease this bitterness. Or simply jump in and embrace the bitter bite as our ancestors did before us. Plump dandelion roots may be roasted in butter with spices such as wild oregano. When roasting the inulin-rich roots, they become sweet, as the inulin is converted to fructose, a readily available energy source when consumed.

Future Harvests

Gather away. Dandelion is in no immediate danger (or long-term danger, most likely).

Cautions

You may do well avoiding bitter dandelion greens if you suffer from active biliary blockage, since this herb is an effective stimulant to bile production.

The flower buds of dandelion can be pickled or eaten in salads.

dayflower

Commelina species

`EDIBLE` entire plant

Found throughout our region, dayflower is an abundant, crisp vegetable with a spicy tuber.

How to Identify

Commelina species all possess three lavender petals (a white lower petal in some species) with a yellow center on the flower. They often grow in dense clusters carpeting the ground, emerging from an edible elongate tuber. They have a somewhat grassy appearance. Although it grows in open areas, dayflower may be found in forests as well. The key identifying feature is the spathe just below the flower. It is often marked with red to purple streaks.

Where and When to Gather

Both native and nonnative dayflower can be found in good numbers from spring to fall throughout most of our region, and at elevations of 4000 to 9000 ft. You may even see it growing as a landscape plant or a weed in your neighborhood if you are at the eastern edge of our region. As they are so variable in their habitat, you can always be on the lookout. Dayflowers require more moisture than your average desert perennial. They can be gathered whenever you find them, as they are perennial.

Top view of whitemouth dayflower (*Commelina erecta*) in flower. Note the pale lower petal.

How to Gather

Simply snip off the spathes (flower clusters) and nibble or toss them into salads. Dig the whole plant, clean off the tubers, and separate them. The roots of whitemouth dayflower are known to be stout.

How to Use

Dayflower blooms make a nice trailside snack. The aboveground portions can be boiled, sautéed, or lightly baked. Once cleaned, the tubers can be eaten raw, although some people claim stomach upset (perhaps due to the tubers' spiciness). The small tubers can also be baked, boiled, or chopped and sautéed; cooking will solve any potential digestion problems. Once boiled, dayflower tubers can be smashed and blended with butter and salt. An infusion of the plant was traditionally used to strengthen tuberculosis patients.

Future Harvests

To maintain populations, never gather more than a quarter of a dayflower stand. As with so many of our herbaceous perennials, dayflower's survival is dependent upon an overall ecology. As long as our forests survive, plants like this will have a future. You can transplant tubers in the fall to your home garden or to a wild place that seems advantageous to dayflower's proliferation.

A plentiful harvest of spicy dayflower tubers and flower clusters, ready for the kitchen.

desert hackberry

Celtis pallida

spiny hackberry, garambullo, granjeno

`EDIBLE` fruit

Desert hackberry can produce tremendous amounts of juicy orange fruit each summer. Fortunately, the birds tend to leave plenty for us to gather.

How to Identify

Desert hackberry is a medium-sized shrub with a rounded crown and smooth gray bark. It is most often around 5 to 7 feet in height, although it can approach 15 feet. It is one of the last desert shrubs to lose its leaves during the dry autumn season. However, it will drop its leaves in response to freezing temperatures and leaf out again in March or April. Its flowers are very tiny and escape the notice of most desert-goers. Desert hackberry's somewhat curved, darker green, and quite full appearance sets it apart from nearly all other desert fruiting shrubs.

The fleshy, round fruit of desert hackberry is orange when ripe.

Where and When to Gather

Desert hackberry occupies seasonal arroyos (washes), and *bajadas* of our desert mountain ranges throughout the southernmost portion of the Southwest. Found in desert riparian areas, it grows underneath mesquite or canyon hackberry. Look for desert hackberry fruit about midway through summer, once the rains have saturated the ground. The ripe orange berries, or drupes, will persist on the shrub through October, often drying on the bush. These dry fruits can be exceptionally sweet.

How to Gather

Simply pick the fruits one by one with your fingers. Due to the plant's thorns, one must pick berries slowly and carefully. There are no simple techniques to remove these fruits. If you could somehow shake them down you'd have to contend with spiny branches to gather off the ground. Bring a bucket, cup, pot, or paper bag, and pick to your heart's content.

How to Use

Desert hackberry fruit is some of the sweetest found in the Sonoran Desert. Nibble off the fleshy fruit and spit out the hard seed, or crunch the whole fruit. The fruits are much sweeter after sun drying and can be stored on the shelf indefinitely. Cook into jelly or make into jam if you like the crunchy seeds. With the addition of warming spices such as ginger, cinnamon, and nutmeg, desert hackberry fruit makes a wonderful sauce that can accompany various meat dishes. Bake the whole fruits into bread for a crunchy surprise, or add to stews when a sweet flavor is desired.

Future Harvests

During good years, foragers will be hard-pressed to pick all the fruit they find, even if they devote every waking hour to doing so—while eating berries along the way for sustenance. When out gathering, toss some fruit in areas where you'd expect desert hackberry to grow well (beneath trees in an arroyo or alongside other shrubs on the hillsides).

Desert hackberry is often found at the edge of seasonal desert washes.

desert willow

Chilopsis linearis

mimbre, flor de mimbre

`EDIBLE` flowers (for tea)

The delicate sweetness of the desert willow flower makes a lovely sun tea.

Desert willow flowers emit an intoxicating scent which permeates the moist, fresh air of spring evenings.

How to Identify

The crown of a mature desert willow tree is often as wide as it is tall. The tree is leafless during winter, but puts out numerous long, thin, green leaves on yellow stems (which can turn purple with age) throughout the summer. There are two varieties of flower colors—pinkish white and lavender-purple. Both have yellow markings on the hairy inner throats of their flowers (as do the devil's claw flowers). Flowers appear in clusters at the branch tips. The tree's bark is light gray and smooth when young, becoming checked with long, dark, vertical stripes with age. The seedpods are long and slender, becoming tan with age while splitting up the side to reveal neatly tucked rows of winged, feathery seeds.

Where and When to Gather

This tree occupies sandy washes, but can

be found in desert riparian groves and at the edges of desert grasslands. You will also find it used in landscapes extensively throughout the Sunbelt. Once you've identified a local population in a wash, or in a friendly neighbor's yard, you can visit there throughout the summer.

Desert willow prefers riparian or desert riparian habitat, and can be found near the edges of desert grasslands.

How to Gather

Begin by gathering flowers recently fallen to the ground (they will still appear fresh) or lightly pull on flowers still on the tree. Pollinated flowers will come off very easily. When there has been no rain, you can also gather recently dried flowers from the ground.

How to Use

One method of making sun tea is to fill a large glass jar about half full with fresh flowers, continue filling the jar with fresh water, and let it all sit in the sun for three to five hours. Strain, cool, and enjoy. You can add sweetener if desired, but many folks love the light, natural sweetness of the blossoms. Once shade dried, the blossoms can be added to a variety of flower, herb, or tea blends. They add a brilliant color to your cup, plus an array of bioflavonoids. The flowers have traditionally been used as a heart or lung tonic; leaves and bark have been used as a medicine for a variety of ailments, including wound wash, cough, poor lymphatic flow, fungal infections, and lung infections.

Future Harvests

This harvest poses no threat whatsoever to the populations of desert willow. A mature tree produces thousands of flowers annually, and picking the pollinated flowers does not affect further formation of flowers, fruits, and seeds. One option is to plant a desert willow near your home where rainwater or transferred graywater is collected in earthen basins, therefore providing shade for your home, habitat for wildlife, and a nourishing tea in season.

Use fresh desert willow flowers for sun tea.

devil's claw

Proboscidea parviflora

unicorn plant, cuernitos

`EDIBLE` immature fruit, seeds

Devil's claw is a unique vegetable with a flavor quite similar to cucumber.

How to Identify

The annual, sprawling herb devil's claw grows to a height of about 3 feet tall, at most. The opposing, broadly triangular leaves are borne on robust glandular stems. Clusters of numerous flowers appear above and below the wide, sticky leaves. These flowers are quite similar in form and color to those of desert willow, with pink, purple, yellow, and white shades. The elongated fruits are most significant in that they possess curling horns at the end, which come to a fine point. The outer flesh of the green pods is sticky and hairy. The dry, split fruits will persist in the area for months if not years, often grabbing your attention by clinging to your shoelaces or socks.

The edible fruits of devil's claw are often found hiding beneath its large leaves.

Where and When to Gather

Devil's claw is found throughout the bulk of our region's western half. It inhabits desert washes, edges of riparian areas, desert flats and *bajadas*, and disturbed sites. The plant germinates with the summer rains or in the spring if there's ample moisture. Fruits quickly form and are available for harvest by midsummer and into the fall if rainfall continues. The seeds are gathered from the mature, dry fruit. The related species *Proboscidea louisianica* (ram's horn) is found from eastern New Mexico into the Oklahoma panhandle and throughout Texas, in grasslands and sandy areas, and can be used similarly. Although quite similar in appearance to *P. parviflora*, its flower petals are dull white to lavender. This species has also been cultivated for making pickles.

How to Gather

Simply pluck the soft, unripe fruit of devil's claw from the stem. Once the fruit becomes fully elongated and stiff it is no longer desirable as food. The mature, dry fruit, once gathered, must be pulled apart and the seeds removed from the two inner chambers. The deepest chamber may require a pointed tool for digging out the soft, white or black seeds.

How to Use

The flesh of the young, soft devil's claw fruit can be eaten raw; the green skin is bitter. Otherwise, quickly simmer the fruit in boiling water to remove the bitterness and prepare as desired—options include whole with butter and salt; sliced and mixed with other veggies; and added into casseroles, salads, burritos, or ferments.

The whole young fruit can be pickled in vinegar. The seeds can be used when making a traditional indigenous trail mix.

Future Harvests

Always leave at least half the fruit in a population for reproduction. There are numerous species and cultivated varieties of edible *Proboscidea* plants. Try cultivating some in your garden or on your property where seasonal rainfall collects.

Closely related to devil's claw, desert unicorn-plant (*Proboscidea althaeifolia*) can be used in the same ways as *Proboscidea parviflora*.

dewberry

Rubus species

`EDIBLE` fruit, leaves (tea)

A tasty relative of both raspberry and Himalayan blackberry, dewberry is ready to pick by early summer in the Southwest.

How to Identify

Arizona dewberry is a woody vine with deciduous leaves that creeps along the ground, well armed with sturdy hooked spines. The stems can be bright red. The three- to five-parted, widely spaced leaves are pronouncedly toothed along the margin. Similar to other *Rubus* species, the underside of the leaf is a much lighter gray-green. The white, five-petaled flowers appear in terminal clusters of one to eight individual blossoms on short, lateral branches. The berries ripen from green to dark red-purple. Southern dewberry (*Rubus trivialis*) is a closely related plant with a similar appearance and similar fruiting habit. Its fruit is also edible and tasty.

Where and When to Gather

Look to shady areas at mid-elevation canyon bottoms, springs, riparian areas, and wetlands. The fruit begins to ripen as the lower elevations heat up to 100 degrees F, usually by the second week of June. Dewberry species of East Texas (*Rubus aboriginum*, *R. trivialis*, *R. apogaeus*, *R. flagellaris*, and *R. lucidus*, for example) can be found beneath tree cover or in open sun, on disturbed ground such as the edges of drainages, or in wooded habitat margins. These species all share a similar appearance.

A Texas native, southern dewberry (*Rubus trivialis*) fruits from late spring to early summer.

How to Gather

Gather carefully, as the unforgiving, ubiquitous spines of Arizona dewberry are relentless in their capture. The fully ripened berries should not be piled high in your bucket or they will crush and spoil quickly in the heat.

How to Use

Dewberries are a delicious foraging nibble. If you're fortunate enough to gather enough to bring home, you can cook dewberries into jellies, jams, syrups, pies, and more. *Rubus* species fruits, in their beautiful simplicity, may congeal and sweeten to perfection when cooked without the addition of any substance, either pectin or sugar. The leaves make a pleasant, tart tea.

Future Harvests

Gather these fruits conservatively where they are sparsely populated. Scatter seeds from ripe fruits to areas which seem suitable for dewberry's growth.

A ripening Arizona dewberry (*Rubus arizonensis*).

dock

Rumex crispus
curly dock, yellow dock, lengua de vaca
Rumex obtusifolius
bitter dock
Rumex hymenosepalus
red dock, tanner's dock, pie plant, wild rhubarb, yerba colorada, caña ágria

`EDIBLE` leaves, stems, seeds, flower stalks

Use versatile dock in many ways: tart greens with garlic and onion, ground seeds as flour, and red dock's stems and flower stalks in pie and tea, respectively.

How to Identify

You may first notice dock in the spring when its bright green leaves emerge looking something like a rolled tongue. All the leaves will be emerging from the ground at this stage. The long leaves have a noticeable yellowish-white midrib which contrasts against the green leaf. Its

Clusters of luscious, young curly dock leaves are perfect for harvesting for food or tea.

margins are wavy. Red dock leaves emerge grayish green with a thick, red-striped midvein. Dock's flowering stalk, or cane, emerges from the center of the basal leaf growth extending above the leaves. In red dock, this stalk is often tinged red. The cane puts out dozens of insignificant and tiny greenish-white flowers which have no petals. In red dock, the seed heads are much more noticeable than the flowers, turning brick red as they mature. Dock plants turn a rusty brown through the summer and into the fall. The potato-like tubers may look tempting, but are high in tannins and inedible.

Where and When to Gather

Dock prefers moist, sandy, well-drained locations, whether streamside, lakeside, in open meadows, or in desert canyons. It can be found throughout our region, with the exception of southern New Mexico and South Central Texas. Red dock is most prominent in the western half of our range. New leaf growth will emerge below maturing seed heads. In addition to the spring gathering season, one can find dock greens re-emerging in mid-to-late summer in response to rain; look for red dock leaves October through April, depending on location. Harvest large, mature red dock leaves for a rhubarb substitute six to eight weeks after they emerge; flowering stalks can be found between January and May. For dock's seed harvest, wait for the whole seed cluster to dry and turn a rusty brown. Mature red dock seeds will appear a few weeks after the plant flowers.

Dock seeds ripen in early summer.

How to Gather

Harvesting dock is as simple as cutting back the leaves at their base. I prefer the leaves closest to the center of the bunch, as they are youngest. You can even harvest leaves which have not yet unfurled; they are the most tender. The leaf and stem can both be eaten. With red dock, you can strip the green leaf and use just the midrib as a rhubarb substitute. Flower stalks can be cut or broken off from the center of the plant. The seed heads can be harvested similarly—simply cut the stalks and collect them in paper or cloth bags or buckets. Seeds can be removed from the stalk later, or you can whack the seed head in the bag to remove it from the stalk, then rub off the outer sheath to expose the hard seed.

How to Use

I was first shown this plant in Guatemala by a *curandera*, or native healer, by the name of Juanita. Doña Juanita told me that I should eat dock greens every day and I would never fall ill. Sautéing them with garlic and onions and having them with scrambled eggs made this sound like a pretty good plan. Simply chop up the whole leaf and add to onion and olive oil or butter in a hot skillet. Spice it up with wild oregano. Cook a large batch with a bit of water, butter, salt, black pepper, and cream (or a substitute) for a classic creamed green. Fresh leaves do contain oxalic acid, so if that is a concern, simply make sure the leaves are always cooked before eating. In addition to the nutritious greens, both the flowering stalk and the seeds of curly dock are edible. Given the name *caña ágria* in Sonora, Mexico, the sour stalk was once made into a refreshing tea during the summer. The flowering stalks are gathered fresh then cut into pieces to be boiled in water. Once cool, strain and add sugar and ice—or simply dilute with honey while the tea is still warm. Red dock's large, fleshy

The reddish midrib at the base of each red dock leaf can be used like rhubarb stems in making pie.

When red dock is in flower or has gone to seed, gather the whole seed head and stalk and chop up for a chilled tea.

red midribs are a flavorful substitute for rhubarb in pies. As a member of the buckwheat family, dock's seeds can also be made into a flour. The seeds, once processed, can go into any recipe calling for buckwheat—biscuits, pancakes, breads, and muffins.

Future Harvests

Dock is considered an invasive or noxious weed in many states, and lots of people would be happy to not have any future harvests. Harvesting the leaves will not endanger a good-sized stand, though, and I doubt you will share the negative view of it once you come to know this plant and its range of edibility. Take no more than a third of the visible flowering stalks. When gathering seeds, harvest no more than half of what you see in a certain patch. Given its numbers across the Southwest, and the concern over its spread, dock is a viable food for a great many people.

Cautions

Fresh dock leaves do contain oxalic acid, and red dock contains tannins as well. These can produce digestive upset for those with sensitive systems. If this is a concern, one may wish to limit their intake of fresh dock.

elder

Sambucus species
elderberry, tápiro, sauco

EDIBLE flowers, fruit

Cherished by bears and birds alike, elderberries are the quintessential intersection of food and medicine. Versatile, plentiful, and a prime food for foragers.

How to Identify

Although this account covers elder and its species and subspecies as a group, there's a good variation in appearance and taste among the elders in our region. They range in height from 12 to 25 feet. All in our area have a characteristic leaf formation, color, and smell. The scent is considered rank by most; in my opinion it smells of skunk and peanut butter—combined. The leaves are pinnately compound with five to eleven (depending on the species) serrated leaflets, ovate to linear in form. The trees grow fast (as much as 8 feet of vertical growth in a season), and the stems and trunks consist of a soft, pithy core. Thus, they are prone to dropping branches and full trunks. The flower clusters consist of dozens of tiny, white to cream-colored, five-petaled flowers that produce yellow pollen in the spring. The clusters of berries are known as cymose panicles. Blue elder is commonly believed to have the tastiest fruit, although this is contingent on harvesting at the appropriate stage of ripeness. American elder (*Sambucus canadensis*) lacks the essential elderberry tartness. Berries from our low-elevation Mexican elder (*Sambucus nigra* subsp. *mexicana*) in the western portion of our region have a tart, sometimes sweet, flavor (with fruit ranging from blue to green to white). American elder can be identified by its darker, shiny fruits.

Where and When to Gather

Elder trees prefer moist habitat: a seasonal desert wash or canyon, an area adjacent to a pond, or atop high mountains where annual precipitation is greatest. Each elder has its own particular flowering and fruiting season. Mexican elder, found in the southwest quadrant of our region, fruits first around the end of June. It can flower any month of the year if it's not too cold and there is ample moisture. As you move north and higher in elevation, the season continues for Mexican elder, culminating in late September and early October. Black elder can be found in the eastern portion of our region, among the confluence of oak woodlands, piney woods, and hardwood forests, and amid swamps and bogs.

Mexican elder (*Sambucus nigra* subsp. *mexicana*), often found at the edge of a seasonal wash.

Elder flowers can be gathered any time they are present. Berry clusters of elder trees ripen in stages throughout the season. There are numerous ways to determine if berries are truly ripe; in fact, I consider ripe a relative term. From year to year, sweetness may vary. A silvery bloom will appear on the ripe berries of blue elder and Mexican elder. The fruits will be blue to dark purple-black underneath the silver. Make sure none of the berries in the cluster are green or red, as they aren't ripe yet. Also, look for red pedicels (the long stems which hold the fruit clusters). Certainly, most ripe fruit clusters will become pendent—although not-quite-ripe fruit clusters also hang down, giving the

tree a droopy appearance. Perhaps the most important characteristic of fully ripened fruit is the relative brittleness of the pedicel. As the fruit becomes fully ripe, the tree begins to usher nutrients elsewhere and the stem becomes dry and brittle and snaps more easily under the weight of the ripe cluster (this test for ripeness may not yield massive harvests, but it will ensure that the berries you gather are fully ripened).

How to Gather

Using a pair of sturdy scissors or bypass pruners, clip the entire flower cluster and place it in a paper bag or basket. Alternatively, you can massage the semi-mature

Note the white bloom (yeast) on ripe blue elderberries.

flower cluster with your fingers, enabling the pollinated flowers to fall off and into your gathering bag.

Once summer arrives, prepare for a bountiful berry-gathering trip by bringing two plastic buckets with handles—just remember you will need to carry them back again when full. I prefer to walk about the grove or population of trees before I begin picking, in order to surmise the harvest and arrange it so I can arrive back at my starting point as the buckets become full rather than having to walk back from the farthest point with full buckets. You'll need no more than your hands for gathering. Simply pinch the cluster of ripe fruits with your thumb, index, and middle fingers, then twist or break it off and toss the whole cluster into your bucket. Another option is to garble berries directly off the stem into your bucket; this way all your processing is done directly off the stem in the field, rather than at home. I feel that harvesting berries on the stem provides a sort of cushion when piled up in the bucket, so they don't get crushed before you begin to process them.

How to Use

Elder flowers make a wonderful, cooling tea and have a variety of medicinal applications. Most culinary uses of the flowers involve using the fresh blossoms. Elderberries can be both food and medicine. Raw Mexican elderberries can cause nausea upon ingestion of even small amounts, and berries from the red elder (*Sambucus racemosa*) may be toxic if eaten fresh—so cook them both to eliminate this problem. Mexican elderberries can also be dried. Cooked elderberries are delicious, and can be fried whole as battered fritters; used in a variety of smoothies and fermented drinks (often with the addition of lemon); cooked into jellies; added to pancakes, pies, compotes, cobblers, breads, and muffins; and even made into ice cream. With the addition of honey, the fresh juice of the berries can be cooked into a delicious and highly regarded syrup. Elderberry wine and mead are traditional across cultures around the world. It is quite possible some of the berries' medicinal qualities are enhanced by fermentation. If you have a surplus of fresh fruits, freeze or dry them for later use. If drying, be careful to spread the fruit out and allow for adequate airflow. A dehydrator is advised, as these fruits mold easily. Elderberries are nutritional powerhouses marked by high levels of anthocyanins.

Future Harvests

Always leave plenty of elderberries for the birds, bears, deer, and other wildlife. They do a great job of planting elder where it will thrive. Elder prefers a certain habitat that normally includes ample moisture. Continuing and rapid loss of the Southwest's ground water has greatly reduced its former range of distribution. High-elevation elder seems to be less at risk. I advise planting an elder tree around your home where graywater- or rainwater-harvesting earthworks have been implemented. This could ensure an annual harvest for you and your family.

epazote

Dysphania ambrosioides
Mexican tea, wormseed, skunkweed
`EDIBLE` leaves

Pungent epazote is known for its presence in pots of Mexican beans. Its high mineral content and numerous medicinal uses are other great reasons to keep it on hand.

How to Identify

Although the doubly serrated leaves of epazote range in color from bright to pale green, and the leaf shape and size vary depending on conditions, all epazote leaves end in a point. The stems develop numerous vertical grooves as the plant matures. Similar to the blooms of the closely related lamb's quarters, epazote flowers are difficult to see with the naked eye—but you will know the plant is flowering by the presence of the blossom clusters near the top of the plant. Tiny hairs, as well as splotches of red, can be found along the stem. For some, the scent alone is enough to identify epazote, a smell expressed

Young epazote greens are prime for picking.

variously as reminiscent of gasoline, kerosene, skunk, lemon, or citronella. You be the judge.

Where and When to Gather

Originally found from equatorial South America north to southern Mexico, epazote has now colonized much of North America. Look primarily to disturbed soil and areas which humans regularly inhabit; it is also found in large numbers along the Gulf coastline. Leaves can be gathered whenever present. In some locations, this is close to year-round.

How to Gather

When young, the tender leafing tips can be broken off. I like to use these for a stir-fry side dish to accompany steak. Otherwise, pluck the needed leaves directly from the stem and more will continue to grow.

How to Use

Either fresh or dried epazote leaves can be used to flavor beans. Use about 1 teaspoon dried leaf per pound of beans, or 4 to 8 fresh leaf sprigs approximately 4 to 6 inches in length. This traditional practice is said to alleviate the gas and bloating which are known to accompany bean dishes. The fresh leaf sprigs can be lightly and quickly sautéed in olive oil with a bit of chopped garlic—a pungent side to accompany a steak or fish fillet. Fresh leaves are also added in small amounts to quesadillas and egg dishes. The decoction or infusion of the leaves is a traditional ingredient in many dishes of Latin America, such as chicken soup and mole. Although much of the traditional medicinal application of epazote involves the distillation of the essential oil from the seed, the leaves can still be used sparingly. Traditionally, the seeds are used as a tea as a vermifuge, for diarrhea, stomachache, diabetes, and respiratory ailments.

Future Harvests

Considering how prolific epazote is, and the small amount we use, there's not much concern here. If you or some other creature introduces it to your garden, you'll soon have more than you'll know what to do with.

Cautions

I caution against using the seed for culinary purposes until you know the plant better, as the concentration of the potentially toxic essential oil is ten times greater in the seed than the leaf.

evening primrose

Oenothera elata

Hooker's evening primrose, flor de San Juan

EDIBLE flowers, leaves, roots, seeds

Evening primrose offers the forager a variety of options throughout the year—from starchy, spicy roots to oil-rich seeds.

An autumn basal rosette of evening primrose is easily identified.

Evening primrose often has flowers and seedpods from spring to autumn.

How to Identify

Look for evening primrose's star-shaped basal rosette of leaves in the autumn or early spring. These leaves are generally 4 to 10 inches long with curled margins. They are clearly distinguished by the milky white midrib, which may have a touch of pink. As spring warms, the central flower stalk emerges, from which appear large yellow flowers with four heart-shaped petals. The stigma or female portion of the flower is shaped like a cross. The flower stalk (2 to 6 feet in height), maturing seedpods, and older leaves will begin to turn brick red in the autumn. Evening primrose flowers always change color as they die back.

Where and When to Gather

Look to desert washes and riparian areas at lower and middle elevations, as well as mountainsides at higher elevations. The tap roots are best gathered in the fall or early spring (look for the small rosettes of leaves). The seeds can be gathered in abundance from large stands in the late summer and early autumn. The tender leaves are best gathered from the flowering stalk. Flowers can be plucked at any time.

How to Gather

Dig up the carrot-like tap roots of evening primrose by excavating and loosening the earth around them. This is easiest in moist, sandy soil. You can keep the attached, spicy leaves as part of your harvest, or compost them at the digging site. The leaves along the budding stalk are most tender. Pluck these off along with the flowers any time either are present. The seeds can be gathered into a paper sack, tub, skirt, sheet, or bucket by whacking plants that have ripened seedpods; use a 2-foot-long stick of about 1 to 1½ inches in diameter. Or simply break off the entire stalk of ripened seedpods, place the stalk in your harvesting container, and process at home. The flowers and leaves of low-growing annual and perennial evening primrose are also edible.

The root of evening primrose is best harvested in the autumn or early spring.

How to Use

For a spicy, starchy side dish, sauté the evening primrose young roots (briefly boil to soften if using midspring roots) in butter with a little salt. Integrate them into a full meal by boiling in soup, purée-ing along with garlic and carrots or beets, or baking the chopped roots with your favorite root vegetables. The young, tender leaves combine well in leafy green salads or can be steamed or sautéed briefly. The flowers, of course, are a beautiful, vibrant addition atop any meal. The seeds are the source of evening primrose oil, commonly found in health food stores for its unique omega-6 fatty acid, gamma linolenic acid (GLA). You can add these to your diet by simply dry toasting the freshly harvested seeds in a pan and grinding, or adding whole seeds to granola, muffins, breads, and salads.

Future Harvests

As a biennial, evening primrose normally produces seeds across a portion of its local population. Keep this in mind when harvesting the roots or seeds, and allow for some to continue their growth cycle, renewing the local seedstock.

farkleberry

Vaccinium arboreum

huckleberry

`EDIBLE` fruit

Farkleberry, a tree-like relative of the blueberry, produces prodigious amounts of sweet-tart fruit.

Farkleberries hang from long pedicels. They can be numerous on a branch, but they don't grow in clusters.

How to Identify

A farkleberry trunk can approach 12 inches in diameter (but is often 1 to 3 inches), with a hue of light reddish brown in the furrows of the scaled bark. The solitary flower pedicels (stems from which the flowers and fruit hang) are often longer than the fruit itself. This is different from highbush blueberry (*Vaccinium arkansanum*), a closely related shrub found in far eastern Texas, on which several flowers and fruits grow from a single cluster. Elliot's blueberry (*V. elliotii*), also found in far eastern Texas, is a deciduous shrub growing from 5 to 10 feet at maturity, with pale pink flowers appearing in clusters near the branch ends. Farkleberry presents the classic *Vaccinium* strategy of maximizing sun exposure by spreading its leaves in a nonoverlapping array.

Where and When to Gather

Look in the relatively acidic, dry, sandy soils of pine woodlands that grow in East and Central Texas and Oklahoma to find this hidden treasure. The farkleberry is not a prolific shrub in its range, but can be locally abundant. The berries begin to ripen in early autumn and continue to ripen into winter. Notice how the pedicels go from green to brown as the fruit ripens. The berries are somewhat mealy and tart even when fully ripe, with a thick skin on the fruit and small seeds.

How to Gather

The berries fall off easily when fully ripe.

How to Use

Farkleberries are a great trailside snack. Bountiful harvests can be dried, made into jelly, cooked in pies, or used in your favorite fermented beverage. Related species highbush blueberry and Elliott's blueberry are also considered to be tasty.

Future Harvests

Make sure there are plenty of these plants in your area before picking. Although there are nearly a dozen native *Vaccinium* species, they are relatively scarce within our range. Oftentimes, doing less or nothing is the wisest action to preserve future harvests. Also consider using this lovely shrub in your private landscaping.

Notice how the leaves of farkleberry splay out in order to take in as much sunlight through the upper canopy as possible.

filaree

Erodium cicutarium

stork's bill, heron's bill, alfilerillo

EDIBLE flowers, young leaves

Frequently occurring filaree often goes unnoticed. The elegant, feathery leaves are quite tender when young.

How to Identify

Filaree often hugs the ground as its stems radiate out three hundred sixty degrees from the central tap root. The slightly hairy stems are reddish brown, while the feathery, pinnate leaves are sparsely hairy as well. The five-petaled, red-lavender flowers are often numerous per plant, while seeds are already forming, or mature. Curiously, the appendage of the mature seeds can coil up before your eyes once it emerges from the fruit (along with four more seeds). Texas filaree (*Erodium texanum*), which is also useful, has dissected leaves similar in appearance to the closely related geranium.

Where and When to Gather

Cultivated fields, waste places, and disturbed ground along the flood plains of

The five-petaled, pink flowers of filaree are edible.

seasonal drainages are all likely places to find filaree. In years of ample winter and spring rains, it can also be found in sizable numbers across mesas. Look to gather filaree when the leaves are young, in the spring. Texas filaree is found scattered throughout our region in dry, open sites below 5000 feet.

How to Gather

In a great field of filaree (not entirely uncommon) one can thin the population by pulling up entire plants. Simply grasp all the stems emanating from the central tap root and pull. The young roots can also be eaten, but best in moderation. Otherwise, pluck tender, green leaves from younger plants. The season can be short, but can come around again with ample rainfall.

How to Use

Add filaree to salads, soups, and stews. I could see it working well with parsley in a tabouleh. Add a few leaves to a cup of tea, particularly in the spring; it has a mildly stimulating effect on the liver. The tea is astringent, but mild.

Future Harvests

As filaree is considered a noxious weed in many locations, gather at will.

Cautions

Excessive consumption could induce constipation.

Filaree's seedpods (or fruits), though not edible, give rise to another common name of the plant: stork's bill. Notice the similarity of filaree fruits to the seedpods of other members of the geranium family.

firethorn

Pyracantha coccinea
scalet firethorn

EDIBLE fruit

A deliciously tart flavor, brilliant red-orange color, and easy access to the main ingredient: all excellent reasons to try your hand at firethorn jelly.

Firethorn possesses sparse foliage and ample fruit.

How to Identify

Firethorn is a woody evergreen shrub with whorls of small dark green leaves clinging to the stem. The leaves have smooth or serrated margins and can end in a tiny, fine point, or not. The branches, covered in smooth reddish-brown to gray bark, come off the main stems nearly at right angles. White, five-petaled flowers appearing in clusters at the branch tips indicate it is a member of the rose family. The correct word for the berries is pomes. They are 1/4 to 1/2 inch in diameter, and ripen to a bright red to reddish orange. The leaf shape and size, serration, height of shrub, coloration of pomes, and overall shape can vary among *Pyracantha* species found in our region, but all have edible fruit.

Where and When to Gather

Native to southeastern Europe, but now used in landscapes throughout the Southwest, this evergreen can occasionally be found as a naturalized escapee. It otherwise prefers parks, yards, gardens, and occasionally waste areas. The fruits ripen in the late summer.

How to Gather

Simply pull off the ripe berries—individually, or in clusters.

How to Use

Firethorn pomes are considered to be high in vitamin C. Their flesh is mealy at maturity, not unlike manzanita berries, with numerous small, angular seeds in the middle. The berries are cooked into a jelly by decocting in water, mashing, then straining the fruit juice before adding the sugar and pectin. The resultant tea will be a reddish brown. Alternatively, use this tart liquid as a base for any sauce or syrup. Add spices such as oreganillo, wild oregano, wild onion or chiltepín, and sugar, and cook down to make a unique accompaniment to roasted meats and vegetables.

Future Harvests

Firethorn pomes are easy to gather from your neighbor's yard (with permission, of course). Or plant one in your own yard.

Cautions

It is recommended not to eat the seeds of firethorn, as they contain cyanogenic glycosides (for example, the cyanide-producing amygdalin in apple seeds is a cyanogenic glycoside). Cooking the pomes and straining out the seeds is the recommended safe method for consuming firethorn.

fragrant flatsedge

Cyperus odoratus
rusty flatsedge

EDIBLE pollen, leaf base, rhizomes, seeds

The rhizome of fragrant flatsedge has a sweet starch which can be chewed or pounded to extract. The tender leaf base is reminiscent of heart of palm.

The flower spikes of fragrant flatsedge turn rusty brown in the late autumn.

How to Identify

This herb is an annual or short-lived perennial occupying disturbed areas with ample moisture. The stems, or culms, form a triangle in cross section, but the leaves (beneath the inflorescence) have a V or W profile. The cyclindric, rusty brown, terminal spikelets of fragrant flatsedge set it apart from other *Cyperus* species. The thin, elongated rhizome is white at the center. Other edible species of *Cyperus* from our region include *C. aggregatus*, *C. esculentus*, *C. rotundus*, and *C. squarrosus*.

Where and When to Gather

One can find fragrant flatsedge throughout our range along shorelines, in disturbed muddy places, and in fresh or slightly brackish marshes. Fragrant flatsedge is scattered throughout our region from the east to the west. The rhizome can be gathered at any time, but is best harvested before the plant flowers. Pollen is gathered in the spring, and the leaf bases are available throughout spring and summer into autumn. The thin, brown seeds (achenes) are gathered in summer.

The tender leaf base of fragrant flatsedge is a sweet delicacy.

How to Gather

To gather the leaf base of fragrant flatsedge, simply pull up on the stalk until it snaps free from the rhizome. Then peel away any fibrous green layers by hand until the tender, white stalk is left. The rhizome must be pulled up from the muck. Hands often work better than a shovel to extract the rhizome, as wet ground is too soft to pry against. In drier ground, a digging stick or shovel works well. The pollen can be gathered into a wide, shallow basket by knocking the inflorescence by hand or with a stick. The seeds can be gathered similarly.

How to Use

Fragrant flatsedge's tender leaf base makes an excellent vegetable, suitable for salad or light stir-fry, or for steaming. The rhizome produces a sweet, starchy flour. You can dry the rhizome, blend, and sift to get the flour. Or pound the fresh rhizome underwater to separate the fibers, then decant and dehydrate the settled starchy powder to save for later use. This flour can be used in breads, biscuits, pancakes, confections, smoothies, or any baked good. The flavor is slightly sweet and sour. The pollen and seeds can be used similarly to the rhizome flour. Seeds of fragrant flatsedge were historically gathered for food by the people of the Cocopah tribe.

Future Harvests

Gather no more than a quarter of a patch's rhizomes in a given year. Allow plenty of pollen to remain, for fertilization and seed production. Harvest no more than half of a given population's seed production in a year, then skip the following year at least.

gooseberry

Ribes pinetorum

orange gooseberry

EDIBLE fruit

A deliciously sweet fruit, gooseberry can taste like thick raspberry jam when fully ripened.

Gooseberry possesses thin, delicate leaves sticking out from a spiny stem.

How to Identify

Gooseberry is a deciduous shrub with long, wispy branches covered in thin, short spines occurring in pairs along the rusty brown stems. The deeply cleft, round to triangular leaves appear in the spring in whorls adjacent to the flowers (and eventually the fruit). The pale orange flowers occur singularly, with the petals reflexed, creating the appearance of a speeding rocket. The fruit is covered in a spiny skin, maturing from pale yellow to a deep purple. Leaves begin to yellow with the first cold nights of late summer.

Where and When to Gather

Gooseberry can be found in coniferous forests of higher elevation in the western portion of the Southwest. The plant likes shady areas, such as beneath mixed conifer canopies and at the edges of high mountain creeks. Find it along roadsides amid aspen groves. The ripe fruits are available midsummer.

How to Gather

Pick the fully ripened, deep purple berries with gloved hands, or lightly touch the fruit first to make sure the spines have softened (the spines become less stiff as the fruit matures). The flavor of fully ripened berries ranges from tart to richly sweet. I believe weather conditions have a lot to do with the development of flavor.

How to Use

I tend to eat most of what I gather right off the bush. When substantial, the fruit pulp can be squeezed out of the spiny skin and laid out to dry as a fruit leather, or cooked with a bit of water to make jam.

Traditionally, the fruits were ground and compressed into cakes, then dried for winter storage.

Future Harvests

Since this shrub is spread largely by bird dispersal, it is wise to leave ample berry supplies for the birds to consume and propagate.

Fully ripe gooseberry fruit is dark red-purple with soft spines on the skin.

graythorn

Ziziphus obtusifolia

bachata, lotebush

`EDIBLE` fruit

The desert shrub graythorn provides another nutritious seasonal berry to forage beneath the shade of towering mesquite trees.

Graythorn is indeed gray when leafless, but takes on a greener tone once it leafs out in response to seasonal moisture.

How to Identify

Its name provides a significant clue about what to expect when looking for graythorn. Drought deciduous, it drops its leaves when the moisture is gone. When leafless, it stands out as a light gray-green zig-zag of short, sharp twigs on a usually tall, upright shrub. Appearing as thorns, the branch tips are sharp and pointed. The leaves are a light green and attach directly to the stem. Leaves can be egg-shaped, elongate, pointed, or blunt, also sparsely toothed or with wavy margins. The ripened berries, appearing mid-spring on short gray stems, are perfectly round and dark blue-purple with a slight bloom (possessing a thin white coating which easily rubs off). This shrub can grow 12 to 15 feet high in shady conditions.

Where and When to Gather

Graythorn can be found throughout our range, primarily in desert grasslands and desert riparian areas. It often grows as an understory in mesquite bosques (forests). The fruits can ripen and disappear quickly—within one week—so don't delay. They will become ripe with the onset of hotter, drier weather in midspring.

However, make sure fruits are ripe before harvesting, to avoid an upset stomach.

How to Gather
Pick by hand. Move about the branch picking the dark blue-purple (almost black) ripe berries; several can be gathered in one pull when they are bountiful. As they are relatively dry berries, they stack well in a small bucket or bag without spoiling.

How to Use
Eat sweet, ripe graythorn berries on the trail while hiking. A good harvest can be used to make jam, jelly, syrup, or sauce. To release the juice, barely cover the berries with water in a saucepan and simmer on low, while smashing the fruit away from the large seeds. Strain and use the brown juice as desired. The whole, dry fruits (including seeds) can be ground into a powder and used in breads and cereals. The seeds are high in linoleic acid.

Future Harvests
Be sure to leave an ample amount of berries for the birds as they are the main dispersal mechanism for these shrubs.

Graythorn berries occur singly or in clusters along the thorn-tipped, gray branches.

greenbrier

Smilax species

catbrier, bullbrier

EDIBLE fruit, leaves, rhizome, shoots, stems

Greenbrier makes for a delicious and tender green wherever it's found.

The tender young leaves, stems, and tendrils of greenbrier.

How to Identify

Greenbrier is a perennial vining plant with spines along the stems and dual tendrils emerging from the leaf bases. The central leaf veins appear parallel as they travel without intersection from the leaf base toward the tip. The leaves are alternate and generally well spaced along the stem, with smooth margins, appearing heart shaped at the base. Clusters of tiny greenish-white flowers arise from the leaf axils, with female and male flowers appearing on separate plants. Thick clusters of blue-black, and in some species red, berries appear on female plants in the autumn.

Where and When to Gather

Greenbrier is only found in the far eastern portion of our region, inhabiting roadsides, the margins of woodland areas, and other disturbed sites. The tender leaves and stems can be gathered beginning late winter through to autumn. The large rhizomes can be gathered any time of year. Berries, though often considered flavorless, ripen in the autumn.

How to Gather

Similar to harvesting asparagus, reach down a tender stem of greenbrier from the tip and bend back where it becomes rigid to break it off. These sections should be free of spines. In the spring, shoots should somewhat resemble greenbrier's distant relative, asparagus. The rhizomes must be dug up, which sometimes can require a lot of digging or even heavy machinery, as they can approach the size of a large child or young adult. However, the most tender and appealing part of the rhizome is the new growth (white) emerging from near the base of the stems.

How to Use

Greenbrier's tender stem tips, new shoots, and still-soft leaves of spring are wonderful vegetables. They can all be consumed fresh, lightly steamed or sautéed, or simmered briefly into soup. Extracting the rhizome starch is far more laborious; some say more energy is burned in the procuring and processing than is gained in the consumption. The rhizome may be pounded underwater to separate the starch from the fiber. The water is then poured off, leaving the wet starch at the bottom. Or, slice or chop the fresh rhizome, dry it, then grind it into a powder, sifting out the fibrous material. This starch has been made into drinks, soups, and jellies, and combined with cereal flours to create bread, cakes, and puddings. The rhizome of a species of *Smilax* was used in the original root beer, known as sarsaparilla. New rhizome growth is white and tender, and can be cooked into soups and stews. The berries can be eaten fresh or made into a jam or jelly if sufficiently sweet. Bland berries with a gummy texture were often used as chewing gum.

Future Harvests

When new greenbrier stems are harvested, the plant resprouts vigorously from the broken point. If gathering rhizomes, ensure there are sufficient plants in the area to warrant the harvest. Gather berries only when plentiful, and consider introducing the seeds into areas which appear to be a good habitat for greenbrier.

Greenbrier's flower clusters emerge from the leaf axils.

ground cherry
Physalis species
tomatillo, husk tomato

EDIBLE fruit

Ground cherries are enjoyed throughout the world for their tart-sweet flavor and the variety of ways they can be prepared.

How to Identify

Ground cherry is an herbaceous annual in our region In general, the plants appear similar to a garden tomato, growing to about 2 feet in height in a rounded form, with mostly upright stems. The flowers and fruit emerge from the leaf axils. The calyx swells over the pollinated ovary, creating the husk around the round, marble-sized fruits which turn yellow to orange when fully ripened. Ripe fruits will be lying on the ground beneath the plant, but the unripe green fruits will remain attached within the enveloping husks. There are twenty-one different species recorded for our region, with only one nonnative species: *Physalis philadelphica*.

Where and When to Gather

Ground cherry can be found in a variety of habitats within our vast region: prairie, desert grasslands, mountainsides, oak woodlands, canyons, coastal areas, and hardwood forests. In general, the fruits ripen late summer to early autumn.

How to Gather

Time it correctly, and you can gather the fully ripened fruits within their handy,

The green, bell-shaped calyx of ground cherry will cover the young fruit as it grows.

biodegradable packaging right off the ground. The fruits will be sweet and yellow to orange color when ripe. If fruits are green or bitter, they are not yet ripe and it's best to at least cook them or allow them to ripen up before eating.

How to Use

Fully ripened ground cherry fruit can be eaten raw or made into a fresh salsa with onions and cilantro, for instance, but may cause irritation in some individuals when eaten to relative excess in the raw state. Otherwise, cook the fruit into jam, sauce, and syrup, or add to stews and soups. They impart a sweet, tart flavor that is delicious unto itself. One of my all-time favorite backpacking meals involves some spicy dried beef strips cooked into a soup with a couple handfuls of ripe, sweet ground cherries and fresh sprigs of wild oregano.

Delicious and fortifying! Indigenous peoples of North America dried the fruits for winter storage, reconstituting them for use. *Physalis* species have also been used for medicine in a variety of ways—mostly topical—throughout North and South America for a very long time.

Future Harvests

Always leave extra fruit behind to be dispersed by animals for reseeding. You may be able to cultivate these plants near your home. Simply scatter the seed before the warm, rainy season.

A peek at an immature green ground cherry fruit within its calyx.

hackberry

Celtis laevigata
sugarberry
Celtis reticulata
canyon hackberry

`EDIBLE` fruit

Sweet hackberry fruit has been foraged since ancient times. The berries make a tasty drink or trailside nibble.

How to Identify

The bark of hackberry is smooth and gray when young, then begins to grow vertical stalagmite-esque ridges with age. The base of the leaf is asymmetrical like an elm tree. The flowers of hackberry are not easily noticed. Its leaves drop during the winter. Although there are two or three species within our range (depends who's counting) there is virtually no difference in how one harvests and eats them.

Where and When to Gather

Hackberry has one of the widest ranges of all our edible plants—particularly tree species. It covers our entire region. In the

Ripe hackberries still present in the autumn season.

western half of our area, look in canyons and mesquite bosques, however in the eastern third of the Southwest, it begins to emerge as a roadside weed and is considered a trash tree—you will find it everywhere. The fruit of hackberry takes particularly long to mature. It can sit on the stem as a green fruit for several months before its sugars ripen. This usually takes place no earlier than mid-September. Fruit will remain on the tree for several months if not eaten by birds; hackberries are a favorite of cardinals.

How to Gather

As ripe hackberry fruits don't readily fall from the tree, one is often relegated to what can be reached from the ground or by climbing up into the tree. Fruits are essentially ready for eating, storing, grinding, or for making tea as soon as they are picked.

How to Use

Although I primarily use hackberries as a nibble while hiking, there are a variety of ways these fruits have been prepared and preserved. Indigenous foragers would often grind the berries into a powder, then form the powder into cakes once moistened. Berries were also mixed with a source of fat, rolled into balls, and roasted by the fire. These could be preserved for a short length of time. Jelly can be made. A sweet, nutritious sun tea is made by pouring boiling water over the berries and infusing for several hours or overnight. Although the fruit contains very little edible pulp, once ground, the whole fruit can be

consumed as an ingredient in *atoles*, breads, and cakes.

Future Harvests

As mentioned, hackberry is considered a trash tree in the eastern third of our range. However, it would be a desired species to have growing near your home in the drier western portion of our region, though it might require supplemental irrigation. Simply allow the birds to eat their share and they will do an excellent job of spreading the seeds under the canopy of mature trees.

Hackberry tree at the mouth of a canyon.

harebell

Campanula rotundifolia
bluebell

`EDIBLE` flowers, leaves, stems

The flowers of delicate harebell lend a splash of vibrant color to a plate of foraged food creations.

Harebell flowers often appear to be in pairs, but are on separate pedicels.

How to Identify

Harebell is an herbaceous perennial that grows from the taproot up to a height of 2 feet. The smooth, thin, wispy leaves occur sparingly along the stem. The nodding, bell-shaped flowers provide a pop of brilliant lavender against the often verdant forest of its surroundings. Harebell flowers are found on separate pedicels and give the impression of blooming in pairs. The lobes of the flower are somewhat reflexed.

Where and When to Gather

Harebell is found throughout the western half of the Southwest within the mid- to higher elevation range (4600 to 8200 feet). Look along moist, shady slopes within coniferous forests, and along embankments above mountain creeks.

How to Gather

Gather the flowers individually by hand.

How to Use

Harebell flowers make a beautiful edible adornment to any plate of food—a wonderful way to brighten up an in-the-field meal made with foraged plants. The flowers can be added to herbal infusions as well. Another idea would be to make harebell syrup or candied harebell, presuming the flower color is retained in the preparation process. The fine leaves and tender stems can be eaten raw in salads or salsa, or chopped and briefly cooked into soup, egg dishes, or a stir-fry.

Future Harvests

When harvesting harebell as a vegetable, be sure your harvest area can sustain the intended amount of gathering. If it can't, move to a different area, harvest minimally, or refrain from gathering. Although this plant can be locally abundant, in some years it may exist marginally in some locales.

henbit

Lamium amplexicaule
dead nettle, giraffehead

`EDIBLE` flowers, leaves, stems

A pleasant-tasting herb, henbit is perfect for salads and adds a splash of vibrant color.

How to Identify

Henbit rarely grows above a foot in height, and possesses the classic mint family attributes of opposite leaves and square stems. The pink flower is elongate and narrow, giving it the whimsical appearance of a giraffe's head. The lower lip of the flower is white with pink spots, or it may be entirely pink. The triangular, ovate, opposite leaves are clearly lobed and show obvious leaf veins. If you look closely, you'll see hairs on the leaves. The stems are often tinged brick red.

Where and When to Gather

Henbit can be found scattered throughout our region. Primarily found in waste places, lawns, gardens, agricultural areas, and

The terminal clusters of pink flowers make this low-growing plant from the mint family most noticeable when in season.

riparian areas (basically, disturbed areas which receive ample moisture). It becomes available during the cool and damp season (winter to spring, depending on your locale). Harvest and eat henbit as long as the leaves are green and healthy. The season normally extends into midspring, perhaps early summer.

How to Gather

Simply pinch off what you prefer to consume and keep it fresh until you're ready to use it—henbit is best consumed fresh within a day or so of gathering. There's no need to harvest the roots unless you're attempting to eradicate it from your garden.

How to Use

Henbit has a wonderfully soft texture, perfect for salads. It also can be steamed, sautéed, or blanched. I would suggest blanching quickly and straining thoroughly before sealing in freezer bags, if you wish to store it for later use. Ready access to quality, nutrient-rich greens is an excellent reason to incorporate this humble plant into the diet. A tea of the plant is pleasant tasting and mildly diaphoretic (it induces sweating; thus, potentially useful with cold or flu) when consumed hot.

Future Harvests

This naturalized European annual is doing just fine on this continent, thank you very much. If you wish to cultivate henbit, you can bring seeds in from wherever you discover it. Sow seeds throughout your garden beds or in the disturbed areas of your yard which retain extra moisture (look to north-facing sides).

Himalayan blackberry

Rubus armeniacus

zarzamora, blackberry

`EDIBLE` fruit, shoots

A wildly popular and widely available food for foragers in some locales, Himalayan blackberry fruit ripens to a juicy, tart sweetness in the heart of summer.

How to Identify

Himalayan blackberry is a many-branched woody shrub with sharply angled canes (in cross section) or branches. It can cover large swathes of terrain, creating impenetrable thickets. The serrated, three- to five-part leaves are green above and greenish white below, with fuzzy white hairs on the surface. Red coloration may be present on the stems and sturdy, recurved thorns. The numerous flowers, each with five white-pink petals, grow in terminal racemes which extend beyond the leaves, seemingly floating above the plant. The aggregate berries are comprised of numerous black drupelets and are a similar size and shape to a thimble. However, unlike other *Rubus* species, Himalayan blackberry does not possess the internal depression made by leaving the protruding thickened stem, or torus, behind. Instead, it is whole.

Where and When to Gather

Himalayan blackberry can be found within moist canyons at middle elevation in the western third of our region. Being an introduced perennial species, it is most likely encountered near old homesteads or around older settlements and roadsides. Look for the ripe berries at the height of the hot, dry summer (June into July). Other edible *Rubus* species known variably as blackberry can be found in Oklahoma, East Texas, and along the Gulf Coast.

How to Gather

Process slowly and carefully. The thorns of Himalayan blackberry are unforgiving. Don't be tempted to extend beyond your reach into the twisted mat of thorny branches. You will be sorry. Although often tart and lacking sweetness, blackberries are best picked (like so many fruits) in the several hot, sunny days following significant rainfall, just before they come into ripeness. Then they will be full, juicy, and decidedly sweet.

How to Use

Besides gorging oneself on the sweet berries beneath the dappled shade of a riparian forest alongside a rolling creek (What could be better?), the berries can be gathered for making jam, jelly, syrup, and wine. Add fresh blackberries to homemade ice cream, quick breads, pancakes, muffins, pies, and cobblers. Mixed fruit creations can be particularly intriguing.

Future Harvests
Rubus armeniacus is a naturalized, nonnative plant, considered an invasive species in some states due to its capacity to colonize vast areas and limit the growth of native vegetation. Harvest at will, and plant in your own yard only with thorough consideration for its known tendencies.

Cautions
Move around the plant carefully lest your clothing (and flesh) get torn to shreds.

Himalayan blackberry leaves are divided into five parts.

horseweed

Conyza canadensis

Canadian fleabane, mare's tail, cola de zorra

EDIBLE young leaf tips

The zesty, aromatic young leaves of horseweed make a flavorful spice and a medicinal infusion.

How to Identify

Horseweed is an annual, emerging in spring as a collection of basal leaves with widely spaced, sharp-toothed margins containing fine white hairs. Oftentimes, the petioles and midribs are red. The leaves are often 2 to 4 inches in length, and the entire plant can grow to 11 feet tall, but is more commonly 3 to 6 feet within our region. After growing for six to eight weeks, the flower buds emerge and the plant elongates and branches at the leaf axils to accommodate more flower heads. The numerous small inflorescences are yellow at the center. There are confounding, closely related *Conyza* species, but they are much shorter and the leaves are much thinner. You will get to know the exact nature of horseweed leaves with practice.

Where and When to Gather

Horseweed is found across North America. Throughout our region it is common as well as locally plentiful. It prefers areas with ample moisture such as river drainages, shady forest margins, roadsides, and garden beds. The young leaves can be harvested from the young plant or at the tips before it begins to flower. Flowering is

Young horseweed plants produce many alternate leaves which are sparsely toothed. The plant likes to inhabit disturbed ground and waste places.

from May to August, depending on your location.

How to Gather
Simply snip off the young, flexible, tender leaf tips of horseweed, or pull up young plants to thin stands. These plants often grow in large patches and produce great quantities of seeds.

How to Use
I have sautéed a bit of the fresh herb with scrambled eggs, dropped it into boiling water, dried it for a spice, and added it to kimchi or other vegetable ferments. Its aroma is similar to our locally prominent false tarragon. Due to horseweed's relatively high quantity of essential oils, this plant is well suited to medicinal applications. Traditional treatments include for rheumatism, internal bleeding, digestive erosions, and as a diuretic.

Future Harvests
Not to worry. So long as we have disturbed ground, horseweed will be with us.

Cautions
This spicy plant can cause contact dermatitis with prolonged direct contact to the skin (for example, if you carry an armload of freshly harvested plant material against bare skin).

Notice the short, fine hairs along the leaf margin, which are also found along the main stem.

Indian tea

Thelesperma megapotamicum

cota, Hopi tea, Navajo tea, greenthread

EDIBLE leaves, flowers, stems (as tea)

The preferred tea of the Southwest, Indian tea is enjoyed hot or cold, sweetened or unsweetened. Generations of native families have gathered this herb for tea, medicine, and dye.

How to Identify

Individual flower heads of Indian tea occur on long, thin, smooth, blue-green stems. The peduncle is barrel shaped and like the flower stems, smooth and blue-green. When opened, the flower top is yellow, comprised of numerous disc flowers. The leaves are opposite and can appear threadlike, especially when the plant is in flower. Longstalk greenthread (*Thelesperma longipes*) is very similar in appearance and can be used interchangeably.

Where and When to Gather

Indian tea occurs throughout the western half of our range, into western Oklahoma. Popular locations are abandoned roadsides, feral gardens, or the occasional clearing in piñon-juniper habitat. Unfortunately for us, Indian tea really likes roadsides. If you know the road well, and it's rarely used, you may choose to gather there. Historically, the herb was foraged for tea, medicine, or dye before the summer rains arrived—in other words, during the hot, dry season.

The composite flower clusters of Indian tea are found at the end of long pedicels.

How to Gather

Clip Indian tea from the base and bundle to dry. Follow the traditional gathering technique by folding several flowering stems of the fresh herb (4 to 5 inches long) upon each other. Then wrap the thin ends of the stems around, to tie the bundle together. Bundles can be hung or placed in a basket to dry, out of direct sunlight.

How to Use

Use one bundle of the herb per quart of water for tea. Simmer 10 to 15 minutes and strain. Drink hot or chill. Sweeten if desired.

Future Harvests

If your location is appropriate, introduce the seeds into your garden or around your home. They can establish themselves through seasonal rainfall. Scatter them during the dry autumn season, or sow directly after winter rains have moistened the ground significantly. Although Indian tea is a perennial, always leave plenty behind in order to reseed for the future.

Bundling Indian tea stores the herb so it can be used to make tea any time of the year.

ironwood

Olneya tesota
palo fierro, tésota
`EDIBLE` flowers, seeds

Regal, frost-sensitive ironwood disperses great quantities of peanut-flavored, edible seeds across the hot, parched desert floor in the month of June.

How to Identify

Although ironwood may live for many centuries, its height rarely reaches above 25 feet in the hot Sonoran Desert. Ironwood usually possesses several trunks with light gray bark in long, thin strips. The deciduous leaves consist of numerous tiny, oval, pointed leaflets that fall off in response to a lasting freeze or significant drought. Short spines dot the smooth, gray bark of the younger branches, often falling off as the branch ages. Branch tips are often yellow-green. The white-pink (with a bit of yellow) flowers cover the leafless trees in the dry, hot spring, lending them the appearance of twilight in midday. Streaked, constricted pods that are a pink-orange hue dangle from the tree in the longest days of summer.

Where and When to Gather

Ironwood trees are found in the frost-free zones of the lower Sonoran Desert, in central and western Arizona, along with barrel cactus, cholla, jojoba, palo verde, and saguaro. The flowers and seedpods are gathered from early spring to early summer.

How to Gather

Both individual flowers and seedpods of ironwood can be plucked by hand from the tree. Oftentimes, clusters of seedpods can be gathered in one pull.

How to Use

Ironwood flowers make a lovely tea, and can be added to salads or atop any dish for a dash of color and vibrancy. The immature seeds can be eaten fresh from the tree once shelled, but may be too astringent to eat. Roast lightly in a dry cast iron pan once shelled. This halts the maturation of the seeds and lends a wonderful flavor reminiscent of roasted peanuts. Ironwood seeds make the cornerstone of a hearty Sonoran trail mix or granola recipe. Once seeds are mature, soak them overnight and allow them to sprout for a firm, tasty snack or salad ingredient.

Future Harvests

These ancient trees have withstood harvesting by numerous creatures and foragers alike, possibly for millennia. But if you're hearty enough to be gathering seeds

Ironwood seeds are ripening as the saguaro fruit is maturing.

by the bucketload in 105-degree heat, you may be in a class unto yourself.

Cautions

Cautions here are more environmental than culinary. Mind your immediate environment when harvesting from these desert centenarians. Tall cactus, short cactus, spiny shrubs, and snakes may be underfoot or at your side.

Ironwood blooms as the dry, hot summer commences.

jewel flower

Streptanthus carinatus

silver bells, golden bells, lyreleaf jewelflower

EDIBLE flowers, leaves, seedpods

All parts of tasty jewel flower are tender and highly palatable—a forager's delicacy when eaten raw.

How to Identify

This many-branched, herbaceous member of the mustard family (annual or biennial) is often noticed for its bell- or urn-shaped, creamy white, purple, or golden flowers which are found at the top of the plant. In fact, this rounded portion of the flower is the calyx, and the petals (if one inspects closely) are creamy white and tinged with purple. The fleshy, smooth, green leaves with milky white veins are pointed at the tip and clasp the purplish-green, ashen stem quite voluptuously. The flowers are followed by elongated green seedpods that are split into two cells (internally) and resemble somewhat flattened bean pods. The seedpods are about 2 inches long. The plant stands 2 feet tall.

Where and When to Gather

Jewel flower is found throughout the southwestern half of our region, after ample winter rains. Find it scattered through the desert on hills, in canyons, and along desert washes. For most locations, this means it's available as a food from February through April.

Jewel flower is unmistakable for its creamy white (occasionally yellow), bell-shaped flower base.

Note the milky veins of jewel flower on its pointed, clasping leaves.

How to Gather

The leaves, flowers, and green seedpods can all be pulled from the plant. If you coppice from a small population by taking a little from each plant (as opposed to pulling up entire plants), the population will continue to grow and the seed stock will remain abundant.

How to Use

All fleshy parts of the plant are delicious raw. You can also lightly steam, blanch, or sauté the green seedpods as you would green beans. The flowers make a beautiful garnish to any vegetable dish. The leaves can be sautéed or added to soups and vegetable ferments, and are perfect in salads.

Future Harvests

Gather seeds in mid- to late spring and scatter in areas which appear similar to where you've harvested them. Also scatter seed around your home, particularly in areas which accumulate water, such as in basins, near berms, or within depressions.

The bean-like seedpods of jewel flower belie its membership in the mustard family.

jojoba

Simmondsia chinensis
goat nut, coffee berry

`EDIBLE` nuts

Roasted and ground, the acorn-like jojoba nut makes a deliciously rich drink.

How to Identify

The evergreen jojoba shrub possesses elliptic, thick, leathery, grayish–green leaves which point straight up in response to the hot sun. Depending on growing conditions, jojoba can be a few feet to over 10 feet tall. Male flowers begin to appear in the autumn and open in late winter, followed by the female flowers (on separate plants). When present, the nut capsules hang downward and are a cinnamon brown.

Where and When to Gather

Jojoba is found in the far west of our region. It generally prefers gravelly

A female jojoba plant with ripe nuts remaining into the fall.

hillsides, or spaces among boulders, below 5000 feet. Look in southwestern Utah and in the Sonoran Desert of southwest Arizona, amid the cactus forests and desert grasslands. The nuts begin to ripen as early as mid-May and could persist on the female shrubs for several months. Javelina are regular browsers of these nuts. Jojoba is dioecious, meaning there are separate male and female plants. Only the female plants bear seed.

How to Gather and Process

Simply pick the nuts one by one from the shrub, or off the ground. The unshelled nuts can be rubbed across a rough surface to remove their light capsules, and then are easily winnowed.

How to Use

To prepare the nuts for a roasted drink, simply place in the oven at 300 degrees Fahrenheit for about 30 minutes. Allow to cool, then grind. For espresso-style brewing, leave as a coarse grind. Continue to a finer grind if a percolation or boiling method is desired. This is my preferred way to use jojoba nuts as food. The nuts can also be eaten raw, although due to the high tannin and wax content, they may cause an upset stomach. They are generally not considered a food among indigenous peoples of the region.

Future Harvests

Jojoba is not always an easy plant to grow. Look to local nurseries for transplanting at

Male jojoba flowers prepare to open in late winter.

your home or neighborhood garden. It normally takes about five years to ascertain whether a plant is male or female. Large stands often produce great amounts of seeds.

Cautions

Raw nuts may cause digestive distress due to their high tannin content.

juniper
Juniperus species

`EDIBLE` fruit

Juniper berries, noted for imparting a distinctive taste to gin and traditionally cured corned beef, possess a range of flavors from sweet to pungent.

How to Identify

Juniper trees are dioecious; plants have male or female flowers, meaning some trees will have fruits and others none. The fleshy, soft fruits go from green to red or bluish brown, perhaps yellow or orange, when mature. These berries, or cones as they're referred to botanically, can contain from one to several seeds. They often appear with a yeast covering known as a white bloom. There are junipers with tall, straight trunks unbranching for several feet—and there are junipers that send out numerous branches just above the ground, appearing like a bristly ball of green across the hillsides and mesas they inhabit. Trees can grow from 10 to 35 feet in height— then there is the prostrate or low-growing common juniper (*Juniperus communis*), which rarely exceeds 4 feet and is found at high elevations in the Southwest. Juniper leaves are made up of short scales, which can feel prickly to the touch. They will be rounded (not flat) in profile, with the exception of common juniper, which has awl, or needle-like leaves.

A dominant tree throughout Central Texas, Ashe's juniper (*Juniperus ashei*) is also found in Oklahoma.

Where and When to Gather

Look for juniper in desert grasslands, piñon forests, high plains, hill country, mixed conifer forests, and at the margins of oak groves. Junipers are varied, plentiful, and widespread throughout our region.

Although the berries become ripe beginning in late summer in some locales, they can be found on the tree for several months thereafter. Most of our junipers ripen to maturity within one year of flowering.

How to Gather

You will have to pick the berries one by one, or you can knock the berries to the ground by hitting the branch with a stick, if your timing is right. Place a sheet or tarp under the tree (where possible) in order to collect the fallen fruits. Gathering is easiest among softer-leaf varieties, and can be unpleasant with the sharply pointed leaves of common juniper. Use fresh or dry for storage.

How to Use

The flavor and texture of juniper berries vary tremendously from species to species and between locations. I have tasted everything from sweet pick-and-eat berries to those with a pronounced resinous flavor. In either case, you will have a valuable spice. Use the berries to flavor meat marinades, salad dressings, or vegetable ferments. Utilize the native yeast bloom (which presents as a white coating) to jumpstart a wild ferment or "beer." The yeast bloom can also season soups, stews, and vegetable dishes calling for some zing. Be aware that if you use whole berries in a dish, there are hard seeds within each berry. You can also process the fruit to remove the seeds if they're not being used strictly for flavoring. The sweetest fruits qualify for trail mix recipes. Get to know your local juniper berries, and how to best work with them to create the flavors you want.

Future Harvests

Don't damage populations by harvesting all the fruits available. If you live in an area favorable as a juniper habitat, consider planting some on your property.

Cautions

The most resinous berries should be used sparingly. Also, avoid the use of landscaped juniper berries (*Juniperus oxycedrus*, *J. sabina*) until you are sure of the species, as some cultivated species are believed to have toxic berries. This toxicity is, however, relatively mild, and even if you ate one fruit, the toxic effect would be quite limited.

The small maturing fruits of one-seed juniper (*Juniperus monosperma*) appear reddish purple in the early autumn.

lamb's quarters

Chenopodium species

goosefoot

`EDIBLE` flower clusters, leaves, seeds

Lamb's quarters leaves are both nutritious and delicious. I like to sauté them with a little bacon fat and favorite herbs.

As fall approaches at higher elevations, lamb's quarters goes to seed. The bountiful seed crop can be harvested for a variety of food applications.

How to Identify

The name lamb's quarters is perhaps misleading because of one of the plant's most striking features: the distinctly webbed-foot shape of its leaves. The leaves may be quite hairy, particularly in our desert climate, or they may be entirely free of hairs. The plant grows erect until it begins to branch, at the time of flowering. The flowers are practically invisible, but you will notice the dense clusters forming at the top of these annual plants, at which time the leaves become more sparse. The plant often takes on a marked brick red tone at this point in its life cycle.

Where and When to Gather

Lamb's quarters is found within a wide range of elevations, often in disturbed areas. It resides in agricultural fields, along trails, or in ground disturbed by livestock. At lower elevations it prefers desert riparian zones or shaded areas along hills and mesas. The leaves usually taste best before the plant goes to flower, although the mature leaves of some species, such as *Chenopodium album*, are still good as the plant ages. The immature inflorescences are gathered as they appear. The seeds are harvested once the plant begins to dry and die back.

How to Gather

When harvesting young leaves of lamb's quarters, snap them off where the stem becomes rigid. When gathering leaves from mature plants, pluck off the leaves

Young, tender tops of lamb's quarters, found in the disturbed ground of a canyon.

individually, or pinch with a thumb and forefinger and run your hand up the stem to remove the leaves. Break off the tender lengths of flower clusters with your hand. The seeds are gathered en masse once the plants begin to turn beige-brown. Simply shake the tops of the plants (or bat them with a short stick), allowing the seeds to fall into a wide mouth basin, paper bag, or skirt. You can also break off whole inflorescences to be processed and winnowed at home.

How to Use

The young leaves of some lamb's quarters species are eaten raw, while others are more palatable after cooking, such as New Mexico goosefoot (*Chenopodium neomexicanum*). I prefer to boil the leaves for a few minutes, strain them, and then combine them with already cooking sliced onion and bacon grease in a hot cast iron pan—a preferred way to prepare many wild greens. The taste and texture is very similar to spinach (and its nutrition is on par). Steam, bake, sauté or boil the flower clusters much as you

would broccoli. A close relative of quinoa and amaranth, lamb's quarters is our North American version of these gluten-free pseudocereals. To help remove the saponins (which may irritate your stomach), run cold water through the seeds for several minutes, then boil and discard the water. Toast and grind these seeds, or sprout as you might quinoa. Use the seed preparation as breading, combine it with other vegetables, or form it into cakes to fry or bake.

Future Harvests

Chenopodium album is considered an invasive weed across North America and it is often exceedingly profuse. To harvest in a specific location, scatter the seed from your favorite lamb's quarters patch into an area that appears to have similar characteristics.

Cautions

The saponins may irritate one's stomach for a short time, so process seeds and older plant parts in water first.

lemonade berry

Rhus aromatica
fragrant sumac, aigrito, limita
EDIBLE fruit

Tart and refreshing when just picked, lemonade berries make a delicious, cooling drink.

Tart, ripe lemonade berries.

How to Identify

Lemonade berry is a variable woody shrub, absent of foliage throughout the winter, then leafing out following a modest flowering in the early spring. The branch tips are often covered in a fine, soft fuzz resembling the texture and appearance of antler velvet. The three-lobed leaflets are often aromatic (hence, the species and varietal name) and they always lie below the flowers and fruit. The foliage of lemonade berry turns a vibrant yellow in the autumn. This species now contains a couple dozen varieties after being merged with a distinct species. They may all be eaten and used the same. Other edible species within our region include smooth sumac (*Rhus glabra*), Kearney's sumac (*R. kearneyi*), prairie sumac (*R. lanceolata*), littleleaf sumac (*R. microphylla*), and sugar

Prairie sumac, a related plant to lemonade berry, can be found throughout our region, but is predominantly located in Central Texas. Its berries are also edible.

bush (*R. ovata*). Fortunately, despite clear differences in leaf shape and formation, the fruits of these species all share a very similar color, shape, size, and formation, making them relatively easy to spot even when the species is not a familiar one.

Where and When to Gather
Moist canyons, oak woodlands, and rims of canyons in piñon-juniper forests are all likely places to find lemonade berry within our region. Fruits ripen as early as the beginning of summer, often remaining on the plant through fall (although progressively losing flavor as they sit).

How to Gather
Pick the fruits one by one by hand.

How to Use
Lemonade berries can be eaten or prepared fresh, or dried or cooked for storage. Most commonly, these refreshing yet nonjuicy, sour fruits are eaten raw to allay thirst, or

Notice the leaves of lemonade berry in three parts, with clusters of unripe, green berries.

were leached at some point to remove some of the tannins present. The fruits can also be cooked into a jam with the addition of water and sugar. Closely related fruits (*Rhus coriaria*) in the Middle East are cleaned, dried, ground, then added to the popular spice mixture za'atar, which includes salt, sesame seeds, and other herbs. This spice blend is commonly added to meat and rice dishes. Perhaps a southwestern za'atar could be made with our wild oregano, algerita berries, salt, and lemonade berry. The inner bark of lemonade berry was also traditionally chewed for nourishment. One could perhaps extract a flour from the bark similar to the preparation used for box elder bark.

Future Harvests

Harvest no more than a third to half of the lemonade berries you find, depending on how bountiful the local harvest is. Consider cultivating this showy plant with attractive fall foliage in the home landscape.

Cautions

Beware of botanical relatives poison ivy and poison sumac (both *Toxicodendron* species), neither of which have red berries. Poison ivy is found widely dispersed throughout our region, and poison sumac is only in the peat bogs of eastern Texas.

used to prepare a summer drink closely resembling classic lemonade. Traditionally, they have been pounded and ground into flour, with the flour being made into sun-dried cakes (for storage), mixed with powdered manzanita berries for a refreshing drink, cooked into soups, boiled with meats, and added to fresh mescál or cornmeal *atole*. I assume the ground fruits

London rocket

Sisymbrium irio

tumble mustard, hedge mustard, mostaza

`EDIBLE` flowers, seeds, young leaves

London rocket is a greatly overlooked, spicy green with health-enhancing qualities. It rivals horseradish in its pungency.

How to Identify

London rocket leaves are deeply divided almost to the milky white midvein, causing the leaves and stem to appear like a thick-toothed comb. As the plant matures, it sends up a central flowering stalk which becomes crowned with clusters of small, four-petaled, yellow flowers. Shortly thereafter, the seedpod emerges from the flower, elongating to several times the length of the flower. The plant turns a purplish beige once it has fully matured.

Where and When to Gather

A naturalized plant, London rocket is likely to be found in disturbed soils (gardens, roadsides, vacant lots, alleys, front yards, and such) throughout our range. The leaves are best gathered before the plant goes to flower. The time of year depends upon location, but the season lasts one to three months, depending on weather conditions. The flowers can be gathered at any time, and the mature seeds are harvested once the pods are no longer green and are beginning to dry.

How to Gather

Leaves and flowers can be snipped by your fingers. The seeds are perhaps best gathered by swatting the dry plants with a flattened piece of wood, while collecting the seeds in a wide bowl (or piece of fabric) below.

How to Use

As London rocket leaves are rather pungent and spicy, they are to be used sparingly—probably best as not the only greens in a salad, for instance. Several leaves chopped fresh and added to soups provide a vibrant piquant spice and a host of vital micronutrients. The leaves make a wonderful spicy pesto that's perfect to have on hand for the cold and flu season. The seeds are slightly sulphury (think cabbage, a fellow member of the mustard family), and after being toasted and ground, they make an excellent breading for various meat cuts. Combine with butter, olive oil, bacon fat, other freshly ground nuts and seeds, and your favorite spice.

Future Harvests

No worries—there is plenty of London rocket. However, if you manage to pick out most of the plants in your yard before they go to seed, the population may considerably diminish over several years.

A basal rosette of young London rocket leaves—the perfect stage to harvest greens for soups, stews, pesto, and additions to salad.

London rocket produces prodigious amounts of seed. Simply thresh into a bucket and winnow out the seedpods.

mallow

Malva species

common mallow, malva, cheeseweed

EDIBLE buds, flowers, leaves, seed capsules (pea), young roots

Our mallow lends a moistening sensation like that of its cousin okra, and presents many possibilities in the kitchen as both food and medicine.

How to Identify

With ample moisture, mallow can grow from 1 foot tall to over 6 feet, with a typical spread of 2 to 7 feet. Mallow produces round leaves with scalloped margins arising from long petioles, first from a central stalk, then later from peripheral stalks as the plant grows and branches off from the main, central stalk. There are tiny, fine white hairs dispersed along the stalk and stems. The tiny white to pinkish-lavender flowers are found nestled within the papery green calices, in clusters at the leaf axils. The seedpods, or peas as they're often called, are round and ribbed, some say resembling a cheese wheel. Depending on conditions, the stalks and maturing seedpods may be tinged with a purple-maroon color.

Mallow leaf (*Malva neglecta*) is reminiscent of marshmallow, hollyhock, and okra—other members of the mallow family.

Where and When to Gather

Mallow loves disturbed ground, roadsides, and waste areas, so gather this plant wisely, avoiding areas prone to toxic accumulations. You probably have some in your yard, which is an ideal place for harvesting if you know the conditions there to be safe. At our lower elevations, mallow thrives through the winter into spring, while elsewhere it is a plant of the summer into autumn. Gather the roots when the plant is still young.

Known as mallow peas, the immature seed capsules are found at the base of the leaf stem. They are eaten as a nutty snack, cooked as a vegetable, and whipped up into a creamy treat.

How to Gather

Pluck the young leaves on their stem by hand or clip with pruners. The flowers can also be gathered for decoration on a plate or within a salad. The largest seedpods are plucked off the stem individually—or strip the whole stem with your fingers when there's a large amount of mature seedpods and few leaves. Conversely, cut back whole branches and harvest the desired parts individually. The roots can be gathered just before the plant flowers to ensure they are most tender.

How to Use

A basic approach is to add young mallow leaves to a salad, stir-fry, or soup. I prefer to use them sparingly in a dish, for they are slightly rough when raw or a bit slimy (for some) if used in excess in a cooked dish. Boil the young roots and purée them until smooth. Add other vegetables for flavor and color. But there is so much more one can do with mallow. Meringue pies, gumbo, and thicker sauces or creams are just a few ways to amaze your friends in the kitchen with mallow. You can also make mallowmallows: a tea of the green fruits which is whipped into something akin to marshmallows. See the book *Edible Wild Plants* by John Kallas for a detailed recipe. A tea of the mallow leaf lightly sweetened with honey can be pleasing on a hot, dry day in the desert and is also relieving to a sore throat or cough.

Future Harvests

Don't pick all the plants in your garden if you'd like to see them come back again. Mallow enjoys a wide range, and as an annual plant, it often germinates robustly in disturbed ground. Simply scatter seeds over disturbed soil which receives moderate moisture if you are looking to introduce it to your yard.

Cautions

Because mallow favors roadsides and waste areas, avoid foraging in places where spray or soil contamination or toxic runoff are possibilities, or where pets frequent (unless you're foraging after a good rain).

manzanita

Arctostaphylos species

big bearberry, pingüica

EDIBLE fruit

The tart sweetness of fresh manzanita berries refreshes during the dry, hot weather that spurs their ripening.

Ripe fruits of pringle manzanita (*Arctostaphylos pringlei*).

How to Identify

Manzanita is a woody evergreen shrub ranging from 4 to 15 feet in height. The beautiful contrast of its smooth maroon bark with the gray-green of its foliage and the pinkish hue accompanying its new leaf growth allows this plant to stand out in its habitat. The pointy leaves are smooth and leathery and often point upward to avoid high sun. The flowers droop in clusters and resemble those of blueberry and whortleberry, other members of the heath family. Its yellowish-green, immature berries are somewhat juicy before ripening, when they become dark red-maroon, and more mealy and dry.

Where and When to Gather

Manzanita abounds throughout the West, often found across the dry, mountainous

Nearly ripened fruits of pointleaf manzanita (*Arctostaphylos pungens*).

How to Use

Since the moisture content of manzanita berries is already quite low, some choose to gather the green, or yellowish, unripe berries. These berries have more moisture, and lend themselves better to preparation of cider, jams, and jelly. The name manzanita is Spanish and refers to the resemblance of the fruit to tiny apples. You can mash the berries manually (or blend with enough water to cover) to extract the juice, before straining out the seeds and skins. Add honey or sugar for your favorite fermentation recipe. A boiled tea of the dry manzanita berries, soaked overnight, provides a refreshingly tart beverage, or an addition to your favorite summertime drink. Make a stronger tea and turn it into jelly with sugar and pectin. The leaves serve as a very useful astringent medicine for the urinary tract, akin to its botanical relative, uva ursi.

areas of our region. This rugged plant colonizes bare, disturbed ground, terrorizes lost hikers with its unforgiving branches, and gives shelter to ground-dwelling birds and rodents. Visit open, exposed hillsides and the edges of their drainages from 3500 to 8000 feet elevation, from late April through June. Take a stroll to discover which plants have managed to produce fruit that season, and take account. You may be in luck and fruits may be ready to gather, or you can revisit the spot within a week or so to see how ripening has advanced.

How to Gather

It is possible to gather manzanita berries at different stages of ripeness. Some prefer the still-green berries, while others wait for berries to be fully ripened. Possibilities exist for each. I suggest you bring a one- or two-gallon bucket, perhaps strung around your shoulder to free up both hands. With one hand holding the branch, pull down a cluster of berries, or pick them off one by one to avoid gathering unripe berries within the cluster. Some choose to wait until the whole bunch is ripe for ease of harvesting.

Future Harvests

Manzanita is alive and well in its current habitats. It serves the purpose of pioneer plant in much of the area it inhabits, making it a most adventitious grower. If your habitat is appropriate, consider planting seeds at home or looking into local nurseries dedicated to cultivating native vegetation.

mariposa lily

Calochortus species

Papago lily, covena

`EDIBLE` entire plant

A sweet, moist bulb, mariposa lily was once relied on heavily by indigenous peoples throughout the West.

How to Identify

As a member of the lily family, mariposa lily possesses flower parts in multiples of three, and long, thin leaves which appear grasslike. The plant rarely attains a height of more than 1 to 2 feet. The two-tone flower bud shows the alternating petals and sepals. Mariposa lily flowers occur in clusters of one to four and grow taller than the leaves. The colors of the delicate petals can vary widely within species, and from species to species. This plant possesses no aroma.

Where and When to Gather

Only found in the western half of our range, mariposa lily first emerges in early spring in the low desert throughout cactus forests and desert grasslands, and continues its season through the summer as you move

The brilliant orange blossom of desert mariposa lily (*Calochortus kennedyi*) delights in early spring.

up in elevation. *Calochortus* species are nearly impossible to find when not in season, as the leaves quickly wither and the seedpods are inconspicuous.

How to Gather

Nibble the flowers at your leisure, but have a digging tool ready in case you have an opportunity to harvest the bulbs. As the plants are often found in hard, clay soils, the anxious forager will easily cut the long, lithe stem before arriving at the moist bulb buried deep below the glaring heat of the sun. Gradually loosen all soil around the base of the plant to a depth of 8 to 12 inches, then pull the bulb out gently.

How to Use

A delectable trail treat on a hot, sunny day, mariposa lily bulbs are perfectly edible raw. Harvested in numbers, these starchy bulbs were once stored for extended periods of time as a main food source, often after pit roasting and sun drying. If you come across some, you may wish to roast or boil them as you would new potatoes. Porridge was made with the dried and pounded bulbs, and was used as a medicine for sore eyes and as a birthing aid among the Navajo.

Future Harvests

Due to the practice of fire suppression in western forests over the span of the twentieth century, we saw a significant decrease in the population of such plants as mariposa lily. So much so, in fact, that many foragers must have wondered how indigenous peoples harvested enough to sustain themselves. Studies have now revealed that periodic fires are essential to reestablishing populations of plants such as mariposa lily.

Sego lily (*Calochortus nuttallii*) is found in the northwest corner of our region.

melonette

Melothria pendula

creeping cucumber, Guadalupe cucumber

EDIBLE green fruit

The green fruit of melonette possesses a burst of sweet and sour, cucumber-like flavor.

How to Identify

Melonette is in the cucumber family, so it resembles many of the conventional garden plants found in that family, such as cucumber, melon, squash, and gourd. You are likely to find it creeping up fences and shrubs, clinging with its small, spiraling tendrils. The leaf is about as wide as it is long, and pointed at the tip. The tiny flowers are yellow with five notched petals. The small fruits are not much longer than 1 inch and hang down from the attached vine. The young, edible fruit is speckled with white.

Where and When to Gather

Melonette is found in the far eastern portion of our region; look to slightly disturbed areas with a bit of sunlight and ample moisture. You may find it growing along fences or at the margins of forests. It is possible to find this plant in fruit most of the year in the milder climate of our eastern edge. Only pick the green, unripe fruit—once melonette has ripened to a purple-black color, it is known to be a strong laxative.

How to Gather

Simply pick the green, unripe fruit of melonette from the vine (and eat on the spot if you so desire).

How to Use

Although there is no processing needed to enjoy these tiny fruits, an ample amount can be harvested for consuming at a later date.

Future Harvests

Since melonette seems to do well along margins, it is likely to increase in numbers as we continue to build more and cut forests. If you would like to increase your odds of finding this tasty treat, simply scatter some seeds near your home's fence line or root a cutting to plant near your home.

Cautions

The point cannot be stressed enough: green, unripe melonette fruit is completely safe to consume, however, the ripe purple-black fruit is said to be an emphatic laxative.

Melonette growing at the Houston Arboretum in early October. Pick only the green, unripe fruit; do not eat the fruit once it turns purple-black.

This cross section of the edible melonette fruit shows the immature seeds.

mescál

Agave species

árbol de maravillas, pitera

EDIBLE base of flower stalk (heart), leaf base, leaf buds, flower buds and flowers, flower nectar

An essential traditional wild food for the Apache in the Southwest, imported mescál can still be found in supermarkets today. Its taste is smoky sweet with a rare richness.

Mescál flowers once in its lifetime, then dies.

How to Identify

Mescál is a succulent plant with rigid evergreen leaves formed in a rosette, often thickened at the base, each ending in a sharp spine. The leaf margins are covered in curved teeth, with the exception of shindagger agave (*Agave schottii*). Flowering once in its lifetime, each individual plant extends a rapidly growing, pithy flower stalk often exceeding the height of the leaves by several times. The yellow flowers are sweet, aromatic, and numerous. The dry fruit capsules contain flattened, black seeds. Approximately thirty-six native and naturalized species of *Agave* can be found growing in the United States and nearly two dozen of these can be found within our region. The uses listed below overlap among all the species found within our region.

Where and When to Gather

Various *Agave* species can be found from the northwest corner of our region (southern Nevada) down to the southern tip of Texas. Although the leaf bases and hearts can be gathered at any time of year, they are best and sweetest just before flowering, or whenever fully moistened by recent rains. The flower stalk, flower buds, and flowers are only available in the spring, during the single flowering event of the plant's life.

How to Gather

The leaves can be severed with a compact handsaw, sharp machete, or long-bladed knife. The unopened flower stalks can be cut similarly. Gathering the heart will require digging up the entire plant (or wedge-cutting the base), then cutting off all the leaves but two (to use as a handle when tied). You may need a ladder to harvest any flower parts.

How to Use

All parts of fresh agaves contain a caustic agent, which is removed by boiling or roasting. The processed hearts can be mixed with other foraged foods (berries, seeds) and pressed into cakes for storage. The fermented drinks mezcal (not the same as mescál the plant) and pulque are prepared from this roasted heart. With the addition of water, the sugars are fermented and drunk (pulque), or distilled into mezcal. The leaf bases and unopened flower stalks can be roasted and the sweet juice extracted from the tough, indigestible fiber. The flower buds and flowers can be boiled, strained, and added to soups. Desert inhabitants have long known how to survive without water by consuming the partially roasted leaves or flower stalks of various *Agave* species. Additionally, *Agave* species possess a high concentration of inulin, an indigestible starch, or prebiotic, considered to benefit the health of our digestive microflora.

The traditional preparation of agave hearts requires a labor-intensive pit roasting. First, a wide, shallow pit is dug to accommodate the harvest. Then, a substantial wood fire is set. The fire is either within a rock-lined pit, or the rocks are piled on top of the wood to be burned. Once the fire has burned down to coals, and the rocks are sufficiently hot (up to several hundred degrees Fahrenheit if done correctly), a pile of fresh plants or cacti is placed onto the rocks, and the prepared hearts are in turn placed on that pile. This steam-cooks the agave hearts. The entire pile may be covered with heaps of green vegetation and soil, or with corrugated metal sheets. The roasting lasts from one to seven days, depending on the size of the roast and temperature. Once cooled, the hearts are removed and sliced. They may be pounded, dried, and stored indefinitely.

Future Harvests

Keep in mind that whenever you harvest the heart of this plant, you kill the entire plant. If you gather the flowering stalk, the plant will die without reproducing.

Considering that these plants live for ten to twenty years or more before flowering, substantial harvesting can and has caused significant disturbance among wild populations. Seek permission from landowners before harvesting mescál on private lands.

Cautions

The entire plant possesses caustic, irritating substances when fresh. Heating or drying destroys these substances. Reactions to fresh agave juice vary from species to species, and from person to person. But a residual rash may linger for several days and be quite uncomfortable.

A pit-roasted heart of cultivated mescál, with leaves removed.

mesquite

Prosopis species

`EDIBLE` flower buds and flowers, sap, seedpods

Globally bountiful mesquite is naturally sweet and ready to eat right off the tree.

This velvet mesquite (*Prosopis velutina*) is in prime historic habitat along a desert wash. As the dry spring and early summer begin in the desert, velvet mesquite flowers profusely.

How to Identify

A member of the bean family, mesquite is related to mimosa—look for long spikes (catkins) of tiny white flowers (appearing yellow when full of pollen), and pairs of rounded, elongated leaflets along the leaf stem. Mesquite can appear like a small shrub or even ground cover in the Chihuahuan Desert. It also inhabits desert riparian areas growing to heights of up to 40 feet.

Where and When to Gather

Due to the dominant presence of cattle in the Southwest over the past two hundred or so years, and their appetite for mesquite

Processing Mesquite Beans and Cooking with Mesquite Meal

Ripe mesquite pods broken down and ready for storage.

Sifting the flour from the seeds after hand-grinding the pods.

Although mesquite beans are edible directly off the tree, they do require specific processing to create a meal, or fine flour, for culinary creations. Traditionally, this was all done by hand with a stone or wooden mortar and pestle.

Today, we have access to industrial, gas-powered hammer mills. For those without access to an industrial mill, a heavy-duty blender or coffee grinder (all metal working parts, no plastic) may be your best option. The seeds are very hard and can wear out or break a standard kitchen appliance. Once the seeds are ground, you can pour the meal through a strainer whose fineness corresponds to your desired flour consistency. Continue to grind until all the loose, non-seed material has been fully ground.

seedpods, the plant has spread over a great swath of our terrain. Look to desert washes and grasslands, riparian areas, backyards, urban promenades and parking lots primarily, as trees in these locations will likely produce many more pods. There has been a recent outpouring of evidence that mesquite pods can harbor *Aspergillus flavilus* fungus, leading to a relatively rapid formation of aflatoxins in the seedpod. Best current practices suggest harvesting before rainfall, or only from trees which you know have remained dry during the full ripening of the seedpods.

How to Gather

Mesquite pods become pretty loose once fully ripened. If you have to tug too hard they are not quite ripe, and as with all fruits, they ripen best on the mother tree itself. If you know the location well (your backyard, for instance) you can gather pods from the ground as they fall—but be sure that the ground is not moist, or that no rain has fallen during the ripening of the pods to avoid aflatoxin exposure. The translucent, light-colored sap is gathered from branches which have been cut. Allow the sap to slightly harden for ease in handling.

Mesquite meal ground in an industrial hammer mill.

Community groups may have access to funding for the purchase of a hammer mill for processing mesquite beans into flour (see Resources). At a community milling event, one can grind roughly five gallons of mesquite pods within fifteen minutes to obtain one full gallon of meal. The consistency will be coarser than all-purpose flour, but finer than almond meal. A finer flour can be achieved by cleaning the mill piping, or by grinding further at home. This meal is shelf-stable for several years, but the freshness and longevity can be increased by storing in the freezer.

When using mesquite in the kitchen, there are a few things to keep in mind. The flavor of mesquite is stronger than most flours or meals. Using one hundred percent mesquite in any recipes will create a powerfully flavored creation. Also, mesquite meal burns easily due to its high sugar content. For both baking and stovetop creations, adjust customary temperatures downward to avoid burning. And because mesquite is fully digestible raw, consider the meal in such foods as smoothies and raw food desserts. The complete protein of the bean pod makes mesquite a very nutritious and widely available food source across the Southwest, and beyond.

Apple-carrot bread made from gluten-free mesquite flour.

How to Use

One of the great things about mesquite is that the pods are edible straight off the tree. Numerous methods exist to further process them for their sweet, complex starches and ample protein, which presents a complete amino acid profile. (See the accompanying sidebar, Processing Mesquite Beans and Cooking with Mesquite Meal.) Simply boil the pods in a pot of water to create a pudding or *atole*. This syrup can also be used as a substrate for decocting medicinal herbs, with numerous applications. The seeds within the pods are so hard as to be winnowed out of most grinding methods. An industrial hammer mill can create about a gallon of meal from five gallons of pods. Use this meal, or flour, in a variety of preparations, such as baked goods (breads, biscuits, cakes), granola, smoothies, sauces, frosting (fine flour), fruit bars, tortillas, and pancakes. The flower buds and young flowers were used as food by the O'Odham people of the Sonoran Desert (and likely others, as well). The sap can be dissolved directly on the tongue as a traditional candy, or into solution for medicinal syrups, ointments, or demulcent drinks.

Future Harvests

Plant seeds from sweet-tasting mesquite in areas which receive ample water, such as swales and berms in a rainwater-harvesting home landscape.

Cautions

Mesquite beans in any form (including the flour) have been reported to cause severe flatulence.

The petals of the corolla of mesquite flowers are white, but the yellow pollen is so plentiful, it can cause the blooms to appear yellow from a distance.

Seedpods of Texas honey mesquite (*Prosopis glandulosa*) are almost fully ripened in early autumn.

Mexican palo verde

Parkinsonia aculeata

retama, Jerusalem thorn

`EDIBLE` flowers, green seeds, leaf sugar

Found the world over, Mexican palo verde's protein-rich, sweet bean can be prepared a variety of ways.

How to Identify

The bark of Mexican palo verde is smooth and yellowish green on young growth. It becomes fissured, furrowed, and gray-brown-beige with age. The long, slender rachis (leaf-bearing stem) clearly identifies this palo verde over all others— even when not present on the tree, the thin, needle-like rachises will be littered on the surrounding ground. The numerous tiny green leaflets reach out like tiny thumbs from the rachis when there's moisture, then quickly fall off as drought approaches again. These leaf features lend the tree an appearance similar to weeping willow when fully verdant. The yellow flowers contain a splash of orange on the top petal, or banner, and will often cover the entire tree, even when nearly leafless in the early spring. The pods are reminiscent of yellow palo verde in that they clearly constrict around the maturing seeds within, but will split open to spread the seeds locally.

Where and When to Gather

Mexican palo verde's habitat has been creeping up in elevation, unlike other palo verdes. We now see Mexican palo verde at

Mexican palo verde flowers for several months each year.

around 5000 feet elevation, occupying roadsides and waste places, primarily. It has naturalized north of its natural habitat due in large part to cultivation for landscaping in those areas. The tree is found across the globe, where it is commonly used for food and medicine. The flowers can be gathered whenever present, and the green seeds are mostly available during our spring season. During the warm, dry spring, sugary globules (called honeydew) from insects can be gathered off the long rachis.

How to Gather

Simply pull the flowers or green pods off by hand. Once the pods have begun to turn beige they are getting past the stage of being edible raw. Once mature, they become dry and hard and can be processed further for food. The honeydew can be carefully picked off the leaves and eaten there on the spot.

How to Use

The young beans of Mexican palo verde can be eaten raw, or can be blanched or steamed and served with butter. They also make an excellent brine ferment within a week. The flowers have a sweetness to them, and they brighten up any plate. The dry beans can be soaked and cooked for several hours to render them soft and edible. The honeydew on the leaves can be eaten on its own or used in wild fermented drinks (if you can gather enough). There is interest in Mexican palo verde beans as an arid-land food crop, due to their high (41 percent) protein content.

Future Harvests

Mexican palo verde can be viewed as a scourge, or as pretty landscaping, depending on the environment. There's little worry that any weedy populations will be disturbed, even with robust harvesting of the flowers and seeds. It finds a way to reproduce.

Note the splash of reddish orange on the top petal of the Mexican palo verde flower.

milkvine

Sarcostemma cynanchoides

climbing milkvine, fringed twinvine, guirote lechoso

`EDIBLE` immature fruit

Milkvine's uniquely sweet fruit will remind you a bit of asparagus.

How to Identify

You will always find mature milkvine growing up something—a bush, tree, or fence. The leaves grow opposite each other along the thin, trailing stems, and like most other plants in the milkweed family, they exude a milky sap when broken. The flowers appear in umbels like other milkweeds—clusters of cup-shaped corollas (five to thirty flowers), tinged with purple. The leaves are elongate with a heart-shaped base. The fruits appear in midsummer and can be 3 ½ to 6 inches long.

Where and When to Gather

Milkvine likes disturbed soils, fields, roadsides, and river bottoms. Look to the margins: along fences, and up trees and large shrubs. After ample summer rains the vines can grow in a robust manner. The fruits should begin to appear midsummer; gather them before they split down the center; they'll toughen up with age. You'll get the feel for it once you've sampled enough fruits.

How to Gather

You can simply pull them from the vine, or bring along a pair of pruners to clip them off.

How to Use

When young enough, the inner portion of milkvine fruit can be enjoyed directly from the vine. Most of the time this fruit is

Once cooked, milkvine fruit can be sliced and simply eaten, or added to soups, stews, or other creative recipes.

This small harvest came from a milkvine growing on a honey mesquite tree in West Texas. Milkvines often grow up trees or along fences.

sweet; sometimes it is a little bitter. To prepare older fruit, boil for several minutes and strain. Slice the fruit and serve with butter and seasonings, or mix in with other available vegetables. It makes an interesting garnish to soups and stews. Milkvine fruit will also keep in the refrigerator for several days.

Future Harvests

This native plant seems to have an advantageous survival strategy in our current climate, as it can be found throughout our region in relative plenitude. If you would like to keep milkvine close to your home, simply press the seeds (gather these in November) into disturbed, moist soil in the late winter or early spring.

Cautions

Milkvine should not be confused with some species of milkweed (*Asclepias* species) which contain cardiac stimulant properties, and would not make a good food. However, these species are not vines, and bear very little resemblance (other than milky sap) to milkvine.

miner's lettuce

Claytonia perfoliata

winter purslane, Indian lettuce, verdolaga del invierno

EDIBLE leaves

This humble native salad green has a satisfying crunch and pleasant flavor.

Miner's lettuce grows in large clumps in wet, shady areas.

How to Identify

The first leaves of miner's lettuce are long and thin, but the secondary leaves become more oval or spade shaped. It grows as a low ground cover in most areas. It has a succulent texture and you can often find red pigment in the stems. As it begins to flower, the central stem appears to pierce through the cauline (on the stem) leaves, looking something like a lily pad in midair.

The tiny white flowers with five petals are about ¼ inch across. Miner's lettuce is a relative of purslane. A related edible species, Virginia spring beauty (*Claytonia virginica*), is a trailing plant with slender leaves and pale pink or white flowers.

Where and When to Gather

This plant is found toward the western end of our range, in Arizona, Utah, and Nevada, occupying agricultural landscapes and urban areas. It is also often with other native vegetation in cool, moist areas. Miner's lettuce is often found under trees, in moist areas where it can take advantage of winter and spring rains. Gather the young greens for salad from early February through early April. In areas where it persists later into the year, boil or steam, as native peoples have done. *Claytonia virginica* can be found in eastern Texas; its root, or corm, can be gathered and cooked like a potato.

How to Gather

Gather miner's lettuce leaves by placing your fingertips at the base of several clumps of leaves and pulling or pinching. Once you've collected enough leaves (in a basket or a clean cloth), scurry back to the kitchen.

How to Use

Miner's lettuce is edible fresh or cooked. The leaves make wonderful salads—alone or in combination with your favorite greens and other salad ingredients. Toss the fresh greens into hot soups just before serving. As the greens age they lose some of their tenderness, but are still suitable for salads and perfect for sauté, soups, or casseroles. Blanching and freezing will allow you to take full advantage of a good harvest, but the greens will lose their characteristic crispness. The fresh herb was used by Native Americans as a poultice to relieve rheumatic pains. Its high Vitamin C content also made it a treatment for scurvy.

Future Harvests

The best way to maintain miner's lettuce populations is to circulate where you harvest from year to year, never gathering more than a third from the patch. Seeds are also available for purchase (as well as off the plant) to scatter about your favorite local shady glen or in a garden bed in your yard. Allow it to take over as a ground cover, cutting back as you see fit.

monkeyflower

Mimulus guttatus

basómari

`EDIBLE` young leaves, flowers

Monkeyflower is often profuse in riparian areas after the rainy season. Best cooked, it is traditionally made into a creamed green.

Monkeyflower grows opposing leaves which are often tinged with red at the stem.

How to Identify

Monkeyflower is an annual with opposing leaves along a squarish stem tinged, or fully colored, red. The leaves can vary from triangular to slightly heart shaped, but usually possess teeth, or serrations, along the margin. The small, yellow flowers emerge on long stalks above the leaves. The plant turns beige-brown after drought or protracted freezing temperatures.

Where and When to Gather

Look to springs, creeks, rivers, and moist desert washes along the margins. Monkeyflower comes and goes seasonally with available moisture. It can be available spring, summer, fall, and winter if moisture is present and the temperature is not too cold. Gather the fresh green growth before plants flower and the leaves become bitter. Patches will emerge and mature

Yellow monkeyflowers are often dotted with tiny red points on the lower lip.

sporadically, depending on when the rains arrive.

How to Gather

Snip off the young, tender leafy stems and leave the flowering stems to produce seed.

How to Use

It's best to wash all monkeyflower greens before consuming, especially if they are found within stagnant water. Some people enjoy the raw greens in salads, but I think cooking improves their taste. Blanch, then sauté in bacon fat or simmer in a bit of water, stirring as you cook. Add butter or cream, salt and pepper, and maybe a bit of wild oregano or oreganillo to arrive at a dish of creamed greens. The leaves have also been dried and burned to make an ash, which can be used in small quantities as a salt substitute.

Future Harvests

Monkeyflower is usually plentiful, but in lean years be sure to let a significant portion of the stand go to seed for future seasons' growth.

Cautions

Wash all harvested monkeyflower material, whether you intend to eat it raw or cooked.

Mormon tea

Ephedra species

jointfir, stick tea, canutillo, popotillo

EDIBLE seeds, stems (as tea)

The leaf stems of Mormon tea make an invigorating, mineral-rich drink once used as a substitute for coffee.

The copper-toned, unopened female flowers of Mormon tea encircle green stems.

Where and When to Gather

Mormon tea can be found throughout the western two-thirds of our region. Look in desert plains and grasslands, rocky *bajadas*, at the edges of seasonal washes, and more sparsely across mesas and rocky hillsides. It can abound locally, with great distances between populations. The stems can be gathered year-round for tea and the seeds are gathered in early spring to midspring.

How to Identify

Unique among desert plants, Mormon tea is leafless—rather, its thin green stems act as leaves, providing food for the plant via photosynthesis. Botanically, it is more closely related to pine and juniper trees than the plants which often surround it. Look for the distinct, thin joints along the stems marked by their contrasting color. Mormon tea can be a short, sprawling shrub, or more upright, taller than it is wide. Its average height is around 4 to 5 feet. In the spring, flowers appear at each joint, or node, with male and female flowers on separate plants. Before opening, they appear to be tiny cones—which they are.

How to Gather

The tough, fibrous stems of Mormon tea are not easily broken, so you will need a pair of pruners or a sharp knife to cut off the younger, more verdant stems. The seeds are perhaps best gathered in the traditional way, carrying a basket in one hand and a small paddle or stick in the other, gently batting stems to release the seeds from the ripened cones.

How to Use

Chop and boil a tablespoon or so of stems for a cup of tea. Simmering longer extracts more minerals. This tea provides much relief for some folks who suffer from symptoms of seasonal allergies such as shortness of breath or a tight chest. The seeds can be roasted, ground, and made into *atoles*, tortillas, cakes, or bread.

seed harvests where populations are diminished or during years of low production.

Future Harvests

If you enjoy what Mormon tea has to offer, you may consider bringing it into your yard. It is a slow-growing plant which can provide food and medicine for many decades over its lifetime. As usual, restrict

Cautions

Although this plant's genus is *Ephedra*, Mormon tea has very little to do with the synthetic pharmaceutical, ephedrine. It will not produce heart palpitations or high blood pressure. It is safe to use.

Notice the unfolding pinkish-beige, papery scales of the mature fruit of the female Mormon tea plants as the seeds have ripened and are ready for gathering.

mountain parsley

Pseudocymopterus montanus
alpine false spring parsley, wild parsley

`EDIBLE` flowers, leaves, roots, seeds

Pungent mountain parsley and its brilliant flowers can lend color
and flavor to your backcountry salads.

When mountain parsley is in full bloom, it's a perfect time for harvesting flowers and leaves.

How to Identify

If you've ever grown a member of the
carrot family in your garden, you will
recognize mountain parsley for its similar
appearance to common parsley, carrot, and
cilantro. The deeply divided, sparse, dark
to bluish-green leaves of this herbaceous
perennial arise from the base of the plant.
Its flowers may be yellow, orange, or ochre
red. Mountain parsley grows to a height of
12 to 20 inches.

Where and When to Gather

Mountain parsley is relegated to the
western half of our region. Look to high
mountain coniferous forests, mid-
elevation canyons, or oak-juniper woodlands. Any part of the plant can be gathered
when present or apparent. Roots will be
sweetest in the spring before the plant
flowers, or post-seeding in the autumn.

How to Gather

The leaves, stems, flowers, and seeds can be gathered easily by hand. You may wish to employ a pair of pruners or a knife to sever the desired plant parts. Otherwise, bring a digging stick, hori-hori, or small spade to unearth the sweet, pungent tap roots.

How to Use

Add the fresh leaves or flowers of mountain parsley to salads, egg scrambles, or vegetable ferments. Mix the leaves with other foraged vegetables to make a nourishing stock. The leaves were traditionally cooked with cornmeal to make porridge. The seeds can be added to soup, potato salad, or sauerkraut for a piquant flavor. The pungent roots are a nice addition to meat soups and stews; grind or finely chop them first.

Future Harvests

Any carrot family plants of the high mountains should be harvested conservatively. Although mountain parsley leaves can be gathered more liberally, collect no more than ten percent of the roots from a given area, and always leave an ample number of seeds for replenishing.

Cautions

A traditional use of this plant is to induce vomiting. Eat in moderation.

mulberry

Morus microphylla

Texas mulberry, mora

EDIBLE fruit, young leaves

Packed with a burst of sweet-tart flavor, mulberry is a treat to find in the desert.

The young leaves, female flower, and ovaries of mulberry.

How to Identify

Mulberry is a many-branched, deciduous shrub with mostly smooth, gray bark. Although it is often found at 8 to 12 feet in height, it can grow to nearly 25 feet. The toothed, alternate leaves vary in form from egg shaped to triangular to deeply lobed. The undersides are rough to the touch. A dioecious shrub, mulberry produces non-showy male and female flowers on separate plants. The small fruits ripen from green to yellow to red to purple. Then clusters of smooth, light orange-red seeds begin to appear. With edible relative red mulberry (*Morus rubra*), shades of red appear in the furrows of the bark, and the leaves are typically unlobed, except perhaps on young trees. Sweet, delicious red mulberry fruits are red to dark purple.

Where and When to Gather

Mulberry can be found throughout our region in canyons and along streams. It prefers limestone and igneous slopes. Rarely out in the open, mulberry prefers the shade of either large boulders or an upper story of larger shade trees. The prime time for gathering depends a bit on where you are. Berries generally ripen within two months of flowering (which often happens in the early spring). Red mulberry can be found within the eastern third of our range (Texas and Oklahoma), scattered throughout shaded woods, and along ditches, river banks, streams, and ravines.

How to Gather

Mulberries are picked one by one, slowly and carefully.

How to Use

Mulberry fruit is often eaten with glee when found. In fact, many foragers are compelled to eat all they've gathered right on the spot. The trick is to find enough to have some left to take home. Prepare mulberry jam, jelly, pies, breads, or cakes. You can also sun dry berries for storage, if you are so generously blessed. Combine the dried fruit with dates, nuts, and foraged seeds to create your own energy bars, or mix with animal fat for a traditional pemmican. Mulberries can also be made into wine.

Future Harvests

We often head out a week or two into the ripening cycle, allowing the birds to gorge and disperse seeds ahead of us. Bringing mulberry into your landscape is another great way to ensure and simplify your own future harvests.

Ripe mulberry fruit is on the right, the seed cluster is on the left.

nettle

Urtica species

stinging nettle, ortiga, ortigüilla

EDIBLE seeds, young leaves

Nettle is a nutritional powerhouse—rivaling all edible greens—and its medicinal effects are legendary. Have no fear of the nettle sting!

Notice the strands of drooping flower clusters, all emerging from around the ridged stem at the base of the leaves on this *Urtica dioica* plant. Not all species of *Urtica* have such long flower racemes.

How to Identify

If you touch a vibrantly green plant and moments later feel a sharp sting like that of an ant bite, you have likely encountered stinging nettle. The various nettle species have toothed leaves, which can be triangular to long and thin in shape. Looking closely and you will find short, stout, translucent spines (trichomes) along both sides of the leaf and along the main stem. Inconspicuous greenish-white flowers hang down from the base of the leaves, and some species produce flowering clusters much longer than others. Flowering is followed in the fall by tight clusters of tiny seeds about the size of a spider egg, if female flowers were produced.

Where and When to Gather

In the Southwest, you're looking for moist soil in order to find nettle—such as the high elevation terrain along watercourses in the western half of our region. Look for nettle in the South Texas Plains and the

Gulf Coast. However, there are annual and perennial as well as introduced and native species throughout our range. They're all edible. The leaves are best gathered before flowering. The seeds are usually collected in the fall, or in winter or spring in gardens or low elevation.

How to Gather

Harvesting nettle is not as dangerous as it may seem. A long-sleeved shirt and gloves will protect you from stings. Grab from the base of the plant with a gloved hand and cut the stem below the lowest green leaves. Then hang the plant to dry in the shade. Once dried, strip the leaves (if your skin is sensitive, you may wish to use gloves here as well) to store for later use. Green leaves can be plucked from the stem, rolled in the palm, and eaten fresh without incurring any stings. Take care to fold the leaf onto itself by pinching the top of the leaf with the thumb and forefinger.

How to Use

The leaves are rather bland and their texture ranges from tender to coarse. Steam, blanch, sauté, or boil the fresh leaves; dried leaves are best added to soups or made into a nourishing morning tea. Nettle pesto is an excellent way to use fresh leaves. Dried nettle leaf stores well in the freezer. Nettle is also a phenomenal pain reliever, and I have seen people intentionally come in contact with the plant for this very reason—though it does raise welts on the skin where the contact occurs. However, once dried, cooked, or rubbed against itself, nettle loses its sting.

Young sprouts of dwarf nettle (*Urtica urens*). The great sting of the spines (or trichomes) on the leaves and stems is negated by cooking or drying.

Future Harvests

Once you understand nettle's preferred habitat in your area, you can disperse collected seed in the fall or before the rainy season arrives. In other parts of the country nettle is considered an invasive weed, but not in the Southwest—here it's a rare treat. Bring it into your home garden if you have ample water.

Cautions

Fresh nettle stings, but it's not a real threat. Drying or cooking solves the issue.

New Mexico locust

Robinia neomexicanum

uña de gato

EDIBLE blossoms

Closely related to the black locust of the East Coast, our New Mexico locust blossoms possess a similar sweetness.

New Mexico locust blossoms range from white to dark pink.

The reddish-brown bark is smooth when young, and becomes furrowed in long strips as it ages. The pinnately compound leaves are on a bristly stem, and possess oval-shaped, odd-numbered leaflets. The clusters of blossoms appear at the ends of the branches and may reach up or hang down. They range in color from white to pink. The young buds and the bean pods are covered in tiny glandular hairs.

Where and When to Gather

Found throughout the western half of the Southwest, New Mexico locust can also be seen in planned landscapes, on occasion, in Central Texas. Look to canyons, juniper woodlands, margins of coniferous forests, and the first growth coming in after large fires. The blossoms can be gathered early summer to midsummer, depending on your location.

How to Gather

If possible, gathering from above on a steep embankment may give you the best shot at reaching New Mexico locust blossoms. Otherwise, a ladder may prove useful. Break off the whole cluster of blossoms (ideally, half of the cluster is

How to Identify

The deciduous New Mexico locust tree, a member of the bean family, grows to a height of about 25 feet when fully mature.

New Mexico locust blossoms fried in mesquite meal and butter.

open, and the other half closed) and stack them loosely in a cloth bag, bucket, or basket. They will need to be removed promptly to remain fresh.

How to Use

Perfectly edible right off the tree, the about-to-open flower buds are sweeter than the opened flowers (which are more astringent). They make a beautiful addition to any type of salad or fresh plate of food as an edible garnish. Dip in egg batter and mesquite flour, then fry in butter for a delicious fritter. Top with saguaro or prickly pear syrup for the ultimate Sonoran delicacy. Add the blossoms individually to stir-fry dishes, or just as steamed vegetables are finishing cooking.

Future Harvests

A pioneer tree, New Mexico locust thrives in disturbed and fire-damaged areas. It is also an excellent honey-producing tree that can do well in your landscape, if you're in the right location.

ocotillo

Fouquieria splendens

coachwhip

`EDIBLE` flowers, nectar, seeds

Often confused with cactus, spiny ocotillo brings sweetness to the Sonoran Desert.

How to Identify

Unmistakable ocotillo is a woody shrub armed with stout spines along its sap-covered, leathery barked, upright branches. The branches are often numerous, coming right out of the ground, or there may be a single trunk that is several inches in height. The branches are highly flexible and springy, often measuring 1 1/2 to 3 inches in diameter. Small green leaves appear all along the stem in response to moisture, then quickly turn yellow and fall off once the moisture is gone. The emergence of the brilliant red flowers (occasionally yellow or pinkish purple) creates an image of the hills ablaze.

Where and When to Gather

Ocotillo likes hillsides and trailing *bajadas* in both the Sonoran and Chihuahuan deserts, from grasslands to cactus forests. It also prefers open areas; you won't find it under tree cover. The inflorescences appear in early spring to midspring (varying four to six weeks by location) and gradually open over one to two weeks. In the very low desert, blooms may even emerge in early winter. It is best to gather ocotillo flowers for tea once they are fully

In response to ample moisture, Ocotillo produces many leaves within several days. It is otherwise leafless throughout the year.

open. The seed capsules can be harvested roughly six weeks later.

How to Gather

It's nice to have a harvesting partner when gathering ocotillo blossoms. One person

One of the most deliciously sweet substances found in the desert is the clear nectar of ocotillo flowers.

can carefully pull down a stem (being mindful of the spines) until an inflorescence is within reach. Simply snap off the entire flower spike. The nectar must be gathered carefully at just the right time. It is most plentiful during days of full sun, following a period of good moisture. Pick the globules of clear, rich glucose right off the flowers. The seed capsules are harvested similarly. You will then need to break open the seed capsules and winnow the capsule fragments from the seeds.

How to Use

My favorite way to prepare ocotillo flowers is as a sun tea, with either fresh or dried blossoms. Fill a gallon jar with flower spikes, then pour water over the flowers, filling the jar again. Set out in the midday sun for about four hours. Strain and enjoy. If you pick the flowers when fully open, the tea will be sweet due to the presence of the nectar. If you harvest the blossoms while they are still closed, the tea will be exceedingly tart—not as tasty. You can also decorate salads, baked goods, or chocolate desserts with the fresh blossoms. Add the tea to kombucha during the second ferment for exquisite flavor. The seeds were traditionally parched and ground, to be made into mush and cakes.

Future Harvests

Ocotillo populations are often high where it grows. Perhaps due to this hardiness, wild populations have been dug up for the landscaping industry, and wild ocotillo is now a protected plant. Only harvest what you can use, and be sure to leave a

significant portion of flowers during lean years, so that insects may access the pollen and nectar they depend upon. Ocotillo stems are easily transplanted by simply being buried 12 to 20 inches in the soil—a practice which also creates a living fence.

Ocotillo flower sun tea is a reviving drink in the hot desert sun.

Cautions

When gathering foods which are over your head it is wise to have a look around before you begin. Ocotillo often grows beside various cacti so you may not like what you bump into.

oreganillo

Aloysia wrightii
beebush, mintbush, Mexican oregano, vara dulce
Aloysia gratissima
whitebrush
Aloysia macrostachya
Rio Grande beebush

EDIBLE flowers, stems, leaves

Sweet, piquant oreganillo can grace your burger, salmon fillet, or pizza. Known for spicing up dishes.

How to Identify

Oreganillo is almost completely unnoticeable once all its leaves have fallen in response to drought or freezing temperatures. It takes a practiced eye to notice the wispy beige-white puffs lining the south-facing wall of a canyon or dotting a desert hillside. Oreganillo responds to winter or summer rains, bringing canyons and hillsides alive with its fragrant white blossoms. You're likely to smell it before you see it when it is in bloom. If you catch a whiff of the sweetly intoxicating blossoms, look up and scan the hillside for the vague, feathery grayish-green shrubs. Leaves are opposite each other along the stem, and the tiny white flowers emerge at a 45-degree angle from the leaf axils (base of leaf stem).

Where and When to Gather

Found across the southern tier of our range, this delightfully scented native shrub is often difficult to spot even when one is standing before a hillside covered

The young leaf of oreganillo. Shoots grow quickly in response to summer rain.

with dozens of the plants. Oreganillo is often found covering north-facing sides of ravines, replete in desert camouflage. However, the sweet scent of its blossoms will draw the forager to its location. Whenever ample rains fall, oreganillo leafs out with tender foliage and blossoms that beckon the culinary minded. Whitebrush (*Aloysia gratissima*), with white flowers,

Oreganillo in Sonoran Desert habitat.

Whitebrush (*Aloysia gratissima*) is a species used for spice and tea.

and Rio Grande beebrush (*Aloysia macrostachya*), with pink flowers, are found in South Texas and can be used similarly.

How to Gather

Gather the tender new stem growth whenever present by clipping with scissors or pruners. These young stems will have large leaves packed with aromatics. Use these leaves fresh, or dry in the shade. To dry leaves, loosely stack them in a paper bag or spread them out on an open surface when the weather is damp.

How to Use

The robust flavor of oreganillo stems and leaves combines sweet pungency with a mild bitterness, which diminishes upon drying. Combine the fresh herb with apple cider vinegar and store on the shelf to dress salads and season meats. Or combine the herb vinegar with wild honey for a delicious elixir known as an oxymel. Used fresh, oreganillo lends itself to the variety of culinary roles played by its

not-too-distant mint family cousins oregano, marjoram, and thyme. Add the dried herb to pasta sauces, pizza, salsas, meat seasonings, salad dressings, soups and stews. When a cold strikes or joints become achy during the cold and damp season, add a pinch of oreganillo to your favorite herbal blend. Native peoples use oreganillo internally for headaches, rheumatism, and infections, and recent scientific studies have pointed to its antidepressant-like effects.

Future Harvests

Oreganillo is a perfect candidate for dryland landscaping, as it serves as both food and medicine, attracts pollinators, needs little to no supplemental irrigation, and contributes a beautiful aroma when blossoming. The seeds can be harvested in the fall and sown during the warmth of spring and summer in moist, well-drained soil. Once you get to know its preferred habitat in your area, you can scatter the seeds where it may grow best.

palo verde

Parkinsonia microphylla
yellow palo verde, foothills palo verde
Parkinsonia florida
blue palo verde

`EDIBLE` beans, flowers

Many culinary options can be derived from this desert legume: a fresh nibble, edamame-like snack, hummus-style dip, or fermented tapas-like delicacy.

How to Identify

Yellow palo verde (*Parkinsonia microphylla*) prefers drier hillsides (although it may occupy desert washes at lower elevations) and possesses no thorns. These two features can distinguish it from the desert riparian blue palo verde (*Parkinsonia florida*), which possesses tiny thorns along its blue-green stems. Yellow palo verde's tiny bi-pinnate leaves quickly yellow and fall off due to drought. The top flower petal, or banner, on yellow palo verde is a pale white. Most significantly, the maturing seedpods of yellow palo verde constrict around the seeds so one can clearly count the seeds within a pod,

Note the constricted pods of the yellow palo verde.

whereas blue palo verde's seedpods do not laterally constrict around the seeds. (See profile for Mexican palo verde).

Where and When to Gather
Desert washes and desert foothills are often home to both yellow and blue palo verde. These trees occupy the southern half of Arizona, extending northwest through the state. Blue palo verde can also be found in southern Nevada. Blue palo verde flowers in early spring, followed two or three weeks later by yellow palo verde. As the beans mature at roughly the same time with each species, you can expect the immature yellow palo verde beans to be available as the blue palo verde beans fully ripen.

How to Gather
Pick the flowers individually, by hand. Same goes for the green seedpods. Green seedpods of blue palo verde can often be gathered several at a time by pulling down the branch to its tip in a stripping motion. The tiny thorns point out in the direction of the pull, and are not often found near the ends of the branches. Clusters of the green seedpods of yellow palo verde can be captured in one hand motion when they are particularly plentiful. Ripened seedpods can be gathered from or beneath the trees before the rains arrive. Imma-ture bean pods are readily opened by twisting opposite ends with both hands, rotating forward simultaneously (like pedaling a bicycle).

How to Use
Palo verde beans provide many options. After being blanched and shelled, they can be puréed into a bean dip, frozen, canned, brined, fermented, or eaten in salads. The blanched, shelled immature beans can also be cooked and eaten like edamame (and taste quite similar). The beans are even edible raw. Mature seeds can be toasted and ground into flour for *atoles*, breads, bean burgers, and the like.

Future Harvests
Expect a bountiful harvest where the trees grow. Plant trees in appropriate areas of your private landscape to bring the foraging to your doorstep. The trees are not long-lived and grow quickly with adequate moisture.

Blue palo verde (*Parkinsonia florida*) seeds ripen before those of yellow palo verde.

pamita

Descurainia species

tansy mustard

`EDIBLE` leaves, seeds

A prolific wild seed crop rich in oils, pamita is traditionally used to aid in digestion.

As pamita goes to seed, its pods turn purple-brown, then beige.

How to Identify

Like all plants in the mustard family, pamita has four-petaled flowers. Most are annuals, however, some *Descurainia* species are biennials. They generally grow upright with tight clusters of yellow flowers prominent at the top. The seedpods may be short and curved, as with western tansy mustard (*D. pinnata*), more elongate like flixweed (*D. sophia*), or linear like blunt tansy mustard (*D. obtusa*).

Where and When to Gather

Look for large stands of pamita growing along seasonal watercourses up on the banks. In years of ample moisture, dozens to hundreds of these plants can sprout and grow in a very small area, making gathering a bit easier. Look to the coloration of the maturing seedpods (visible at a distance while hiking a wash or driving down the street)—they should be turning purplish brown when dry, almost ready to burst open.

How to Gather

When the miniscule seeds are ripe, harvest them by batting the plants with a flattened stick or lightweight tool, while catching the falling seed in a basket (or long poncho or apron). Sure, you'll miss a good deal, but you'll still gather plenty in a dense area, and those which fall will reseed for next year. Winnow out the lightweight seedpods in a light breeze.

How to Use

Pamita leaves are a soft green. The seeds, which get slightly slimy when wet, can be stirred into water and sweetened to make a refreshing drink traditionally used as a digestive aid. In my experience, these seeds do not have the sulphur-spicy flavor of most seeds from the mustard family. Instead, they're rather bland, slightly nutty-oily. You can parch them on a hot skillet, then mill them to a powder. This flour can then be used in breads (helps cohesiveness in gluten-free recipes), sprinkled on salads, made into traditional *atole*, or used as a breading on meats. Mustard family plants are widely cultivated for the nutritious oils present in the seeds.

Future Harvests

I have successfully established this plant in my yard and garden simply by winnowing seeds in the yard. It is a prolific annual that always responds to seasonal rains. The method of harvesting described above helps ensure a future seed bank.

pápalo quelite
Porophyllum ruderale
yerba del venado, yerba porosa, broad leaf

EDIBLE leaves

The herb pápalo quelite has a unique aroma and a flavor reminiscent of cilantro. Some people love it; others avoid it.

Pápalo quelite grows in large numbers near the border regions in Arizona, southwest New Mexico, and southwest Texas.

How to Identify

Pápalo quelite is a summer annual with opposing, smooth, oval, blue-green leaves that have notches along the margin. The entire plant is smooth to the touch. The tiny flowers appear at the end of a long peduncle (flower head). Upon maturity, the blooms open up to a dandelion-like seed puff. Upon being crushed, the herb emits a unique, pungent odor.

Where and When to Gather

Pápalo quelite is unique to the southeast corner of Arizona and the southwest corner of New Mexico after the arrival of summer rains. Look to canyons, desert washes, and the margins of desert grasslands. Gather when still young, tender, and flexible.

How to Gather

Clip pápalo quelite beneath the most tender tips—or in a large stand, the entire plant can be pulled up. It's likely you won't be gathering very much. A little goes a long way.

How to Use

In Mexico, where *Porophyllum* species are more widespread and culturally integrated into the food system, they are used in a variety of ways: in fresh salsas and tacos, added to guacamole, and on salads and sandwiches. Add fresh, chopped pápalo quelite to yogurt sauces, or try substituting it for cilantro (a bit at a time). I make a tomato, onion, and chile salsa with fresh pápalo quelite that is often well received.

Future Harvests

A bountiful summer annual where it is found. Seeds are also available for sale; cultivate in your garden or in a suitable desert landscape fed by seasonal rainfall.

pecan

Carya illinoiensis

nuéz

`EDIBLE` nuts

The rich, nutritious fats available in pecan nuts are a forager's dream.

How to Identify

Pecan is closely related to our hickory species (*Carya*) and black walnut (*Juglans* species), and the three trees share several characteristics. All possess pinnately compound leaves with an odd number of leaflets—they end in a single lone leaf. Generally, the leaflets of pecan are wider and appear larger than walnut, and are more numerous (seven to fifteen) than hickory species. The fruits of pecan are elongated and look something like an old leather football. They mature from green to brown, at which point they split lengthwise, revealing the brown–beige–streaked nut within. The nutmeat is within this shell.

Where and When to Gather

The true native North American pecan tree is a beautiful member of gallery forests across the South. Within our range, wild pecans can be found in river bottoms and floodplains from West Texas to East Texas, and north into Oklahoma. Their native range extends east from there. They are otherwise cultivated throughout the Southwest and can be found at sites of old homesteads, or in perennially wet areas where they've become naturalized. They begin to ripen as early as September, and the harvest extends to November. You'll need to beat the javelina and wild hogs to the feast!

A mature pecan tree at an old homestead in southern Arizona along the Gila River.

How to Gather

Pick up whole fruits or nuts from the ground and place in your bucket. You can also pick open fruit from any low-hanging branches which may be accessible. Large trees are prolific and can produce hundreds of pounds of nuts. Pecan's dependence upon extensive irrigation in drought-stricken habitats across the Southwest further demonstrates the need to utilize our wild populations of pecan for food.

How to Use

Once you've picked enough pecans you can begin to appreciate pecan pie. The nuts store well in the shell for later use, or you can crack them on the spot to savor the unique, oily sweetness of freshly shelled pecans. These tasty nuts combine well in breads, brownies, granola, trail mix, and various other baked goods. Blend them with fresh dates to make a crust for pies.

Future Harvests

Habitat destruction and the rapid loss of groundwater threaten the pecan more than anything else. If you own land which could support pecan's water needs, gather the fruits from trees that produce large and especially tasty nuts and plant them on your land in the appropriate location.

Ripened pecan fruit still on the tree, but ready for picking.

pellitory

Parietaria species

rillita pellitory, Florida pellitory, cucumber weed, hammerwort

EDIBLE leaves

Pellitory is a delicate, tender green with a clearly cucumber flavor.

How to Identify

A small, delicate plant, pellitory requires close inspection to be identified properly. It is light green and possesses very tiny, faintly coarse hairs on its leaves. The plant grows upright for 8 to 12 inches and can easily fall over on itself due to its tender stems. The small seeds, or achenes, turn brown once mature.

Where and When to Gather

In the western half of our range, pellitory prefers moist, shady alcoves along arroyos (often to the north side of boulders). Here, look to harvest pellitory leaves from shortly after winter rains arrive until April. At our eastern edge it can be found in weedy locales, borders, fields, roadsides, and sandy shores. In these places, the season extends and pellitory leaves can be gathered throughout the spring and summer.

How to Gather

In large pellitory patches (which I find often in wet years), I simply grab a handful of plants here and there, along with the tiny roots, thinning out the patch gradually. These annuals have stored up significant seed caches over millennia.

How to Use

Pellitory leaves were one of my daughter's favorite trail snacks when she was 2 years old. She would nibble away like a little rabbit. I recommend you consume it raw if you like the cucumber flavor. If you'd prefer a bland green with most of the nutrition intact, you can steam, blanch, boil briefly, or sauté pellitory. Plants such as pellitory provide an opportunity to make unique salsas, toppings for stews and soups, or flavorful sandwiches, wraps, or burritos that will have your friends asking, "What's that flavor?"

Future Harvests

If you particularly enjoy this flavor, gather some seeds in the summer once they've turned brown. Scatter in your yard. If you're in the drier western portion of our region, you'll need to care for them a bit more by providing extra moisture and shade.

Pellitory (*Parietaria hespera*) in its habitat in the Sonoran Desert, early spring.

pennywort

Hydrocotyle species

marsh pennywort, large-leaf pennywort

EDIBLE leaves

In the far east of the Southwest, one may have to look no further than the front lawn to find this edible treasure.

How to Identify

Pennywort grows singular, coin-shaped, flat leaves from tall stems. These tall stems come up from tiny white rootlets found all along the trailing stems, as they emerge from the ground and grass clumps. A somewhat distant relative of ginseng, pennywort puts out small, pyramidal umbrella clusters of creamy white, five-pointed star flowers.

Where and When to Gather

Pennywort inhabits perennially wet grounds and marshy areas in the eastern edge of our region. Find it all along the Gulf Coast, from sandy soils to manicured lawns. It can be available year-round.

How to Gather

The stems grow rather strong once mature and may not break before you pull up some

Large-leaf pennywort (*Hydrocotyle bonariensis*) grows along the Texas Gulf Coast in grasslands and moist, sandy soils.

rootlets as well. This is fine; simply replant the rootlets elsewhere. Otherwise, clip with pruners below tender stems.

How to Use
Clean the freshly gathered leaves well, and chop or add them whole to soups and stews. The young, tender leaves add a nice splash of flavor to salads.

Future Harvests
Pennywort is a native plant that favors marshlands. It will continue to inhabit them as long as we don't greatly alter the ecology. Harvest with care for the rootlets to remain for replanting, and this plant will continue to thrive.

Whorled pennywort (*Hydrocotyle verticillata*) grows in a marshy area in Sonora, Mexico. It is traditionally eaten as a cooked green.

peppergrass
Lepidium species

pepperweed, pepperwort, cress, cowcress, pennycress, kardamo

`EDIBLE` entire plant

A spicy, sharply flavored native herb, peppergrass can heat up sauces, eggs, vinegars, and salads.

How to Identify

As members of the mustard family, *Lepidium* species have white, four-petaled flowers with two stamens. In this case, the plants produce ovate, or egg-shaped, seedpods. The leaves may be toothed or entire, and occur along the stem as well as at the base of the plant. These annuals generally don't grow above 3 feet in height, but can be much smaller. A few perennial *Lepidium* species exist.

Where and When to Gather

Peppergrass is found throughout our range, with limited representation in far eastern Texas. Look in disturbed areas, from deserts to woodlands to riparian areas, from high elevations to low.

How to Gather

Pinch the newest tender leaf growth and pull off. Pluck the largest leaves from the base of the plant. When plentiful, you can pull up the entire plant. Use the plant fresh, or hang or spread it out flat to dry, strip the seedpods, and prepare or store as a spice.

How to Use

Use large peppergrass leaves in salads or blends. Chop the fresh plant—including the leaves, flowers, tender stems, and green seedpods—and add to soups, egg dishes, and sauces. Make a pesto-like dish by blending pieces with olive oil, garlic and other spices. Use green seedpods to flavor an herbal vinegar or to give your dressings an added kick. Use ripened seedpods like black pepper. Once dried, grind the seed and apply to marinades, seasoning blends, sauces, and dressings. The dried seeds are often mucilaginous, similar to pamita, so they make a refreshing spicy drink. This relative of horseradish can also be used liberally in the kitchen to help abort the early onset of any respiratory illness.

Future Harvests

Peppergrass is often an abundant plant seasonally. Take care to leave numerous seeds from each harvesting location to allow restocking of the local seedbank for the future.

Cautions

The sharp spiciness of peppergrass can burn the tongue slightly, like a good horseradish, but this bite wanes quickly.

Lesser swinecress (*Lepidium didymum*) is naturalized on every continent but Antarctica. Populations of peppergrass are easily identifiable in the autumn and winter by the flat, circular form of the seedpods.

pigweed
Amaranthus species

bledo, amaranth, quelite, carelessweed, cat's tail, callaloo

seeds, young leaves

Savored across the globe, tender young pigweed greens are highly nutritious, and can be spiced up with garlic, onions, and chiles.

How to Identify

The veins on the young leaves of pigweed stand out—they are deeply impressed into the leaf and are a contrasting color (either red or tan). Additionally, the side veins appear parallel, as they reach out from the center vein before they curve up at the leaf's edge. Occasionally, the upper leaves will have smudges of white, ashen gray, or reddish purple that seem to have been sponge painted on. Most leaves reach straight out from the plant, nearly horizontal—however, at high temperatures they will look droopy. The stalks of pigweed often appear red at various stages of development. Many of our species of *Amaranthus* have male and female flowers on separate plants; you will only be able to harvest seeds from the female plants. The tiny flower spike has been referred to as a cat's tail as it emerges.

Where and When to Gather

Pigweed pops up in disturbed soil in yards and gardens, along floodplains and dry arroyos, and in forest clearings and margins. It can first appear in March, or later, with the first rains of summer. However the greens can be harvested

These young, tender tops of pigweed are at the perfect stage for foraging.

through early September on older plants. In early autumn the spikes of seed clusters ripen to a brown-beige, signaling the onset of the seed harvest—for humans and birds alike.

How to Gather

Tender pigweed greens are simply pinched off. Feel down the soft, flexible stem until it becomes less pliable, bending it as you go, then snip it off. This whole portion, stem and leaf, is eaten. When collecting seed from the female plants, use care—the flower (seed stalk) is rimmed with spikelets that poke.

How to Use

Cooking with pigweed greens is quite simple, and limitless variations exist. Fresh greens can be sautéed with garlic and onions, added to soups, and tossed into omelets. Leaves and stems can also be blanched and frozen for later use. Dried parts can be powdered and baked into breads, added to smoothies, and—well, you get the idea. Seeds are often roasted soon after processing. After roasting, seeds can be ground or left whole; I prefer them whole for storage. Combine ground seed meal with other grains, milk, cinnamon, and honey for a delicious *atole*. Mix the toasted whole seeds with honey, puffed rice, and chocolate chips for cookies.

Future Harvests

Amaranthus palmeri has developed resistance to glyphosate (Roundup®), resulting in hundreds of acres of agriculture in the Southeast being compromised. I don't think pigweed is going anywhere soon. And no, I wouldn't forage any plant growing on chemically treated soil.

Female pigweed, full of ripened seeds.

Gathering and Processing Pigweed Seeds

Gather dry pigweed seedpods with leather work gloves.

Shake or strip dry pigweed seedpods into a paper bag.

Harvesting the seeds of *Amaranthus palmeri* involves multiple steps, and there are several options. Start with a paper bag and a pair of leather work gloves. Clippers are optional. Later in the process, you will need a bowl, preferably a fairly wide one.

1. If plants are not fully dehydrated, you can bend them over into the paper bag and shake the plants while holding onto the main stems. This should allow the mature seeds to fall out of the seedpods and into your bag (there will be other debris that falls into the bag as well).

Alternatively, you can simply snip off the whole top of the plant (or the majority of seedpods). Gather a good number of seedpods.

2. Strip the remaining seeds into the bag. Holding the stems in or over the bag, pinch the stem and run your fingers out toward the thinner end of the stem, removing all attached seeds as you go. Collect all of this stripped material in the paper bag. Take some time to rub all the seedpods vigorously between gloved hands to help disintegrate the plant matter further (essentially making it lighter).

4. The ideal condition for winnowing is to have a gentle unidirectional breeze blowing. Either sitting on the ground or with the bowl on a waist-high surface in front of you, lightly toss the contents up into the air (careful not to lose those tiny seeds!) and allow the breeze to carry off the lighter plant debris. You can also pick up handfuls of the mixture and drop it from an appropriate height back into your bowl, allowing the wind to blow the lighter debris away.

In this time-honored process, you gradually arrive at a debris-free bowl of seeds. However, employing only the wind can take quite some time. Another option is to pour your mostly winnowed mixture into a bucket of water, and stir with a long stick. The seeds will descend to the bottom while the lighter plant debris floats to the top. This allows you to scoop it off and discard. Repeat the process until the water is clean, then pour most of the water off the top, and pour the seeds through a very fine strainer or clean cloth. Dry the seeds in the sun, or place them in a cast iron skillet on medium heat to toast lightly, imparting a fine flavor. Store seeds in a glass jar in the cupboard, or in the freezer for greater longevity. Grind seeds as needed, or use them whole.

Winnowing the fine pigweed seeds and dry plant material requires a gentle breeze and several pairs of busy hands!

3. Next, it's time to winnow! It must be in our DNA—a simple task that our ancestors perfected at some point along the evolutionary path. Winnowing can be done either on the spot as you're harvesting, or later. Either way, transfer the contents of your paper bag to the bowl.

pincushion cactus

Mammillaria species

nipple cactus, fishhook pincushion, cabeza de viejo, biznaguita, coyote's paws

EDIBLE fruit, stems

Although they look like small peppers, the fruits of pincushion cactus are tangy and sour with tiny, crunchy seeds inside.

How to Identify

There are a variety of *Mammillaria* species found throughout our region. They all contain tuberculate stems (with nipples along the stem) where the spines emerge (at the areole). The stems grow single or clustered to a height of about 6 inches. The central spine may be hooked (as with *M. grahamii*) or straight, and the flowers are pink or white. Look for the opened flowers several days after the summer's first rain.

Where and When to Gather

Mammillaria species (about thirteen total) can be found throughout our region with the exception of East Texas and the Four Corners area. All of the species have edible fruit, but *M. grahamii* is considered choice. The fruits are generally available in the late winter through the spring within our region.

How to Gather

Pincushion cactus fruits can be carefully plucked from the cactus. They come off easily when ripe.

How to Use

The hollow, tart fruits of pincushion cactus make a refreshing nibble along the trail. Chopped up, added to water, and soaked for several hours, a refreshing tart beverage can be made. Some species may be bland. Various tribes in the Southwest roasted the stems and ate the flesh once the spines were removed.

Future Harvests

Eat no more than half the fruits you find, to provide food for wildlife and seeds for reproduction. Cactus seedlings have a very low survival rate in the wild.

Fruits of *Mammillaria grahamii* ripen from late winter to early spring in the Sonoran Desert. Under certain conditions, fruits can encircle the whole cactus.

pine

Pinus species

piñon

EDIBLE inner bark, needles (tea), nuts, sap (chewing gum), pollen

With several edible options, pine provides some of the tastiest and most nutritious foods for the forager's table.

How to Identify

Pine is a conifer. Like many conifers, it possesses needles. However, the needles found on a pine tree are always fascicled, that is, they are bundled together in a small, thin sheath—even if there's only one needle. This is true of no other conifer within our region. There are many different versions of the pine tree throughout the Southwest, from wind-beaten scraggly shrubs, to stately trees in tremendous stands reaching heights of more than 200 feet. All pines bear seed cones, which may persist on the tree or fall shortly after maturity. The bark of pine trees varies, but is often reddish brown, butterscotch brown, or gray brown.

Pine trees are often found oozing clear, aromatic sap as the weather begins to warm.

Where and When to Gather

Pine trees are found throughout our region with the exception of low deserts, river valleys, the high plains of the panhandles, and coastal areas. Pine trees prefer acidic soils. The pollen is available from mid-spring to early summer, depending upon your location and any given year's weather patterns. Pine nuts are the most cherished and infrequent offering, being produced every two or three years. Several species are preferred for their sweet, oily, edible seeds including *Pinus edulis, P. monophylla,*

Gathering pine pollen from a lodgepole pine (*Pinus contorta*).

P. cembroides, and *P. remota*, all collectively referred to as piñon. Although subtle differences occur amongst species, the shape of the cones will be similar with brown seed shells becoming visible as the cones mature. These nuts will be ripe in the early autumn of harvest years. Inner bark, sap, and needles can be harvested year-round.

How to Gather

Pine pollen is very fine, and is gathered by shaking the open male cones over a basket, or into a plastic bag or open jug. As for the nuts, it is estimated that a family of four can gather around 200 pounds of piñon nuts in one day (in a good harvest year). The nuts are found in mature, unopened or opened female cones, on the tree or on the ground. Many still harvest piñon nuts in the Southwest by banging the tree with sticks to cause the nuts and cones to loosen and fall onto a tarp on the ground. Unopened cones will open in time on their own, or they can be placed among hot coals to force them open and roast the nuts. Soft or hardened sap is gathered from the bark, or off stones or fallen branches beneath the tree. Gather the inner bark from freshly fallen trees or cut back the outer bark on trunks to access (only in emergency situations). The youngest needles, at the tips, can be cut back and used fresh or dry for tea.

How to Use

Pine pollen is used as a nutritional supplement and is considered an invigorating food. It can be consumed raw from the tree, or

The edible nuts of pine discolor and are encased in hard shells.

used like cattail pollen when baking. I mix it with local honey and ground saguaro and barrel cactus seeds, then form the mixture into 1-inch balls. Toasted or raw, the nuts can be eaten as a snack, but they also make the most delicious addition to cakes, muffins, and other baked goods; any nut butter preparations; gravy; stuffing; the aforementioned seed balls; and soups and stews. Sap can be used as a chewing gum, as well as a medicinal substance applied directly to wounds to disinfect and hasten healing. The inner bark is chewed to extract the sugars, or dried and pounded to separate the starch from the woody cellulose. Pine needle tea is aromatic, warming, and delicious.

Future Harvests

Harvest what you can use and pine populations will continue to provide for us all.

pony's foot

Dichondra species
silver pony's foot

EDIBLE leaves

Pony's foot is a wild, crisp green without a hint of bitterness. You may even have some growing right now in your yard.

How to Identify

Pony's foot is so small, you've probably overstepped it without a second thought. The round to kidney-shaped leaves occur in pairs on relatively long petioles. The base of the leaf is often heart shaped. This feature and the blunt tips help distinguish pony's foot from pennywort or violet. Pony's foot possesses tiny hairs which are flattened across the leaf and stem. Similar to strawberries and pennywort, they send out runners from which they continually leaf out. Tiny five-petaled white flowers emerge from the leaf axils.

Where and When to Gather

Look for pony's foot in your lawn, city parks, or other moist, shady areas with a tree canopy. Although pony's foot occurs throughout our region it may be more common in the far eastern portion. The leaves can be gathered at any time. In certain locations, this may be year-round.

How to Gather

You're going to have to get low to gather pony's foot. Pinching a few at a time is about as efficient as it gets. If the temperature is above 80 degrees Fahrenheit, you may want to have a cooler handy to keep the leaves fresh.

How to Use

Pony's foot is great on sandwiches, as a solo salad or with other greens, for garnishing chili or tacos, or used like any mild-tasting green. Pony's foot is best eaten fresh.

Future Harvests

If you enjoy the experience of harvesting and eating your own pony's foot, there's a good chance you could establish it in your yard anywhere throughout our region (below 6000 feet elevation).

The pony's foot leaf is considered reniform, or kidney-shaped.

prickly pear
Opuntia species
Indian fig, nopál, tuna (fruit)

`EDIBLE` flowers, fruit, pads

Do not be dismayed, there are trouble-free ways to handle prickly pear, allowing one to enjoy a multitude of tasty preparations and the fruit's vibrant color.

The bright flower of *Opuntia ficus-indica* appears in the spring.

The pink-red fruit of *Opuntia phaeacantha* is delicious.

How to Identify

Throughout our range, prickly pear pads are round to ovate to elongate. Some pads contain spines; others don't. Glochids may be sparsely present or numerous, ranging from a light color to dark and thick as a beaver's coat. The pads are mostly green, but can appear brown-beige-purple depending on weather conditions. Flowering occurs in the spring followed by ripening of the fruit, which requires from two and a half to five months. Fruits are a range of red-purple colors. The inner flesh of the fruits can be a deep wine red to a melon green when ripe. Fruits are spiny or spineless, but always contain glochids, in my experience. The cactus can spread out close to the ground or grow upright to over 5 feet (10 to 15 feet with cultivated *Opuntia ficus-indica*).

Where and When to Gather

Prickly pear covers a wide range of habitats; this quintessential cactus of the southwestern deserts can be found throughout our range. In Arizona, the 3000- to 4000-foot elevation range is often most heavily colonized. The pads are gathered in the spring as they emerge; collect them when they are still flexible and a brighter green than older pads. Harvest the flowers for tea once they dry on the green fruit. Gather the fruits once they are fully ripe (see accompanying sidebar for more information).

Ripening coastal prickly pear on Mustang Island, Texas, in the early autumn.

Once fully processed, freshly processed or recently thawed prickly pear juice can be used to create fruit leather.

How to Gather

Use a knife and a pair of tongs to collect prickly pear pads. Hold a pad with the tongs and use the knife to cut across the base of the pad (within 1 inch of the joint), then place the pad in a large bowl nearby. Pick the dried flowers out of the apical stem (from which the flower emerged) and place them in a paper bag. To gather the fruits, use tongs again; the fruits should come off easily. If unripe, they will be difficult to remove and will taste bitter and excessively sour. Place the fruits in a handled plastic bucket.

How to Use

Prickly pear pads are a classic vegetable in traditional Mexican and Southwest cuisine. They are boiled, roasted, sliced, sautéed, dehydrated, pickled, and canned. They make a perfect accompaniment to meat dishes. The flowers create a lovely, tart tea with medicinal attributes (studies and anecdotal evidence indicate antibacterial and anti-inflammatory effects). The fruits make a low-glycemic juice, and pads are a similarly low-glycemic food—both useful in the improvement of insulin resistance. The juice can be consumed fresh, frozen, canned, added to kombucha ferments, or made into jelly, syrup, fruit leather, vinegar, or wine.

Future Harvests

In many areas, prickly pear is advantageous and grows quite prolifically (especially since grazing arrived on these lands). If you find a fruit you're particularly fond of, bring seeds and a pad to your property. Pads are simple to cultivate—simply bury a third of the lower pad and walk away.

Cautions

Rare cases of chills, fever, and hallucinations can accompany the consumption of small amounts (2 to 4 ounces) of uncooked prickly pear juice. It is as yet unclear, but this indicates an allergic response in my opinion, if not a clear sign of microbial shifting in our ecology. Indigenous cultures have consumed raw prickly pear fruit, en masse, for generations and generations.

Processing Prickly Pear Fruit

Prickly pear is a hearty, bountiful, trans-desert native cactus—a splendid food source (and medicine), worthy of supplying a variety of staples in the forager's cupboard. However, there appears to be much confusion surrounding the processing of prickly pear fruit. It can, however, be accomplished quite simply. Many sources direct the forager to burn off individual spines and glochids over an open flame, or peel each fruit individually. Neither of these tedious methods is necessary if one intends to extract the juice, which is the most effective way of accessing the flavor and nutrition of the fruit. Once you've arrived home with a bucket of ripe fruit, here are three options that offer straight-forward, efficient approaches.

Option 1. One of the simplest techniques for processing prickly pear fruit is the freeze and thaw method. There is no burning of spines, no peeling of fruit. Simply fill a pillowcase (or similar bag dedicated to the task) with fresh (cleaned, if necessary) prickly pear fruit. Place fruits directly in the freezer, or in a bowl or storage container that is a shape which will fit inside a strainer. Once the fruit is fully frozen, pull out the bag and place it inside the strainer. Set the strainer and its contents inside a slightly larger bowl or bucket, where it can rest at the top with space below to drain. In hot weather, place the set-up outside to expedite the process. You'll soon notice that as the prickly pear fruit thaws,

it shrivels and smooshes, essentially juicing itself. Freezing and thawing helps break down the cells of the fruit, allowing it to passively release most of its juice. Once the fruit is fully thawed, you'll have passively extracted 40 to 60 percent of the fruits' juice. To remove the last amount of juice, apply adequate pressure with a potato masher or similar tool and push the remaining liquid through the pillowcase. Note that the tightness or looseness of the fabric's weave can either restrict liquid passage or allow unwanted particles (like glochids and spines) through.

Freezing and thawing prickly pear fruit is a simple and efficient way for foragers to process small batches at home.

The main drawback (or benefit, depending on your perspective) of this method is that with an amply dense filter, you get a very clear juice, devoid of any pulp (or particulate) and, perhaps, pectin. Pectin is attributed with providing some of prickly pear fruit's healthful qualities. Discard the mash (filled with seeds, spines, and glochids) which remains, or spread it out on screens to sun dry and use later to make a well-strained infusion. The juice can be used fresh, stored in the freezer, hot packed and canned for storage, utilized in any of the ways suggested in the prickly pear plant profile.

Option 2. Another method, often preferred by those with large harvests or limited freezer space, is to blend and strain the fruit. This method also does not involve any burning of spines at the stove, meticulously peeling the fruit, or sweeping them across the desert floor with brooms. This technique does, however, require a blender or similar machine, several bowls, and a ⅛- to ¹⁄₁₆-inch mesh strainer. Begin by processing whole ripe fruit—a few to start—in the blender. As juice accumulates, add more fruit (this allows for more efficient blending). Pulse-blend to help break down the flesh of the fruit without pulverizing the seeds or shredding the skin too much. Strain the blender contents in the mesh strainer. Using this method, 99 percent of seeds, skin, spines, and glochids will be filtered after the first pour-off. Perform a second filtering; you may want to use a strainer that is slightly finer. Perfectionists (or sloppy pourers) may desire a third strain. The result will be a pulp-laden juice which is ready to consume, heat, can, freeze, or use otherwise. As with Option 1, discard the mash, or sun dry it and strain later for an infusion.

Option 3. A third method, also low tech, is to simply slice the fresh fruit crosswise and lay it out in the sun on screens to dry. However, this method does not extract the delicious juice, which is much of the fruit's content. It also does not separate the seeds, and requires that the fruits be thoroughly cleaned of spines and glochids before cutting. Therefore, it is probably more labor-intensive up front, but certainly requires far less equipment. The dried fruit segments are best rehydrated to make an infusion or tea.

A very simple option is to slice fresh prickly pear fruit and set it out to dry in the sun.

purslane

Portulaca oleracea

verdolagas

EDIBLE entire plant

A tart summer green, purslane is loaded with nutrition and makes a variety of unique, tasty dishes.

The yellow flowers of purslane open in the late morning, once the sun is high.

How to Identify

The succulent, spatulate (shaped like a spatula) leaves of purslane attach directly to the thick, copper-colored stem. Tiny yellow flowers emerge from within a cluster of leaves near midday, often not visible first thing in the morning or late in the afternoon. Purslane predominantly spreads across the ground, rising up to perhaps 4 to 5 inches in height. If it has purple flowers, it is not our purslane.

Where and When to Gather

Introduced from Europe, purslane is found nearly everywhere the ground has recently been disturbed. Emerging in the summer with the arrival of moisture, this annual can be gathered any time it is present. Toward the end of its life cycle, the greens are less palatable.

How to Gather
Pull up whole purslane plants when found in significant numbers (for example, hundreds of plants at your feet), or snip stems from a large plant you are coppicing in your garden. It will grow back.

How to Use
Fresh purslane can be blanched, sautéed, boiled, pickled, used in salads, or added directly to a bowl of hot soup. I like to add it to a sauté of other seasonal vegetables, such as onions, tomatoes, summer squash, chile peppers, or chiltepín. Add meat or beans if desired, and stuff peppers, tacos, or burritos—or serve as a stand-alone meal with rice or tortillas. For an extra-tart experience, combine purslane with sliced nopales and your favorite desert seasonings. A small amount in a salad goes a long way—add a splash of lime or balsamic vinegar. If oxalates are a concern for health reasons, blanch purslane for a minute and throw out the water; most of the oxalates should disperse in the water. The plant has been traditionally oven-dried to store for use as a winter green.

Future Harvests
As purslane is considered to be the sixth-most-common plant distributed globally, eat it to your heart's content. It is resistant to heat and drought, and one of the most nutritious and hardy plants we have available. I suggest encouraging its growth in your garden if you enjoy eating plant foods.

red bay
Persea borbonia

EDIBLE leaves

Red bay is a delightfully sweet, aromatic spice not unlike cinnamon, but with an entirely unique flavor.

How to Identify
Red bay is an evergreen tree which generally grows to a height of about 20 feet, but it can also be found to heights over 60 feet. Its dark green leaves are long, thick, and shiny with smooth margins, not toothed. The leaves are yellow at the stem and along the midvein, have flattened, rusty brown hairs on the underside, and possess a pleasant aroma when crushed. The white flowers with yellow centers are in three parts. Red bay is known to have galls (growths shaped like small, green beanpods) on the leaves, or in place of berries.

Where and When to Gather
Within our region, the range of red bay is limited to southeastern Texas and along the Gulf Coast. It prefers moist areas, but usually just out of the swamp, where bald cypress or tupelo may be growing. Red bay is also found in coastal dunes where southern live oak once flourished. Gather the healthy green leaves any time of year.

How to Gather
Simply pluck the leaves from the branch ends.

How to Use
I would suggest using red bay leaves sparingly, as other culinary bay leaves are used. A member of the Lauraceae family, red bay makes a wonderful, spicy addition to soups, stews, or slow-cooked roasts such as the Mexican dish, *bírria*. The sweet, fragrant aroma of red bay comes through in a hot infusion of the leaves, creating a wonderful tea for a chilly evening. It can also be drunk cold on a hot day to help one cool down. Use three or four dry leaves for a pint of tea. Red bay leaves were recorded as being used medicinally by coastal peoples of the Southeast.

Future Harvests
Along the Atlantic coast (South Carolina to Florida) the red bay ambrosia beetle has wreaked havoc on the local populations. This pest has not yet affected eastern Texas, but please plant a tree or two if you have suitable habitat for growing red bay.

Cautions
Use red bay sparingly (just as you would bay leaf) as it has a history as an emetic at much higher concentrations.

Red bay leaves make a wonderful, fragrant spice.

Healthy red bay leaves may be gathered any time of year.

red date

Ziziphus zizyphus

jujube, Chinese date, hong zao

`EDIBLE` fruit

Crunchy like an apple but very sweet when fresh, red date has a rich tradition of culinary and medicinal use.

How to Identify

In our desert environment the red date tree grows 15 to 20 feet in height, with gray bark that develops into strips laid tightly against the trunk. The thick, shiny leaves turn yellow in the fall and reappear in the spring; they possess small, irregular teeth around the entire margin and have three main, raised, yellow-green veins, which run from tip to base. The new stem growth is gray-green, and the thorns are found at the base of the leaves. Tiny yellow-green flowers appear from the leaf base in the spring, turning into elongated green fruit by early summer. These fruits come in a variety of shapes and sizes ranging from marble sized to 2 to 3 inches in length and an inch across, and possess a linear crease at the base. They ripen from green to yellow to brick red.

Where and When to Gather

Red date can be found scattered through-out our region in urban and rural settings. This semi-naturalized tree is native to Asia, but is both drought and frost tolerant, allowing it to flourish in a wide diversity of climes—particularly the Southwest. Look for it in vacant lots, disturbed ground, city parks, or old homesteads. The fruits ripen midsummer. In Thailand, this is the last fruit of the season to ripen and its name is translated as "come late" (*poot-saah*). It is often applied to those who have a habit of arriving late to events.

The immature fruit of red date is edible.

When fully ripened, red date is at its optimal sweetness.

How to Use

Store red date fruits in the refrigerator to maintain their freshness. They have a unique sweetness when fully ripe and can be eaten like a fresh apple or pear. Red date fruits become softer and sweeter just before they dry and harden. Prepare red date jelly or syrup, ferment the fruit into wine, pickle it, or candy it when fresh. Otherwise, dry it for tea, or for use in soups and stews as flavoring and nutrition. Red date fruit is also used for wide-ranging medicinal treatments, and is a common ingredient in traditional Chinese broths.

Future Harvests

As you may notice, red date trees proliferate readily once introduced. Interestingly, they don't seem to spread widely, but reproduce locally and well via root suckers. Cultivate this frost- and drought-tolerant tree in the appropriate place for continued fruit supply.

How to Gather

Simply pull red date fruits from the stem. The yellowish-green or chartreuse fruits are just beginning to ripen, but are certainly edible. At this point, they are the most crisp. If you wish, wait until the sweetness concentrates further and pull the fruits off the tree when they are fully red, or pick them up off the ground, as they readily fall when ripening.

red raspberry

Rubus idaeus

American red raspberry, western red raspberry

`EDIBLE` fruit

The full sweetness of red raspberry fills one's mouth amidst chirping birds, swaying conifers, and the sounds of full, rushing summer creeks.

This ripe red raspberry (*Rubus idaeus*) was found in the high mountains of Arizona.

How to Identify

Red raspberry is an herbaceous perennial with red or beige zig-zag branches covered in short spines. Plants generally stand 3 to 4 feet in height, although branches may be up to 12 feet long. The three to five pinnate, sawtooth green leaves often possess a fuzzy underside. Like all of our native *Rubus* species, red raspberry flowers are comprised of five white petals. In the case of *Rubus idaeus*, blooms are found in groups of one to four, hanging down from the leaf axils on growth that is second year and older. The thimble-like, aggregate, hazy to bright red berries appear beneath the five-pointed, dry, brown calyx.

Where and When to Gather

Red raspberry is found throughout our range, though not in Texas. It favors wet, mountainous areas, or coniferous forests. Ripe raspberries can be found through August and sometimes into September.

How to Gather

Lightly touch the fruit with forefinger and thumb with a slight pull, being careful not to squish too hard. If the berry doesn't come off easily, it's not yet fully ripe. Fully ripe red raspberries are very soft. Be sure to empty out your gathering bag or bucket before the fruits pile too high, to prevent berries from spoiling.

How to Use

You can do anything with wild red raspberries that you can with garden-grown or store-bought raspberries. In my opinion, the wild berries taste much better. Red raspberries make an excellent jam without the addition of any sugar or pectin, and, yes, the jam jells beautifully. Bake red raspberries into pies, cobblers, quick breads, muffins, cheesecake, tarts, and certainly anything with chocolate. Cover the raspberries in an equal volume of sugar and set the mixture aside for a day to make a decadent syrup. Red raspberries may also make a good wine. Dried raspberries are a wonderful addition to homemade granola, trail mix, hot cocoa drinks, or herbal tea blends. The leaves of first-year canes (primocanes) make a tasty, mildly astringent tea which is known to help tone the uterus.

Future Harvests

You are welcome to scatter seeds (camping out in a red raspberry locale helps promote this), but numerous creatures are fully engaged in this activity throughout the raspberry season.

Rocky Mountain bee plant

Peritoma serrulata

wild spinach, bee spiderflower, tumi (Hopi), waá (Diné)

`EDIBLE` young leaves, flowers, seeds

An abundant green in the early summer, Rocky Mountain bee plant is often around when no other wild greens are available.

How to Identify

Rocky Mountain bee plant is an annual with smooth, pointed, compound palmate leaves (with three leaflets). It is light in color with a yellowish hue cast across the stem. In midsummer the abundant and showy pink flowers appear with long, exerted stamens and four petals. The plant can grow to nearly 5 feet high under rare circumstances but is most often under 3 feet.

Where and When to Gather

Rocky Mountain bee plant inhabits the entire mountainous western half of our region and up into the panhandles of Texas

The terminal raceme of Rocky Mountain bee plant appears pink to purple.

The young leaves of Rocky Mountain bee plant are boiled in two changes of water before consuming.

and Oklahoma. The terrain is piñon-juniper woodland, dry desert washes, and sagebrush flats. The young plants are available for harvest mid- to late spring. The flowers can be gathered throughout the summer rainy season; the seeds, shortly thereafter.

How to Gather

In large stands of Rocky Mountain bee plant, simply pull up the whole young plant. Otherwise, clip below the tender growth tips. The flowers can be plucked individually, or whole stalks can be gathered from large stands.

How to Use

Boil the leaves for one minute. Strain and taste. If the flavor is still too strong, boil in clean water once again. The second boiling should mellow the flavor considerably. Then sauté leaves in oil with onion, or cook via any other preferred method. Leaves may also be dried for future use. The flowers are used for their sweet nectar and their beauty as a garnish. The seeds are a pungent spice. Rocky Mountain bee plant was often integrated into traditional three sisters agriculture in order to attract bees as pollinators for food crops.

Future Harvests

Like so many wild greens, when Rocky Mountain bee plant is plentiful, harvest abundantly. When scarce, allow a significant portion of the population to mature to seed.

saguaro

Carnegiea gigantea

sahuaro, giant cactus, hashaan

`EDIBLE` fruit, seeds, flowers

Saguaro is found only in the Sonoran Desert, and its fruit is the epitome of sweetness. Its rich caramel juices blend with the oily crunch of its seeds to create the ultimate desert candy bar.

How to Identify

Saguaro, the tallest cactus in the United States, is a pleated columnar cactus with a single central trunk. You will find the white flowers with creamy yellow centers from late March through early July, and the brilliant red fruits throughout June and into early July. Saguaro begins flowering around 40 or 50 years of age.

Where and When to Gather

Saguaro is found exclusively in Arizona (rare outliers exist in Southern California), near the central portion of the state, toward the southwest corner, and south of the Mexican border in Sonora, Mexico. It likes to grow on rocky, south-facing canyon hillsides and down the *bajadas*, or gradual slopes, that form the bottom slopes of desert mountain ranges. Saguaro is generally found below 4000 feet elevation. Technically, harvesting saguaro fruit is limited to private property (with the owner's permission, of course). However, strolling through a saguaro forest from mid-June to early July in a year of ample fruit production, one may find hundreds of

Saguaro flowers are visited by birds, bats, moths, and bees.

sun-dried fruits, still nestled in their outer rinds, strewn across the desert floor. Just pick one up, remove the fruit from the rind, and chew.

Growing near the branch tips, both fully ripe and unripe fruit can exist together.

Although many run for shelter from the sun during the dry summer of the Sonoran Desert, wise desert dwellers relish this time as the saguaro fruit ripens. In fact, some visitors specifically plan trips to the area then, just to taste the fresh fruit. Several workshops and private camps are offered to the public for harvesting during this time.

How to Gather

Dry flowers can be gathered from the base of the cactus throughout June. Traditional fruit collection methods involve the use of a harvesting cane, or *kuiput*, which is used to pull down ripe fruit into the waiting arms of an agile harvesting partner, who is ready to catch the juicy delicacy. If you lack the equipment and the partner, look for dry, preserved fruit lying on the ground or hung up in nurse trees such as palo verde, mesquite, or ironwood. These trees once shaded the young upstart saguaro, when frost or trampling ungulates posed a real threat to its survival.

How to Use

Saguaro is often referred to as the grandmother or grandfather of the Sonoran Desert. It provided the people who dwelled there the raw elements for syrup, wine, bread, *atoles*, oil, animal feed, medicine, construction material, starting a fire, and so much more. The juice can be turned into jam, syrup, juice drinks, vinegar, wine, ice cream, and popsicles. The oily, nutritious seeds from the fruit can be added whole to salads, breads, muffins, or granola. They also make a delicious flour when dried and ground in a coffee grinder; add the flour to breads, cookies, pie crusts, or other baking endeavors. I regularly use the seed flour in my various acorn bread recipes. Freeze the fresh juice (strained or with seeds) for later use, or cook it down to concentrate the sugars once the seeds have been strained out. Traditional shelf-stable syrup can be made by reducing the fresh juice by ten to fifteen times its original volume, resulting in a molasses-like syrup. Keep in mind, before the introduction of European and African honeybees and the importation of sugar, this was the primary sweetener of the region. I've also discovered that an infusion prepared with the dried flowers resembles the smoky sweetness of the ripe fruit.

Future Harvests

Once you've located private land with permission of the landowners, start your harvest roughly one to two weeks into the season. This allows the foraging birds to gorge themselves and disperse the seeds freely. It is estimated that a saguaro produces 40,000,000 seeds during its lifetime. If even one of those seeds grows to a mature saguaro, the populations will remain relatively stable.

Strained saguaro seeds drying in the sun.

Traditional Processing of Saguaro Fruit

The Tohono O'Odham of the Sonoran Desert have long labored through various systems for the gathering, processing, and storage of a variety of desert plant foods. One such food was significant enough to mark the time of transition from year to year: the ripe fruit of the saguaro (*bahidaj*). During the hottest, driest days of the year in the desert, the saguaro cactus fruit quickly ripens. Just before the rains begin, dousing the parched desert floor, brilliant red fruits explode across the Sonoran Desert. Sufficiently baked by the sun, juice taken directly from the plant's fruit tastes of cooked-down caramel. But this fruit, high in sugar, quickly begins to ferment if rained upon or not swiftly dried by the sun. Traditional processing of saguaro fresh fruit involved cooking batches daily. Follow this simple process to replicate the ways of the Tohono O'Odham.

1. Establish a bed of hot coals (mesquite or ironwood, preferred) on which to cook the fruit and juice.

2. Dump all of your freshly gathered fruit (once removed from the tough outer skins) into a large pot. Add a bit of water to the

Skimming debris off the top of the boiling fresh fruit (with water added).

pot (creating a slurry which is easy to stir) to prevent the juice from scalding. Don't worry about debris attached to the fruit—you'll skim this off the surface once the contents are boiling.

3. Place the pot and its contents on the hot coals and bring to a boil.

4. As the pot's contents boil, skim off the lightweight debris that floats to the top. (Grains of sand and pebbles will sink to the bottom and be removed later.)

5. Decant the juice, seeds (*kaai*), and fiber (*kivc*) through a strainer that will accommodate the pour.

6. Filter the juice again, this time through a fine cloth and strainer. As the juice is strained, sand and pebbles should be removed from the bottom of the pot.

7. Return the refined juice to the pot and place over the hot coals once again. Slowly cook the juice down to a thick syrup (*sitol*); the consistency should be similar to that of molasses, roughly a twelfth of the volume you started with.

8. The thick, dark, shelf-stable syrup you have prepared is as delectable and seductive as any sweetener on the market. The syrup may begin to ferment within one to two years on the shelf. Prolong its stability by storing in the refrigerator, or canning.

The second straining of the cooked juice through a fine cloth and strainer.

salsify

Tragopogon dubius

goatsbeard, yellow salsify, wild oysterplant

`EDIBLE` flower buds, roots, shoots, young leaves

A versatile vegetable, salsify was once cultivated widely, and has now become naturalized.

How to Identify

Salsify is easiest to identify once it's gone to seed, as its plumed seeds grow out in a globose form resembling dandelion. But that's a little late in this biennial's life for our purposes. The long, grass-like, clasping leaves are wooly where they attach to the stem. The flower buds are long and tapered at the end of an extended, hollow stem. Also similar to dandelion, the plant exudes a milky latex once broken. The yellow flower petals are much shorter than the surrounding phyllaries, which appear like green, hairy rays of sun. The tap root is white; tiny rootlets grow from it, taking on different forms depending on the growing conditions.

Where and When to Gather

Salsify can be found throughout our entire range, with the exception of the southeastern and central areas of Texas. Look to disturbed areas at higher elevations or with relatively high moisture levels—forest clearings, meadows, and riversides. The roots are best dug in the fall of their first year or in the late winter or early spring before the plant flowers in its second year. Once the plant has begun to flower, it's too late to gather the root. The young shoots, of course, are gathered earlier, and the unopened inflorescences (flower buds) are found in greatest numbers midsummer. Leaves are best gathered when young.

How to Gather

Most parts of the salsify plant can simply be picked by hand. Gathering the root will likely call for a shovel, digging stick, or trowel. The roots may reach a foot down into the soil. Young shoots, tender leaves, and flower stalks can all be snapped off by hand.

How to Use

The tender young leaves and sweet flower buds can be added to salads. I prefer to lightly sauté the long flower buds in butter and garlic, then salt to taste. They are reminiscent of tender asparagus. The roots can be grated and eaten raw; sliced or grated and boiled, baked, sautéed; or fermented (they are high in inulin). If you are blessed with an abundance, you can freeze any parts, or pressure can the roots.

Salsify flowers appear in the midday sunshine.

Future Harvests

Allow a majority of the plants you encounter to go to seed, and future harvests should continue. Keep in mind this plant is naturalized throughout our region, and is considered a weed by many.

saya

Amourexia palmatifida

Mexican yellow show

EDIBLE flowers, fruit, leaves, roots, seeds

A subtropical relative of annatto, saya contributes a variety of flavors to the forager's menu, since every plant part is edible.

Saya's yellow flowers often cover hillsides in desert grasslands along our border region.

How to Identify

The first thing you will notice about saya is this herbaceous perennial's showy yellow flowers. They feature red spots on the descending orange petals, but not on the singular upright petal. The leaf segments splay out like fingers on a hand (botanical term: palmate), and the edges of the leaves are serrate, with small sawlike teeth. The seeds are black within the mature hollow fruit. Nearly all evidence of this plant will have disappeared upon the arrival of winter.

Where and When to Gather

Look to rocky, southeast- or southwest-facing hillsides in desert grasslands, along the border regions (southeast Arizona and southwest New Mexico, in particular). The best time to identify saya is from mid-July

The roots of saya can be eaten raw or cooked.

Saya's hollow fruit and its seeds are edible.

through mid-August, at the height of the summer rainy season. Once a population is discovered, you can return there yearly. All parts of the plant are edible, so gathering can occur throughout the summer.

How to Gather

You may wish to first nibble a sample of saya's leaves or flowers. Then try the rich, cucumber-like flavor of the young seedpod. When you're ready to roll up your sleeves and break out your shovel, trowel, or pickax, you can collect the root. Begin by clearing the rocks and debris in a 2-foot diameter around the plant. Then start digging about 18 inches laterally from the base of the plant's stem. Once you've cleared an opening about 1 foot deep and 2 feet long, you can begin carefully excavating around the root mass or tap root in order to extract the roots without damaging them. Continue digging around the plant as needed to access the root mass. It is possible to harvest only a portion of the root mass in older plants, allowing them to regenerate and provide opportunities for future harvests.

How to Use

Adorn salads with saya leaves, flowers, and seedpods, or use any of these to garnish a stir-fry. You can harvest enough leaves to make them the base of a stir-fry. Consider adding the young fruits to salsa or fruit salads for an intriguing desert flavor. The fresh root can be eaten raw, or roasted to reduce the spiciness and bring out more sweetness. Alternatively, the root can be grated over cooked vegetables or a raw salad. Wrap the root in foil and place it near the edge of a campfire for a hearty foraging culinary experience.

Future Harvests

Saya is not common throughout our region. However, it is plentiful where it exists. It is a plant, in my opinion, that seems to respond well to regular harvesting. In our region, it was probably used over the centuries as a subsistence food by indigenous peoples. I suggest only coppicing the roots (not harvesting the whole root mass), allowing them to regenerate. This should insure substantial harvests of saya for generations to come.

serviceberry

Amelanchier alnifolia

shadberry, shadbush, Juneberry, saskatoon

EDIBLE fruit, leaves, stems (for tea)

Serviceberry is not particularly common in our region, but when encountered ripe, it is a delicious fresh fruit.

How to Identify

Serviceberry is a medium- to large-sized shrub, usually reaching 5 to 15 feet tall, with long, slender branches drooping off to the side. Look for the characteristic rose family flower with five petals (resembling that of apple, peach, pear, or plum). Your chances of identifying patches of service-berry are enhanced in the early spring, as they will often flower out ahead of the surrounding vegetation, mostly in May throughout our region. Additionally, the white flowers appear toward the branch tips before the leaves emerge. The berries show a crown at the far end. All berries with these crowns are edible.

Where and When to Gather

Serviceberry often occupies the edges of forest clearings just under the shade canopy, or at the upper margins of moist drainages. It is not abundant in the Southwest, as moist forest habitat is decreasing due to drought and epic forest fires. You will find the fruits available starting in July and into August.

How to Gather

If heavy dew is present, allow the berries to dry a bit in the early sunshine, and begin harvesting mid-morning. Pick berries one by one or in small clusters off the plant. Snip the young leaves and stems whenever they are available.

Serviceberry is a shrub of medium to large size.

How to Use

Serviceberry fruits are good fresh, dried, or cooked. In areas where serviceberries flourish, they are mashed and formed into cakes, then allowed to dry in the sunshine for winter storage or later use. In the Northwest, they were mashed into freshly cooked salmon and dried into pemmican. Don't hesitate to cook them up into jam, jelly, or pie. It's likely that the medicinal properties are enhanced through heating. The fruits are rich in anthocyanidins and the leaves and stems contain proanthocyanidins—both of which are healthful antioxidants. The fruits have been shown to relieve inflammation as effectively as over-the-counter pain relievers. Traditionally, they have been made into a deliciously sweet wine. Brew the leaves and stems as a hot infusion.

Future Harvests

Serviceberry "serves" as an apt reminder of what is happening in a much larger ecosystem that encompasses our region and beyond. This plant's important niche has been reduced in our range over the past century. Wildlife management strategies have played a major role in the prevalence of its alternating abundance and lack thereof. Look for ways to enhance its microhabitat in your local environment, or for opportunities to integrate it into your private surroundings. This will help secure future harvests as well as improve your connection to the local environment.

Ripe and unripe serviceberries with morning dew. Notice the serrated leaf margins.

sheep sorrel

Rumex acetosella

EDIBLE leaves

Pleasantly tart, the leaves of sheep sorrel make a lively addition to salads or the base of a piquant soup.

How to Identify

Sheep sorrel is a naturalized, perennial herb often found growing as an extensive carpet. It rarely reaches 1 foot in height in the Southwest. The leaves of the small rosette appear spear-shaped and have pointed segments angled diagonally near the base. The thin inflorescence extends upward, dotted with tiny flowers that adhere closely to the stem. All parts of the plant gradually mature to a brick red (a common characteristic in the buckwheat family). Sheep sorrel possesses shallow, fibrous roots. Fiddle dock (*Rumex pulcher*) is a close relative found predominantly in the eastern half of our region. Its leaves are also edible and it is similar in appearance, but has spiny seed capsules.

Where and When to Gather

Sheep sorrel can be found in nearly every state and province of North America. It regularly occupies both the eastern and western halves of our region. Look to disturbed areas, gardens, sandy and muddy shores, waste places, and open meadows. Its leaves are available for gathering from late spring through summer.

How to Gather

Get down low. Sheep sorrel requires squatting, emphatic bending, or lying on your belly. I suppose you could rake it up, but that seems sort of nonforager-like. Gather with your fingertips.

How to Use

Grace your summer salads with this delicacy, add a bit to pickled creations and vegetable ferments, or go classic French style and use sheep sorrel as the base for a tart or soup with butter, onions, stock, and cream. A wonderful, unique flavor for the forager's kitchen.

Future Harvests

Forage and collect as much as you want. Sheep sorrel is a naturalized nonnative plant. It is considered invasive in Arizona.

Cautions

References to sheep sorrel containing oxalic acid are true. To be on the safe side, I would moderate intake to less than several handfuls of the fresh leaves per day (or boil and discard the water) if you are prone to kidney stones, have gout, or have overt kidney disease.

Tiny sheep sorrel turns red as it matures.

Siberian elm

Ulmus pumila

`EDIBLE` inner bark, young samaras, mature samaras, young leaves

Often viewed as a weedy nuisance tree, Siberian elm adds a variety of sweet, soothing elements to foraged meals.

How to Identify

Siberian elm's alternate leaves possess tiny crenulations (rounded teeth) along the margins, and are often stiff and crinkly with prominent raised veins on the underside. An asymmetric leaf base (resulting in unmatched sides when leaves are folded at the midrib) is a common characteristic shared by all elms. As the season progresses, the following spring's flower buds will emerge at each leaf axil. Siberian elm bark often appears in long, narrow strips and is gray in color. The flowers and fruits, or samaras, appear before the leaves emerge. The samaras mature with crepe-like wings surrounding the seed inside. Siberian elm's leaves turn yellow before falling in the autumn.

Where and When to Gather

Siberian elm can be found throughout the western portion of our region, mostly at elevations above 4000 feet. Cedar elm is found throughout Central Texas. Winged elm (*U. alata*), American elm (*U. americana*), and slippery elm (*U. rubra*) can all be found within our region from Central Texas eastward. The young samaras of Siberian elm are available in the early spring before the tree is leafed out, but the

You will find Siberian elm (*Ulmus pumila*) across our region, except in Texas, where cedar elm is prevalent.

mature samaras can be harvested at any point afterward. The leaves are best gathered when still young as they are most tender then. The inner bark is sweetest in the spring before the tree flowers or in the

Stately cedar elm (*Ulmus crassifolia*) is found abundantly throughout Central Texas.

The green, unripe seeds, or samaras, of *Ulmus pumila* (and all *Ulmus* species) are sweet and slightly nutty.

fall once the leaves have turned color; harvest during these times.

How to Gather

Young samaras of the Siberian elm can be gathered by hand from hanging clusters along the low branches. Look to harvest from trees growing in the open with a wider crown. The mature samaras are often found on the ground beneath the tree. If you visit the trees often enough you can gather them shortly after they've fallen. Young leaves can be plucked from the branches. Young branches are harvested to procure the inner bark. Refer to page 76 for a discussion on how to harvest bark.

How to Use

The young samaras are sweet and nutty eaten fresh. The mature, cream-yellow samaras can be eaten raw once the papery outer covering has been removed. The young leaves can be eaten raw, or lightly steamed, boiled, sautéed, or blanched. The inner bark is boiled and strained to produce a pleasant, demulcent tea, or it can be boiled longer to cook the liquid down to a sweeter syrup. Alternatively, the dried bark can be pounded and powdered and the fibers sifted out to arrive at a sweet, starchy, fine flour. This flour can be used to thicken soups and stews, or added in small amounts when baking.

Future Harvests

Harvesting from *Ulmus pumila* should be encouraged wherever it grows. It is often viewed as invasive, but is rarely appreciated for the gifts it offers. Other native elm species of our region should be harvested with caution, as the Dutch Elm disease has been known to affect more than just slippery elm. Get to know your local populations by visiting them throughout the year and only harvest bark and seeds from stable or growing populations.

smartweed

Polygonum species
knotweed, dotted smartweed

`EDIBLE` entire plant

The peppery spice smartweed can add an extra kick to your freshly foraged creations.

How to Identify

Smartweed is an herbaceous perennial plant, growing to 6 feet in height, found exclusively in wet soil. The long, linear, alternate, smooth-edged leaves possess contrasting yellow venation on the upper surface (especially the midvein). The tiny white flowers, tinged with pink, droop down heavily from yellowish stems along the long terminal spike. The whole plant turns a brick red through the autumn and winter. Signature red sheathed joints along the stem reveal it as a member of the buckwheat family. The plant's common names of smartweed and knotweed are both widespread within the genera *Polygonum* and *Bistorta*, which are found across the United States (both native and nonnative species).

The new growth of *Polygonum punctatum* possesses numerous joints along the stem.

Where and When to Gather

Smartweed can be found throughout our region in swamps, marshes, riparian areas, reservoirs, lakes, or any perennially wet soil. The edible, nonnative marshpepper knotweed (*Polygonum hydropiper*), and lady's thumb (*P. persicaria*), can be found in the eastern portion and throughout our region, respectively. American bistort (*P.

bistortoides*) and alpine bistort (*Bistorta vivipara*, formerly *P. viviparum*) can be found at the high elevations within the northwest quadrant of the Southwest; they possess similar inflorescences to other bistorts, with jointed stems and alternate leaves.

How to Gather

Smartweed's young, tender leaves can be plucked from the stem tips at any time.

Roots are gathered in the fall. The seeds can be stripped off the flowering stem in a way similar to dock.

How to Use

Use fresh, chopped smartweed leaves in salads, salsas, soups, and stews which require a spicy zing. However, go easy on this pungent ingredient until you're familiar with how it flavors dishes; it has a strong peppery presence. You can also dry and powder the leaves to use as a spice. Add the fresh leaves to a forager's kimchi. The entire plant has traditionally been used for a range of ailments, including internal bleeding, stomach aches, and leg pains; employ sparingly for these purposes. The roots of American bistort are edible when soaked and cooked to remove the bitter tannins. The roots of alpine bistort can be eaten raw or cooked. Both can be made into a purée, and the seeds—toasted or not—can be ground into flour. The seeds of nonnative prostrate knotweed (*Polygonum aviculare*), black bindweed (*P. convolvulus*), and the native Douglas's knotweed (*P. douglasii*) all have a long tradition of being used as food.

Future Harvests

Gathering smartweed leaves as a spice poses no threat to its presence. When gathering roots or seeds, take care to locate flourishing stands before proceeding. Only gather what you can use, and leave the rest for regeneration, wildlife, and other foragers.

Cautions

Smartweed has been known to produce contact dermatitis in some individuals. Most people will show no response to gathering a few leaves for seasoning. Those who have known sensitivities may choose to wear gloves before harvesting. Although it's unlikely one could actually eat enough to aggravate high blood pressure, in theory, this plant could exacerbate it.

The long, flowering racemes of *Polygonum punctatum* tend to hang downward.

snakewood

Condalia warnockii

condalia, frutillo, Mexican crucillo, Mexican buckthorn

`EDIBLE` fruit

Snakewood is a prickly desert shrub with shiny black berries that possess a thick, sweet, soft pulp.

The shiny black fruits of snakewood appear singly along the spine-tipped, dull gray-brown branches.

How to Identify

This spiny-branched, evergreen shrub has tiny, linear to spatula-shaped leaves with a wrinkled look on top. The diminutive yellow-green sepals of the flower persist on the ripened berries. The flowers may appear at any time of the year when the proper conditions present themselves. The globose fruits hang on short green stems and mature to a shiny, dark blue-black.

Knifeleaf (*Condalia spathulata*) and bluewood (*C. hookeri*) are closely related species that also produce blue-black, sweet-tasting berries; the plants are stout desert shrubs with spiny branches.

Where and When to Gather

Snakewood is found in southern Arizona and southern New Mexico, as well as scattered throughout Texas. It may be found in open desert areas, washes, canyons, or within the canopy of mesquite and other riparian-area trees. Snakewood berries are available in the early autumn. The other *Condalia* species can be commonly found in the Southwest border region, or in the South Texas Plains.

How to Gather

Just like other spiny desert shrubs, you'll have to pick each snakewood berry by hand. Yes, some people beat the shrub with a stick to knock the fruits onto the ground, but in my experience, that makes many of the berries inaccessible—unless you are a kangaroo rat.

How to Use

Snakewood berries are a pleasant treat when eaten fresh. I imagine they would make a nice jam, jelly, or syrup (especially with their thick, full texture), perhaps even baked into breads and pies. I would suggest fermenting them in an equal amount of wildflower honey as soon as they can be harvested.

Future Harvests

Gather no more than what you can use, and leave a substantial amount for wildlife and reseeding. A general rule of thumb, in locations with robust berry production, is to harvest no more than a third of what you see.

Cautions

Be aware of the thorny nature of this shrub. It is unforgiving, so approach with slow, patient movements.

Solomon's plume

Maianthemum racemosum (syn. *Smilacina racemosa*)
false Solomon's seal

EDIBLE shoots, rhizomes, berries

A denizen of deep forests, Solomon's plume is another wild vegetable with a flavor similar to asparagus.

A signature terminal raceme of flowers easily distinguishes Solomon's plume from other related plants.

matures, the wide, glossy, alternate clasping leaves extend laterally from the main stem. The plants often grow in clusters, arching forward. A tight terminal cluster of numerous, showy, bright white flowers differentiates this plant from other *Maianthemum* species within our region. The terminal berries are a deep red when fully mature.

Where and When to Gather

Solomon's plume inhabits lush sections of our conifer forests. Look to the shady areas on the north side of a mountain or canyon bottom. The shoots are gathered in the early spring, but the rhizomes can be foraged nearly any time (as long as the ground is not frozen). The berries mature mid- to late summer.

How to Gather

To gather the shoots, dig or loosen the soil around the base of the shoot. Reach your fingers down and pull up firmly until the shoot snaps. You can also extend a sharp knife through the loose soil to slice off the shoot while pulling from the top. The berries can be picked from the end of the plant. Although the rhizome is widely

How to Identify

There are different characteristics to look for depending on when one encounters Solomon's plume. In the early spring, a singular, erect, overlapping cluster of blue-green leaves emerges from the soil (this is our preferred vegetable). As it considered an appropriate part of Solomon's plume to forage, I largely discourage it in our region due to the plant's limited availability and the possible consequences to future populations. That said, if you wish to gather judiciously, the rhizomes can be dug by hand from the loosened soil (loosen with a trowel, hori-hori, or small pickax). The rhizomes grow laterally, so feel down from the stem to see which direction they extend before digging into the adjacent soil and accidentally cutting into the small, tender rhizome. Enough rhizome to feed two people as a small side dish could potentially provide enough medicine (made into tincture) for an extended family for several months to a year, so only gather from areas of plenty. The berries can be picked from the end of the plant.

How to Use

I prefer to quickly blanch the young shoots, then sauté them in garlic, butter, and olive oil for one to two minutes. Add some bracken fern shoots or wild mushrooms, perhaps even fresh cholla buds, to considerably round out the texture and flavor. The rhizomes can be boiled to relieve some of the bitterness and soapy taste, then eaten whole, mashed, or roasted. If you manage to find a bounty of berries, they can be made into syrup, jam, or jelly. Cooking the berries should diminish their potential purgative properties. Solomon's plume is a potent medicinal plant, but can be used as food with moderation. Medicinally, the alcohol tincture is used to alleviate joint pain, address connective tissue injuries, enhance breathing, expectorate mucus, and stimulate digestion.

Future Harvests

I have attempted to propagate Solomon's plume populations by re-planting rhizome sections (the end with the recent stem; after harvesting for medicine), or burying ripe fruit in shady areas which appear appropriate Solomon's plume habitat.

Cautions

Consume Solomon's plume in moderation. It contains feeble cardiac glycosides which may temporarily increase blood pressure if taken in excess. Also, please abide by the sustainability practices suggested above.

This young shoot of Solomon's plume is at a perfect stage for harvesting.

sotol

Dasilyrion species

desert spoon

EDIBLE flower stalk, root crown, seeds

Sotol's unripe seeds taste like fenugreek or maple syrup, and its flower stalks roast up deliciously sweet.

A ripened sotol seed stalk in the low desert sun of December. Seeds are only found on female flower stalks.

Roast and eat young sotol flowering stalks for the sugars within; stalks retain their moisture hours after exposure to hot coals.

How to Identify

There is often confusion around sotol among desert foragers. Botanically related to *Yucca* and *Agave* species, our sotol is nonetheless distinct. To tell the difference, push your palm against the end of a leaf. If you pull back from a sharp point, the plant is not sotol, but perhaps one of its botanical cousins. The leaf ends of sotol are splayed and relatively soft to the touch. However, the leaf margins (edges of the leaves) have small, curved spines. Another distinctive characteristic of sotol is its ribbon-like leaf, with a profile that is flat for its entire length—not U shaped in cross section like a *Yucca* or *Agave* species.

Where and When to Gather

In the Sonoran Desert, sotol inhabits a mid-elevation range which begins just as the saguaro reaches its upper limits on the mountainside, and continues up to comingle with juniper, oak, and piñon. Sotol is also often landscaped in cities of the Southwest. The seeds begin to fully ripen in late October and into November, but can be harvested for months. The young flowering stalk may begin to emerge in late April; it should be harvested at its most tender, when it is still under 3 feet tall. The root crown is traditionally harvested just as the flowering stalk begins to show itself, as its sugars are most concentrated at this time—ideal for food or for making sotol's namesake drink (distilled or simply fermented).

How to Gather

Pull the dry female flower stalk down until it snaps, then pull and garble the seeds off the stems. The young flower stalk will need to be cut (or sawed) off as close to the base as one can reach. Wear gloves and watch the spines on the leaf margins. Harvesting the root crown requires considerable effort. Strip all the leaves first, then dig several inches down around the plant's base. A wedge-shaped tool was traditionally used by indigenous foragers of the Southwest to cut into the base of the root crown, removing it from the remaining root mass.

How to Use

Sotol's fresh seeds can be nibbled on the trail once the husk is removed. Dry seeds can be toasted, then ground into flour for baking. Gently rub the toasted seeds between rocks, or use a *molcajete* (Mexican mortar and pestle) to rub the husks loose, then winnow—or leave it all in for extra fiber. I've found that sotol flour adds a peanut butter flavor to baked goods. The young flowering stalks must be roasted at relatively high heat (at least 350 degrees Fahrenheit) to break down and remove bitter saponins, and be made palatable. Additionally, the leaves can be woven into mats, hats, and baskets. Root crowns are traditionally pit-baked overnight or for several days to slow-release the sugars within. Once removed from the pit, this food can be eaten, pounded flat into cakes and dried, or fermented and distilled into alcohol.

Future Harvests

Disperse seeds during your harvests, within the general gathering vicinity or in other favorable locations for sotol germination and growth. Use judgment when harvesting root crowns, with permission from the land owner or the presiding agency. Sotol can proliferate on overgrazed lands; harvest accordingly.

Cautions

Sotol's fresh flower stalk and root crown contain bitter and potentially irritating saponins. Always cook at recommended heat and for sufficient duration before ingesting. If the taste remains somewhat acrid or irritating, cook longer.

sow thistle

Sonchus oleraceus
common sow thistle
Sonchus asper
spiny sow thistle
Sonchus arvensis
field sow thistle

EDIBLE entire plant

Found the world over, sow thistle is an unsung hero of the garden, kitchen, and medicine cabinet—a perfect plant ally.

How to Identify

Sow thistle has many similarities to common dandelion; however, there are differences. Both dandelion and sow thistle have hollow stems (where the name *Sonchus* comes from) and composite heads of yellow flowers. They both exude milky sap when broken, taste bitter, and produce light, fluffy seed heads once mature. Like dandelion, sow thistle's deeply incised leaves can be tinged with purple and pink under certain conditions, and leaf tips look something like an arrowhead. Species of *Sonchus*, however, grow considerably taller (by several feet) than dandelion when in flower, and generally have spinier leaf margins—especially spiny sow thistle (*Sonchus asper*), whose spines are more substantial and numerous. Field sow thistle (*Sonchus arvensis*) can also be found within our region. Interestingly, sow thistle is *not* a true thistle (as plants in the *Cirsium* genus are).

Spiny sow thistle in flower.

Where and When to Gather

You will find sow thistle almost everywhere in the Southwest. This underutilized and relatively unknown and unsung plant hero is probably hanging out right under your nose, in disturbed areas, lawns, garden beds, and forest margins, and along trails and roadsides. In some locations, sow thistle can be harvested year-round. It likes relatively cool and moist conditions, so follow your local weather patterns to identify its optimal season. Generally, in lower elevations it prefers autumn to spring. It is a summertime plant at higher elevations, and in places with particularly cold winters.

How to Gather

Sow thistle's leaves and flowers can be picked with your fingertips. Prune an entire flowering stalk to harvest the stem. You can continue to harvest leaves from the same plant under appropriate growing conditions. Once the root is harvested, however, that's it.

How to Use

The leaves, stems, and flowers are eaten raw or lightly cooked. Use the stem like celery. The root is somewhat stringy and more bitter than the leaves. *Sonchus oleraceus* leaves are much more tender than those of spiny sow thistle (*Sonchus asper*). I prefer to cook the leaves of spiny sow thistle before eating. You can add sow thistle fresh to stir-fries, soups and stews, as well as fermented vegetable recipes such as kimchi. You can also dry its parts for future use. Once lightly steamed and coated with butter, the flowers taste very much like artichoke hearts. Sow thistle is thought to possess revitalizing properties, having been used traditionally to enhance digestion and support liver health; it is now being studied for its hypoglycemic effects.

Future Harvests

There is plenty to go around (the world!). Simply rejoice in the fact that you have some to harvest and allow propagation to take its natural course. This plant is a survivor, at least for now.

Look for sow thistle's characteristic clasping leaves.

Texas persimmon

Diospyros texana

chapote

`EDIBLE` fruit, leaves for tea

Texas persimmon fruits are delicious when ripe, with a hint of rich molasses.

Texas persimmon fruits occur individually along the stem and are dark purple-black when ripe.

How to Identify

This member of the Ebony family has smooth, white to light gray bark, making it stand out in the oak forests it calls home. Primarily an understory shrub or small tree, Texas persimmon has alternate leaves (with downturned edges) that are dark green and wider from the middle to the end of the leaf. The plant flowers in the spring and its fruits (covered in tiny white hairs) are ripe beginning in August.

Where and When to Gather

Texas persimmon ranges across the southern half of Texas and is found only in this state. This shrub inhabits edges of prairies, open woodlands in bottomlands, and along rocky hillsides throughout West Texas, the Big Bend area, and the Texas Hill Country. You will begin to find ripe fruits in August and into early October. Various nuts, seeds, and fruits are ripening at this time of the year in southern and Central

Texas, and Texas persimmon helps make for a bountiful foraging season.

How to Gather

Ripe Texas persimmon fruits easily fall off the bush when only slightly brushed or exposed to a light breeze. When gathering, lightly touch the fruit—if ripe, they will fall into your hand. Don't pile them too deeply in your bucket or bowl, as they are quite soft when ripe and vulnerable to spoiling. The leaves can be plucked individually from the stems.

How to Use

Texas persimmon fruits are delicious eaten raw. This fruit has a concentrated, rich sweetness which lends itself to unique creations. If you have a substantial harvest, you can make jams, pies, fruit leather, and various baked goods. Soak pitted fruits in an equal amount of sugar to create a rich syrup. Add your favorite vinegar in an amount that is 20 percent of the syrup's volume to create a delicious, cooling sweet and sour concoction that can be poured over sparkling water. Since Texas persimmon fruits are harvested at the same time that hackberries, walnuts, pecans, mesquite beans, prickly pear fruit, and acorns are all available, the inspired forager can create all sorts of wild-harvested desserts. The fruits are also used as a black dye (if you can bring yourself to use them for non-culinary purposes). Leaves are briefly boiled to make tea. The wood is exceptionally hard and used to make handles for tools.

Future Harvests

Habitat still exists for this shrub, but development and drought threaten its existence in various locations. Save the seeds and deposit them throughout oak woodlands in the abovementioned regions of Texas and at the edges of prairies.

Common persimmon (*Diospyros virginiana*) is found in the eastern half of Texas, most of Oklahoma, and extreme southwest Utah. It is also edible.

thimbleberry

Rubus parviflorus

EDIBLE fruit, shoots, leaves

Thimbleberry's soft, delicate texture and perfect blend of sweet and tart make it a favorite of Southwest foragers.

Thimbleberries on the same branch are often at various stages of ripeness.

How to Identify

The large, palmately lobed, fuzzy leaf of thimbleberry somewhat resembles a maple leaf with a pale underside. The plant normally grows no taller than 3 feet within our region. The terminal raceme of flowers often extends beyond the foliage of second-year and older plants. The five-petaled, bright white blossoms have prominent golden yellow centers, and produce thimble-shaped, fuzzy fruit comprised of numerous pale red drupelets.

Where and When to Gather

Thimbleberry is found in the high-elevation coniferous forests of the Four Corners area and the southern Rockies, south onto the Mogollon Rim and the Sky Islands of southeastern Arizona. Look to shady areas, north-facing slopes, and the edges of mountain streams. Thimbleberries ripen in the early summer around the same time as serviceberries. The shoots are gathered in the spring.

How to Gather
Pick thimbleberries by hand, one by one. They are quite soft, so cannot be piled atop each other for more than two or three hours before being spread out, eaten, or cooked.

How to Use
This sweet-tart berry is an excellent snack while walking forest trails. When many are gathered, they can be cooked up into jam or dried into a fruit leather, either alone or mixed with other berries. Quickly freeze thimbleberries for later use in smoothies. Try mixing them with other delectable rose family fruits such as dewberry and serviceberry. In the Northwest, thimbleberries are often eaten with fish eggs, or mixed into salmon and dried as a sort of pemmican. The shoots can be peeled and eaten raw, or bundled and steamed when fresh in the spring. The leaves can be used as tea (traditionally after turning brown in the fall), or for wrapping prepared foods.

A nice patch of thimbleberry. Berries still may be found underneath.

Future Harvests
Wherever thimbleberry is abundant, gather to your delight. If you plan on visiting the patch regularly, be sure to leave plenty behind at each stage of gathering.

thistle

Cirsium species

flower stalks, flower buds, leaves (midribs), roots

Thistle is easily found throughout our range and is a delectable, starchy root vegetable.

How to Identify

All heights of thistles can be found, from a few inches to 4 feet. We have at least forty-four different species within our region (most of them native). They are biennials or perennials, and they flower once in their lifetime (in a variety of colors). Thus, you will likely find them in one of two stages: as a basal rosette (all the leaf stalks emanating from the root crown), or with an upright flowering stalk. The flower clusters consist only of disc flowers. The typical image of thistle conjures up a spiny plant, defiant to touch, though not all plants commonly referred to as thistle are *Cirsium* species. You will find spines along the leaf and perhaps at the flower clusters of any thistle. They are indeed spiny plants—but don't let that deter you.

The flower head of New Mexico thistle (*Cirsium neomexicanum*).

Where and When to Gather

Thistle can be found throughout our region any time of year—one of the qualities which makes it a favorite of foragers. Depending on your local species, look for thistle in open pastures, mountain meadows, desert hillsides and drainages, and forest clearings. Optimal root harvesting is done in midautumn or early spring—although roots can be gathered any time of year from a basal rosette. Flower stalks are best harvested when 1 to 1½ feet tall, before the flowers open. The flower hearts should be gathered before the flower opens. Leaves (midribs) can be gathered at any time (discard the spines before consuming).

How to Gather

Bring a long-handled or folding shovel to harvest thistle roots. Insert the shovel about 4 to 6 inches adjacent to the plant's center and dig it up. In moist soil, roots should come out easily. The root is removed from the basal leaves and washed. Cut the flower stalk at its base and remove the leaves with a blade. The flower buds are cut off the plant before opening.

Prepped flower stalks (in bud) of New Mexico thistle, waiting for cooking.

How to Use

All *Cirsium* species are edible. The roots are wonderful boiled, then sautéed or roasted in butter. Add local herbs (peppergrass, wild onion, wild oregano) for additional flavor. After cooking, the roots can also be dried and ground for flour. Once the young flower stalk is devoid of spiny leaves and its blooms, you can chew it like fresh sugar cane. Some species possess a wintergreen flavor—delicious! If the plant is young enough and not yet too fibrous, boil or roast the flower stalk like celery. The midrib of the leaf can be eaten the same way (the papery leaf material is often covered in spines, making it practically inedible). The unopened flower buds may be steamed or boiled, peeled, and consumed like diminutive artichokes. Foragers may find a wide range of flavors and preparation options among various thistle species. Additionally, *Cirsium* species are used medicinally the world over.

Identify basal leaves of thistle in the fall so you can come back and harvest in the spring.

Future Harvests

There are active, publicly funded campaigns to eradicate invasive *Cirsium* species. Find out which ones are nonnative in your area and make it a point to harvest roots in the fall and spring. As with other so-called invasive plants, let's choose to learn about thistle as a nutritious, healing resource, so we can avoid any further chemical treatment of our environment.

Turk's cap

Malvaviscus arboreus

wax mallow, lady's teardrop, manzanilla

EDIBLE flowers, fruit, young leaves

A beautiful plant often found in garden landscaping, Turk's cap offers a variety of edible options.

How to Identify

Characteristic of the mallow family, the veins of the leaf are palmate, branching out like fingers from a palm or base of the wrist. The leaves are somewhat soft and fuzzy, especially when young (the best stage for eating). The spiraling red flowers resemble antennae (both male and female flower parts contribute to this effect), making this plant difficult to miss when in bloom. The fruits have persisting sepals, which means the tiny green leaves below the red fruits remain for some time.

Where and When to Gather

Turk's cap is found landscaped and growing wild in the eastern third of our range. This showy plant with its bright red flowers and fruits is native across the southeastern United States and down through Central and South America. You will likely find it growing wild in a shady area beneath forest canopy. Turk's cap is often available all year, particularly the flowers. The new leaves are available in spring, and the fruits are ready in late summer.

A mature Turk's cap growing in its native environment: a flood plain above the main creek bed, amidst yaupon, cedar elm, walnut, and live oak.

Mature, edible Turk's cap fruit is bright red.

How to Gather

Simply pick the flowers, fruits, or young spring leaves. Bringing the plant into your garden will attract butterflies and hummingbirds and provide nearly year-round snacking.

Remember that the flower of Turk's cap is also edible and sweet.

How to Use

The flowers of Turk's cap are sweet and slightly demulcent. They make a nice tea or addition to salads and baked goods. The fruits are also sweet, with a taste similar to hackberry; they lend an interesting flavor to fermentation experiments. Their texture is reminiscent of manzanita berry and apple. The fruits can also be prepared for jelly, jam, or wine. The seeds are crunchy. The leaves are best when slightly cooked (blanched) to improve texture before sautéing or adding to soups or stews.

Future Harvests

Turk's cap is a native plant that lends itself to garden landscaping. Choose a spot that receives part sun and shade, preferably where the soil is well drained. The birds seem to do a nice job of distributing the plant.

violet

Viola species

EDIBLE leaves, stems, flowers

Known across the West for its beauty, folklore, and medicinal and culinary applications, violet is always a welcome sight.

How to Identify

Numerous species of violet appear throughout our region, from east to west. They are herbaceous perennials which produce variously shaped basal leaves in the spring, followed by five-petaled flowers which are predominantly white, purple, or yellow. The leaves can be egg shaped, lance shaped, or shaped somewhat like a heart or kidney, with toothed or entire margins. The flowers may extend beyond the leaves, but in some species they cling to the ground. The leaves are on somewhat rigid, upright stems. The elliptic seed capsules appear in autumn.

Where and When to Gather

Violets can be found scattered throughout our entire region—with the exception of most of western Texas and eastern New Mexico, where their preferred cool, moist coniferous forests are less prevalent. The plants are found sporadically within the wooded areas of the easternmost portion of our region, and are available from winter through spring. At the higher-elevation coniferous forests of the western portion, they are available from spring through the end of summer or early autumn.

How to Gather

A cluster of leaves, stems, and flowers can be pinched and placed in a gathering basket or cloth bag. Skip around within a stand, and leave the roots in the ground. If you pull a plant up by accident, be sure to replant.

How to Use

Violet jelly and syrup are classic preparations with the flowers, as are candied violets. Indigenous peoples of the Southwest prepared violet leaves by first parboiling, then frying them in a pan with grease. The leaves and stems can be added to soups and stews; however, only add them toward the end of preparation and cook briefly. Violet leaves are also an excellent addition to salads. They are mucilaginous which is why they have been commonly used as a thickening agent for soups. Violet leaves are traditionally used, both internally and topically, for a range of complaints from colds and cough to boils, headaches, and dysentery.

Future Harvests

In some forested locales of the Southwest, violets are less abundant and should be gathered with care, if at all. Survey a habitat first before gathering. Then proceed by gathering no more than a third of the leaves you find. In the eastern portion of our region, violets may be more locally abundant.

Cautions

It may be best to avoid consuming violet roots, as they are considered to be mildly toxic (perhaps due to the presence of saponins).

Violet flowers in the spring and late summer.

walnut

Juglans major
Arizona walnut, nogal silvestre
Juglans microcarpa
little walnut

EDIBLE green fruit, ripe nuts

A sweet, oil-rich delicacy is enclosed within the hard nutshells of our native walnut trees.

The unripe fruit of Arizona walnut.

How to Identify

Although walnut leaves are pinnately compound and alternate with an odd number of numerous leaflets, there are several other trees within our region which fit this description as well. I always go by the smell first. Walnut leaves possesses a sweet aroma when lightly touched, and they are velvety soft when first emerging. The hairy, central, yellow-green stem (rachis) of the walnut leaf also distinguishes it from other similarly leaved trees such as soapberry, tree of heaven, sumac species, and pecan. The bark of walnut is smooth and gray when young, then turns darker and checkered as it ages. The male flowers dangle several inches below the branches, whereas the inconspicuous female flowers emerge at the center of the leafing branch tips. This is where the much-loved fruits appear, in groups of one to three, come midsummer. The fruits mature from green to black during the heart of the summer, before falling from the tree.

Where and When to Gather

Walnut is a tree of the riparian zones of the Southwest. It is also found in dry yet well-shaded washes. Arizona walnut is found throughout our region, but is most populous in the western portion. Little walnut is more common in the central to eastern area. Harvest season of the immature to mature fruit occurs within a short span of time, usually late July to late August.

How to Gather

Some trees will lose all their fruit rather quickly, and you'll have to beat the javelina or wild boar to the task of collecting

walnuts for food. Within smaller populations or in years of scarcity, it may be best
to climb the tree and pick them just before
they fall. Gather the immature fruits for
pickling, or making *nocino* before the shell
matures and hardens.

How to Use

For centuries, the Italians have used
unripe walnut fruits to create their
aromatic liqueur *nocino*, which you can
make at home. Soak green fruits in your
preferred spirit for a couple months, then
combine them with a simple syrup to
create your own *nocino*. You may want to
further flavor the drink with spices.
Immature walnut fruits can also be brined
or pickled, then seasoned to be used as
tapas, salad garnish, or an ingredient for
salsa; consume moderately due to astrin-
gency. The ripened nuts are deliciously
sweet and nutty, although it takes some
tedious effort to remove them from their
shells. Alternatively, smash the whole nut
and boil it in water, then skim the shells
from the surface and strain the nutmeats.
Eat the nuts raw or make them into nut
butter, combining them with other foraged
nuts and seeds. These walnuts are great
atop acorn pancakes.

Future Harvests

Riparian areas are the most threatened
habitats in the Southwest. Appropriate
water usage and management of rainfall
will do more than anything else to help
sustain future harvests of our native
walnuts. Installing rainwater and graywater catchment systems at home may
facilitate a healthy environment for walnut
tree cultivation.

Cautions

Wonderful for creating dyes, walnut fruits
will stain your fingers for weeks. Consumption of the fresh green walnut fruit is
not recommended. It is very astringent and
is used medicinally.

Little walnut has tiny nutmeats encased within a thick, hard shell.

watercress

Nasturtium officinale

berro

EDIBLE flowers, leaves

Known as a food plant since time immemorial, watercress is spicy with a touch of bitterness.

Note the four-petal flower of watercress, an herb from the mustard family.

A stand of springtime watercress growing in a calm stream.

How to Identify

There are dozens of seasonal members of the mustard family in the Southwest, but few that appear with such frequency as watercress. Characteristic of all mustards, its white flowers contain four petals. Later in the season you will find an array of nearly horizontal seedpods (known as siliques) growing in all directions from the flowering stem. They will appear like tiny green or beige (once dry) hot dogs on a stick. This is a familiar trait of mustards the world over. Watercress leaves are normally divided into three to nine segments, which range from linear to ovate in shape (they are very similar in appearance to arugula). You will always find watercress growing in water or in sopping wet soil.

Where and When to Gather

Watercress occupies perennial streams and river banks across North America (known to grow native in every U.S. state but North Dakota). Inhabiting canyons and streamsides, it can be washed away on occasion, only to be deposited farther downstream. The tiny, threadlike rootlets of watercress prefer quiet eddies and babbling brooks, where they can anchor into the sandy or loamy banks. Part of the beauty of this plant is that it can be harvested and eaten fresh year-round if the conditions are right (a hard freeze will kill it back).

How to Gather

I prefer to snip the plant back with pruners, scissors, or a knife; fingertips are fine if necessary. Further into the season you will want to cut below the last fresh green leaves, allowing any yellowing or decaying leaves to remain behind. When young, whole segments of leaves can be removed with rootlets attached. Be sure to wash your harvests well with clean water, as various plant debris is likely to be attached to the plant surface.

How to Use

Although some like to nibble on fresh watercress, many sources advise against this. Whenever animal grazing exists upstream (particularly sheep), a liver fluke parasite may be present within the water system, which watercress can pick up. Therefore, it's safest when cooked. Watercress makes a delicious meal when sautéed with onions and olive oil or bacon fat, after a quick blanching. The plant has been revered throughout history and was considered a warming stimulant by the physicians of ancient Greece and Rome. Modern scientific research has pointed to its anti-inflammatory, anticarcinogenic, and antioxidant qualities.

Future Harvests

As watercress readily reproduces vegetatively or from seed, look to gather only what you can eat at a given time. Enable a portion of any patch to go to seed, allowing further dispersal and germination downstream.

Cautions

There are some concerns with watercress regarding streamborne illnesses. To be safe, cook before eating. As with all plants, it's important to know the location from which you are harvesting.

wax currant

Ribes cereum

EDIBLE flowers, fruit

Wax currants are soft and jellylike, with a fragrant, piney aroma—unique among edible berries of the Southwest.

How to Identify

Wax currant is a deciduous, spineless, woody shrub that reaches a height of 6 to 8 feet at maturity. It may be upright and erect, or a bit more laterally sprawling. The margins of the small leaves (less than 1 inch wide) are cleft with rounded lobes. Leaves may be greasy to the touch with apparent glandular hairs, or completely smooth. The whitish-pink to dark pink flowers may grow singularly or more commonly in clusters, sticking out from behind the leaves or hanging down below them. The shiny red fruits are covered in contrasting tiny glands, and hang on short green pedicels. Dry, brown styles (female flower parts) often adhere to the end of an individual fruit. The entire plant emits a piney, spicy aroma. Golden currant (*Ribes aureum*) is a spineless shrub with smooth bark and numerous clusters of bright yellow flowers in the spring. Sticky currant (*R. viscosissimum*) has blue-black berries. The berries of both are edible.

Where and When to Gather

Wax currant is found throughout the northwestern quadrant of our region, extending into southern New Mexico and the extreme western panhandle of Oklahoma. Look to coniferous forests, and dry, rocky montane and alpine slopes. Golden currant is found scattered throughout our region with the exception of eastern Texas and western New Mexico. It frequently inhabits margins and canyons in ponderosa pine forests. Wax currant flowers are available in the early spring, and the berries ripen in late summer to early autumn.

How to Gather

Pick the flowers by hand, sparingly, unless they are plentiful. Wax currant fruits are gathered by hand, off the branches, individually or in pairs. Don't pile them higher than several inches in your gathering basket, to avoid crushing them. Empty out and process within several hours to avoid spoilage.

How to Use

Wax currants and golden currants make a nice foraging snack, and are sufficiently plentiful to warrant gathering some to bring home. The berries are reported to make a delicious wine. Sun dry the berries for storage, or cook fresh fruits into jams, jellies, sauces, mixed berry pies, or stews. The Hopi people consume the fresh berries

A lone wax currant.

Wax currant flowers in the spring.

with their traditional piki, a feathery light cornbread cooked on a hot stone. The Zuni people ate the leaves with animal fat. The fruits of golden currant were traditionally dried, ground, and cooked into a wild-seed-meal gruel.

Future Harvests

Treat as other wild berries, and only gather what you can use. Leave plenty of fruits on the bush for wildlife and seed dispersal. If you live in a wax currant habitat, consider integrating it into your home landscape.

Caution

Some people may experience nausea from eating an excess of fresh berries.

whitestem blazing star

Mentzelia albicaulis

whitestem stickleaf, small-flowered blazing star, pegagosa, buena mujer

`EDIBLE` seeds

An abundant seed crop of the Southwest. Turn an afternoon of foraging into a memorable dish with the unique flavor of whitestem blazing star.

Whitestem blazing star is an annual with semi-succulent leaves.

How to Identify

The annual herb whitestem blazing star possesses sticky, succulent leaves, which clasp the milky white to pinkish-red upright stems. The entire plant is adherent and readily sticks to clothing, hence the common name stickleaf. The short, five-petaled, yellow flowers possess numerous stamens extending beyond the corolla. The small orange seeds are rounded and grain-like. Despite being mostly hairy, the entire plant has a greasy, glistening quality when the sun hits it just right.

Where and When to Gather

Whitestem blazing star can be found throughout the western third of our region. It occupies desert grassland, chaparral habitat, sandy soils, desert washes, and disturbed ground from the Sonoran Desert to the Great Basin Desert. The seeds can be gathered from late spring to midsummer, depending on one's location.

How to Gather

Similar to other seed plants. See sidebar on page 89.

How to Use

The seeds of whitestem blazing star can be consumed raw or ground into a flour to be combined with other pulverized seed flours, creating a mixture for baking ashcakes, breads, and tortillas. The flour can also be liquefied to make an *atole*. Alternatively, toast the seeds in a dry pan over low to medium heat, then grind to a flour when ready to use (or store the ground meal in the freezer). The seeds have also been used traditionally by indigenous peoples of the Southwest to treat burns and toothaches. The whole plant, crushed sufficiently, can be used as an external poultice for bruises and strains.

Future Harvests

Only gather what you intend to use, and leave behind a substantial amount for future reseeding. Gather some seeds and scatter in similar areas or disturbed ground within your home landscape.

The unripe seedpods of whitestem blazing star.

whortleberry

Vaccinium myrtillus
myrtle blueberry
EDIBLE fruit

Taking in the scents of the forest floor, crawling on one's belly, following the particular aroma of fresh whortleberry: this is the life of a forager.

The fruits of our southwestern whortleberry are often found by looking uphill, close to the ground.

How to Identify

Whortleberry is a near relative of the blueberry, but grows closer to the forest floor, beneath stands of giant conifers. The vast green carpet of its alternate, ovate, bright green leaves is pocked with the dark brown humus background in between. The tiny, dangling individual flowers are colored white to pink and exist beneath the shade of their own Lilliputian canopy. Midsummer, the small berries turn from green to blue, almost purple-black. The plant turns yellow and maroon in the autumn.

Where and When to Gather

Whortleberry grows in high-elevation spruce-fir forests, old growth forests, clearings at the edge of forests, and logged areas. At some point in August, the sweet-tart berries will ripen and it will be a race against all the creatures of the forest to savor this foraged delight.

How to Gather

Timing is everything, as certain years are better than others due to flowering patterns. But you're going to have to get down. You will find yourself crawling like a baby, uphill bound, to have a chance at these tasty morsels. As you pull yourself up the mountain, you will feel yourself becoming part of the mountain, smelling the topsoil and moss, feeling it work its way under your fingernails, and viewing the tiniest features of the forest as you never have before. Or, you will opt to buy Washington blueberries from the local market—but, oh, what you will miss!

How to Use

I think you can figure this one out. What you don't eat before you get back to camp or home, you can preserve by canning, drying, or freezing. Boil up into jams, jellies, or syrups, or, of course, bake into pies, cakes, breads, muffins, pancakes, and the like.

Future Harvests

Where whortleberry exists in the Southwest, it is locally abundant. Climate is the specific limiting factor in their distribution. You may, however, choose other *Vaccinium* species better suited to your local climate if you wish to integrate this wild food into your landscape.

wild grape

Vitis species

uva del monte

EDIBLE fruit, leaves

Diverse and widespread, wild grapes offer a distinctive variety of flavors and options for the curious forager.

The growing habit of Arizona grape (*Vitis arizonica*) along the edge of a dry wash.

How to Identify

Wild grape is a vining perennial that can be found climbing high into trees or covering low-growing shrubs or fences. The green, generally palmate, alternating leaves (with teeth along the margin) emerge in the spring; clusters of tiny white flowers appear soon after, opposite the leaf stem. The leaves may be fuzzy, and the undersides may be lighter in color.

Tendrils emerging from the ends of the branches will be split into two parts. Ripe grapes develop in clusters along an extended raceme, and clusters can be found in a scattered arrangement or a more densely packed array. The color of ripe wild grapes ranges from reddish-purple to blue-black. Several different wild grape species can be identified within our region. Canyon grape

Muscadine grape (*Vitis rotundifolia*) has a light-colored flesh and a sweet taste.

(*Vitis arizonica*) possesses a variable leaf shape and long strands of numerous tart berries. Mustang grape (*V. mustangensis*) has a white, downy underside to its leaves and reddish purple flesh. Muscadine grape (*V. rotundifolia*) possesses a heart-shaped leaf with large teeth at the margins and a light-colored flesh.

Where and When to Gather

Our various wild grapes inhabit niches within all habitats of our region. In the western half, look to desert washes, riparian gallery forests, riversides, and mountain canyons. In the eastern half, look to piney woods, limestone ridges, hardwood forests, streambeds, thickets, and floodplains. Wild grapes generally ripen between August and October. Gather leaves whenever they are available (spring to summer), at a size you prefer.

How to Gather

Wild grapes are picked individually, or whole clusters can be gathered when the grapes are fully ripened.

How to Use

Traditionally, wild grapes are eaten fresh, dried for storage, cooked into jelly or jam, boiled to make wine, combined with other fruits to make beverages, or used as a seasoning with other foods. After blanching, use fresh leaves to create dolmades by rolling up into the leaves some combination of rice, fresh mint or parsley, pine nuts, garlic, and raisins; then steam. Try pecans, wild oregano, wild onions, and sun-dried wolfberries as possible foraged substitutes. As a means of obtaining drinking water, the end of a live grape vine can be cut, then suspended within a bucket for several hours to catch the water being pumped out. The water, similar in flavor to coconut water, is then ready to drink.

Future Harvests

Wild grape is locally abundant throughout our region. Always gather no more than what you can use, and allow for abundant seed stock to remain on-site for dispersal and future reseeding.

Cautions

The seeds of some species of wild grape contain an acrid oil on their surface, causing burning at the back of the throat even if they are held in the mouth for a moment. Although this effect is limited, it can be avoided by fully dehydrating or cooking the fruit first.

wild onion

Allium species
nodding onion, cebolla
`EDIBLE` entire plant

A mountain hillside of wild onion is a happy sight for foragers who know the many ways this pungent herb can flavor dishes.

How to Identify

Wild onions are perennial herbs that grow from bulbs (like a supermarket onion) or rhizomes (like an iris). First and foremost, they always smell sulphury-pungent, like an onion. Some leaves are round in cross section, others are slightly V shaped. In high altitudes of our region, there can be some confusion with death camas (*Zigadenus* species) before wild onion flowers; however, *Zigadenus* species do not smell like an onion. Like all *Allium* species, wild onion possesses flower clusters at the end of a leafless stalk, or scape, with parts in multiples of three.

Nodding onion (*Allium cernuum*) is unique in that its blossoms hang down even when in the shade.

Where and When to Gather

Wild onion can be found scattered throughout all habitats within our region. Wherever it grows, wild onion always likes moist soil and cool temperatures. Although it may sprout in the winter at lower elevations, it is relegated to midsummer at high elevations. You can gather wild onion blossoms, leaves, or bulbs any time you find them. Meadow garlic (*Allium canadense*) is found throughout Oklahoma and the eastern half of Texas. Drummond's onion (*A. drummondii*) can be found throughout the eastern two-thirds of our range.

How to Gather

The flowers can be plucked off the top by hand, and the tender leaves can be pinched off. A trowel or small shovel is best to dislodge the shallow bulbs (deeper down in the desert), before you gently pull them up within your palm. Flowering stems (scapes) are often too rigid to use in cooking.

A day's harvest of wild onion. Separating the tender, sulphury stems from the spicy-sweet flowers.

favorite curry, or bone broth. The flowers or chopped leaves also make a nice flavoring for herbal vinegars.

Future Harvests

The bulbs are not necessary to harvest if you wish to include this wild flavor on your menu. Best practices dictate that you harvest the bulbs only when the plant is present in large numbers, which it certainly can be.

Cautions

Toxic look-alikes, from the deadly death camas (*Zigadenus* species) to the rather mild crow's poison (*Nothoscordum bivalve*), exist throughout our range. Be absolutely sure of what you are gathering. When in doubt, seek out an experienced forager for help with identification.

How to Use

I love to garnish a variety of dishes with the fresh, spicy flowers—especially the pink or purple varieties. These flowers can also be soaked in honey for a few days, creating a spicy cough medicine or a secret ingredient for your vinaigrette, barbeque sauce, or fermented veggie condiment. I roast the whole plants over coals when grilling meats at the campfire; this brings out the onions' buttery sweetness. Just like supermarket green onions, dice the greens and place them atop steaming bowls of pozole, chicken soup, your

wild oregano

Monarda species

bee balm, orégano de la sierra, orégano del campo, horsemint

EDIBLE flowers, stems, leaves

Wild oregano is a first-rate seasoning with spicy, sweet, and citrus tones. If I had to choose one cooking spice, this would be it.

How to Identify

True to its form as a member of the mint family, wild oregano has a square stem with opposing leaves. As with other mints, you can often locate it simply by stepping on it. The long-lipped flowers are quite noticeable and sweetly aromatic. Two distinct types occur, which are differentiated by their flowering forms. The bee balm type (*Monarda fistulosa* var. *menthifolia*) normally has one terminal whorl of flowers (often purple) and the *orégano de la sierra* (*M. citriodora, M. pectinata*) type will often have several whorls. Oftentimes one can find last year's dry flower clusters as an identifier in the spring. The leaves are profoundly and pleasingly aromatic.

Where and When to Gather

Wild oregano is widespread throughout our region, but the spicy versions reside in the western portion of the Southwest. These include all of the species mentioned here, with the exception of *Monarda punctata*. Plants can be found from our higher elevations down to mid-elevation canyons and desert washes in our western half, moving out into the plains in the eastern half of our region. As the plants begin to flower in early summer, harvest the entire stem. In the secondary growth of late summer to early autumn, the leafy stems can be harvested again.

Monarda citriodora in flower.

Monarda punctata grows on the Gulf Coast. It does not possess the spiciness of wild oregano from the West.

How to Use

Dry the leaves on the stem, then run your finger over the stem to remove the intact leaves. Store them whole in glass jars or plastic bags—they hold their scent for over a year. Crush this aromatic herb over your dishes within the final minutes of cooking for the most pronounced flavor. Crush over marinating meats and flavored vinegars, or make delicious, warming medicinal teas. Add the fresh flowers to salsa creations for added heat and spice. A honey infusion made from the flower clusters makes a wonderful remedy for dry, sore throats and lends a subtly sophisticated flavor to epicurean breads and muffins. The stems retain their flavor and can be added to pots of cooking beans.

Future Harvests

This herbaceous perennial resprouts from the same spot each year. Simply coppice the stand, allowing numerous stalks to go to flower and produce seeds for the seed bank. You can readily dig up a rhizome to be transplanted in your home garden or landscape if the conditions match.

Cautions

You may not harvest enough to suit your desires and have to anxiously wait several months for new growth to sprout. This has been known to cause irritation among foragers.

How to Gather

Fold and snap stems, or cut with pruners, below the last green leaves. When the plant is in flower, you can pop off the flower heads to be soaked in honey (for use medicinally or in baking recipes). The leafy stems can be left to dry in paper bags before processing. Alternatively, gather several fresh leaves directly off the stem to add to your cooking.

wild plum

Prunus mexicana

Mexican plum, big-tree plum

`EDIBLE` fruit

Wild plum, with its juicy flesh, can be a sweet summer treat in the
eastern half of our region.

Notice the wide leaves of wild, or Mexican, plum.

How to Identify

Wild plum has a single trunk with rounded
crown and can grow to 35 feet in height.
The blue-gray bark develops horizontal
striations and peels up at the edges with
age. All wild plums put out many white,
fragrant, five-petaled flowers at the branch
tips before leafing out. Then the large oval
leaves appear, which curl under considerably at the margins. The underside of the
leaf is noticeably lighter in color. Plums
ripen from yellow to reddish purple, but
with a light, white yeast coating which can
be rubbed off easily, revealing the shiny
fruit skin beneath. Chickasaw plum
(*Prunus angustifolia*) possesses thorns
and has long, thin leaves, and bright red
fruits.

Where and When to Gather

Wild plum can be found in piney woods
and hardwood forests alike, primarily
along the borders. It's found in both Texas
and Oklahoma. Look to bluffs, the edges of

gorges, forest clearings, or areas just above the floodplain. The fruits ripen from the end of summer into fall. Chickasaw plum (and river plum, *Prunus rivularis*) can also be found in Texas and Oklahoma; these fruits ripen near the end of spring.

How to Gather

Get up on a ladder or your friend's back, or just climb the tree and pick away. Wild plums can produce prodigious amounts of fruit, so be prepared with buckets or baskets for gathering.

How to Use

Any sweet-tasting plums make an excellent snack right off the tree. If fruits are more astringent or bland, try giving them more time to ripen in the hot sun, if possible, or commit that harvest to the creation of jelly, wine, or sauce—with the added help of sugar. Sweeter plums can be sun dried for storage (once pitted). Bake with pork roast or chicken, or use in a sweet-and-sour sauce.

Future Harvests

Plant seed from wild plums with preferred flavor wherever you recognize a similar growing habitat. Wild plums readily hybridize and can produce a great variety of fruit. Wild plum rootstock is often used for grafting hybrids.

Cautions

As with other rose family stone fruits, avoid consuming the pits, due to the presence of cyanogenic compounds.

Wild plums are juicy when ripe and covered with a hazy yeast bloom.

wild rose

Rosa species

rose

`EDIBLE` hips, petals

The seductive aroma of wild rose is often its main attraction, but no less appealing is the lovely flavor imparted by the petals and hips.

The fruit of the rose is called a hip.

How to Identify

Wild roses grow from perennial rootstock, often in large stands. The stems may be 3 to 15 feet long, upright, climbing, or trailing. *Rosa* species vary in size but always have stems covered in thorns, both thin and stout, straight and curved. The pinnate leaves possess serrate margins with sharp or rounded teeth, and turn yellow before falling off in autumn. The flowers of wild rose are less complex than the cultivated varieties, but possess a more subtle and intoxicating aroma. Find the white to pale or dark pink petals of wild rose flowers attached at the branch ends. Here, too, you'll find the bright red hips with the stiff green calyx, come late summer.

Where and When to Gather

Wild rose can be found in moist coniferous forests and oak woodlands in the western half of the Southwest, and on old farms, dry hills, and prairies toward the eastern half of our region. The petals are available in the late spring to early summer, whereas the hips mature in the late summer and early autumn. Their flavor and texture improve, however, after the first hard frost.

How to Gather

Gather the unopened flower buds or petals of the opened flowers for tea. Use buds or petals fresh, or dry them for storage. The leaves can be gathered at any time for tea. Hips should be gathered after the first hard frost. Sun dry the hips in a shallow basket or pan.

How to Use

Use the sweeter, darker-colored petals to flavor syrup, jelly, vinegar, wine, honey, desserts, mescál, or sodas. The leaves, flowers, or hips can be used to make a refreshing tea. Purée fresh rose hips to make fruit leather, or simply rehydrate dried hips before running them through a food mill. It's best to strain out the hairy seeds from dried hips before consuming. Otherwise, completely grind the hairy seeds into a powder before using it in food.

Future Harvests

Gather wild roses wherever they are in ample numbers and leave plenty of fruit to replenish the local seed stock.

Cautions

Remove all seeds from dry rose hips (or grind thoroughly) before consuming, as they possess fine, irritating hairs.

Freshly picked wild rose hips after the first freeze of autumn.

wild strawberry

Fragaria vesca
woodland strawberry
Fragaria virginiana
Virginia strawberry

EDIBLE fruit, leaves

A ripe wild strawberry can impart tremendous flavor in one small bite.

Wild strawberry's five-petaled white flower is a familiar precursor to the sweet fruit. The dried leaves make a delicious tea.

How to Identify

Although the wild strawberries of our region are usually one of two species, there are numerous varieties. Appearances vary slightly and taste may have little to do with the botanical features. Like all members of the rose family, each flower possesses five petals, which appear independent. The center of the flower will appear yellow. The stems are characteristically red and the leaves are in three parts—each leaf blade possessing teeth and an obvious midvein. Strawberries grow close to the forest floor, not exceeding 3 to 4 inches in height, generally. Uniquely, strawberries possess seeds on the outside of their skin, not within the fruit as with most members of the rose family.

Where and When to Gather

Wild strawberry can be found in the eastern and western portions of our range. In the western areas, it's found exclusively in high-elevation coniferous forests (aside from garden bed cultivation). Being at the right place at the right time is essential for strawberry harvest, as several other creatures also like these fruits, which are easily accessed by all. Ripe fruit can appear from June to August.

How to Gather

Inhaling the aroma of a ripe wild straw-berry is an exalted experience in its own right. Give a slight tug on a bright red berry; when fully ripe it should release with little effort. Be careful not to pile berries too deeply in your container, as the ripe fruits bruise and rot easily.

How to Use

If you've managed to either pick faster than you can eat, or better yet, more than you can eat, then preserve your wild strawberries as jelly, jam, pie, or dry fruit. (Okay, pie is not really preserving.) The leaves make a very pleasant, tart tea and are a decent stand-in for raspberry leaves when needed as a medicine.

Future Harvests

Healthy populations of wild strawberry are no doubt due to a variety of factors. I have seen populations increase exponentially after severe burns. Yet, they are members of intact climax pine-fir-spruce forests as well. Leave plenty for the local creatures, and make sure the stand is sufficiently large before gathering more than just a taste.

wild sunflower

Helianthus species

common sunflower, girasol, Jerusalem artichoke, mirasol, paleleaf sunflower, sunchoke

EDIBLE flower buds, seeds, tubers (*Helianthus maximiliani, H. strumosus, H. tuberosus*)

The oil-rich seeds and starchy tubers of sunflowers have been known to foragers for millennia.

How to Identify

Sunflowers are nearly unmistakable once in flower. The characteristic yellow ray (or strap-shaped) flowers surround the darker center of numerous disc flowers. The plants can be 3 to 15 feet tall depending on growing conditions, location, and species. Generally speaking (as we have a variety of species), sunflower leaves are often coarse and triangular in shape, coming out to a pointed tip. They are also usually green (except the silverleaf sunflower, whose leaves are, as you might guess, silvery green). The stems often turn reddish with age, and have fine hairs along the entire length. The leaves are generally alternate, but can be opposite toward the top in some species.

The dark brown disc flowers in the center of the sunflower's cluster house the achenes, or shells, of the seed.

turn color, as well as throughout the winter. Avoid digging tubers along roadsides and anyplace where hazardous waste runoff may be an issue. It's best to know your area well.

Where and When to Gather

We find sunflower across our region, covering the landscape in prairies and vacant lots, at roadsides, and on disturbed grounds as the sun steadily gains along the horizon. Harvest the seed heads in the early autumn. The tubers can be dug as the seed heads mature and the leaves begin to

How to Gather

When gathering wild sunflower seed heads, prune the stem below the seed head, leaving a length of stem if you wish to dry the seeds by hanging them. They are best harvested before fully ripe. Bring the seed heads indoors and hang them, or place them in a cardboard flat or over a fine screen to dry and fully ripen—otherwise the birds will get to the seeds first. The tubers will require more work. Bring a large shovel, trowel, or digging stick. The flower buds are best picked in the early spring before they become bitter.

How to Use

Sunflower was an ancient food for the indigenous peoples of the Americas. The sun-worshipping Aztecs held it in such high esteem, they once enshrined its image in gold. The processed seeds can be consumed raw with no further preparation. To separate seeds from shells, crack the shells open with a food mill and place the whole mass in a bucket of clean water. Allow the nutmeats to sink to the bottom and skim the shells off the top with a strainer. Roasting the seeds brings out more flavor and extends storage time. The seeds can be pressed for oil, and the toasted shells have been made into a coffee substitute. The tubers can be consumed raw, roasted, boiled, steamed, or baked. They possess a unique combination that is the true definition of bittersweet. Cover with butter, olive oil, and salt and bake whole in the oven at 375 degrees Fahrenheit until soft. Traditionally, the plant was used in a wide variety of medicinal applications, including the topical use of the root to treat bruises and contusions.

Midsummer at high elevation in Arizona, after the ray flowers have fallen off. Toward the center, the seeds are beginning to ripen.

Future Harvests

Sunflower has been growing near humans for thousands of years—it's not likely to leave us anytime soon. Best to leave an ample supply of seeds for the birds and other wildlife, although that will likely be a choice made for you, rather than by you.

wolfberry

Lycium species

matrimony vine, desert thorn, thornbush, water jacket, tomatillo, cuáveri, frutilla

fruit

Wolfberry is a close relative of the goji berry—and a bountiful wild food in the Sonoran Desert.

How to Identify

Although wolfberry species vary to some extent, there are consistent qualities among them. Look for the somewhat erratic branches spreading in all directions with alternate branchlets ending in spinelike tips. The leaves appear in alternate whorls and are spatulate (elongated and rounded toward the tip). The white, purple, pink, or yellow-green flowers are generally shorter than 1/2 inch and have five petals (*Lycium carolinianum* is one of the rare four-petaled species). The flowers often appear to dangle from the branch. Most species are upright, reaching over 10 feet tall under the canopy of mature mesquite and hackberry trees. In open areas they are often 3 to 6 feet in height and roughly the same width. The egg-shaped orange-red fruits of purple-flowering *Lycium fremontii* are preferred by many.

Where and When to Gather

Wolfberry grows in an assortment of habitats and comes in various forms, so one can find a fruiting *Lycium* somewhere within our region any time of year, whether

Although wolfberry fruits grow abundantly along the stem, the sharp thorny branch tips disallow running your hand along the stem to remove the berries.

growing wild or in a landscaped setting (still counts when you're foraging). Look to mesquite bosques, the edges of riparian areas, the slopes of cactus forests, and along dry washes, open floodplains, roadsides, and piñon-juniper mesas.

Carolina desert thorn (*Lycium carolinia-num*) is found all along the Gulf Coast and is known as Christmas berry. It grows in brackish water. In the Sonoran Desert, several species (*L. andersonii*, *L. berland-ieri*, *L. fremontii*) may flower and fruit two seasons per year (early spring and late summer) or not at all; it depends upon available moisture and other variables in the environment.

How to Gather

Gathering wolfberries is a great job for quick little hands. Due to the thorny nature of the plant, hand-picking can be slow going, though. If you were to encounter just the right bush at the right time, you could possibly knock numerous ripe berries off the plant with a stick, but that is not as easy as it sounds.

How to Use

Wolfberries are often sweeter when sun dried, and these dried fruits make an excellent addition to trail mixes, soups, granolas, breads, or desert desserts. Fill a jar with fresh berries, then cover them with honey. Let the mixture stand in a warm location for several days, until the sugars begin to ferment. Use this as a sweetener or a topping for cakes and sweet breads, or add it to fermented beverages. Wolfberry also makes delicious puddings, syrups, and pies.

Future Harvests

When you find a berry with a flavor you like, save several fruits and plant them in moist soil around your home, preferably in a catchment basin or area that receives ample moisture without supplemental irrigation. Otherwise, simply leave ample berries for the birds to eat and spread around.

Cautions

Avoid eating unripe wolfberries. The berries from the tiny-fruited *Lycium macrodon* were not considered edible by the indigenous peoples of the Sonoran Desert region.

wood sorrel

Oxalis species
lemon sorrel

EDIBLE leaves, roots, flowers

Each tiny leaf of the lemony herb wood sorrel delivers
a burst of flavor.

Freshly harvested sweet wood sorrel roots.

How to Identify

Oxalis species have from three to ten
heart-shaped leaflets. They are attached at
the V of the heart, atop the central stem.
These stems possess no leaves beneath the
top leaves. The five-petaled flowers can be
yellow, pink, or purple. Wood sorrel often
forms large carpets across the forest floor.
At lower elevations it exists within shady
areas, interspersed with other plants.
Wood sorrel's leaves are quite soft and
always possess a lemony flavor.

Where and When to Gather

Wood sorrel can be found throughout our
region in a wide array of habitats, including garden beds and potted plants. It is
possible to find wood sorrel year-round.
Most native *Oxalis* species will be found
growing from early spring to late fall.
High-elevation species with edible bulbs
and bulblets are available spring through
early autumn. You can gather them any
time the leaves appear fresh and vibrant.

How to Gather

Wood sorrel's delicate leaves are easy to
snip off with your fingers. Pinch a small
cluster and gather in a cloth bag or basket.
The tart flavor of the leaves goes a long way,
so you may want to start with a modest
amount.

How to Use

I like wood sorrel atop a mix of salad
greens (wild or otherwise), or as a special

Oxalis decaphylla can have as many as ten leaflets.

The leaves of *Oxalis alpina* are wider than they are long. Flowers of wood sorrel are edible, too.

garnish to a wild foods meal. Make a tart or cooling drink from the mashed or blended fresh leaves. You may wish to add a bit of sweetener, but taste first—the leaves contain a moderate amount of natural sweetness on their own.

Future Harvests

Wood sorrel is another plant firmly established within various ecosystems throughout our region. Play it safe by gathering no more than a third of any population.

Cautions

You won't be surprised to learn that the *Oxalis* genus is likely named after the oxalic acid it contains. If there is a concern, consider limiting your intake to very small amounts initially.

Metric Conversions

Inches	Centimeters		Feet	Meters
1/4	0.6		1	0.3
1/3	0.8		2	0.6
1/2	1.3		3	0.9
3/4	1.9		4	1.2
1	2.5		5	1.5
2	5.1		6	1.8
3	7.6		7	2.1
4	10		8	2.4
5	13		9	2.7
6	15		10	3
7	18			
8	20			
9	23			
10	25			

Temperatures

degrees Celsius = $5/9 \times$ (degrees Fahrenheit − 32)

degrees Fahrenheit = ($9/5 \times$ degrees Celsius) + 32

To convert length:	Multiply by:
Yards to meters	0.9
Inches to centimeters	2.54
Inches to millimeters	25.4
Feet to centimeters	30.5

Useful Internet Resources

Community resources for processing foraged edibles
www.desertharvesters.org

Eat the Weeds
www.eattheweeds.com

Forager's Harvest: Samuel Thayer
www.foragersharvest.com

Foraging and ethnobotany links and books page
www.foraging.com

Foraging Texas
www.foragingtexas.com

Neil Logan: Co-founder FARM Center, Hawi, HI. International expert on food production from mesquite (*Prosopis* species).
www.rnl3.net/ILSDWeb/Projects/kiawe/Projects_Puako_1.asp

Southwest Environmental Information Network. A portal for online botanical information throughout the Southwest and elsewhere in the United States.
www.swbiodiversity.org/seinet/

Urban Outdoor Skills—The Quest for Southern California Flavors: Pascal Baudar
www.urbanoutdoorskills.com

Useful Wild Plants (Texas): Scooter Cheatham
www.usefulwildplants.org/index.htm

Wild Food Adventures—Institute for the Study of Edible Wild Plants: John Kallas
www.wildfoodadventures.com

Further Reading

Cheatham, Scooter, Marshall C. Johnston, and Lynn Marshall. *The Useful Wild Plants of Texas, the Southeastern and Southwestern United States, the Southern Plains, and Northern Mexico, Vol. 1–3.* Useful Wild Plants, 1995.

Epple, Anne Orth. *A Field Guide to the Plants of Arizona.* Guildford, CT: The Globe Pequot Press, 1995.

Hodgson, C. Wendy. *Food Plants of the Sonoran Desert.* Tucson: The University of Arizona Press, 2001.

Kallas, John. *Edible Wild Plants: Wild Foods from Dirt to Plate.* Layton, UT: Gibbs Smith, 2010.

Moore, Michael. *Medicinal Plants of the Desert and Canyon West.* Santa Fe: Museum of New Mexico Press, 1989.

Suter, Mark. *Edible Wild Plants of Texas (Non-woody species).* College Station, TX: Primitive Texas Press, 2013.

Thayer, Sam. *The Forager's Harvest: A Guide to Identifying, Harvesting, and Preparing Edible Wild Plants.* Birchwood, WI: Forager's Harvest Press, 2006.

Thayer, Sam. *Nature's Garden: A Guide to Identifying, Harvesting, and Preparing Edible Wild Plants.* Birchwood, WI: Forager's Harvest Press, 2010.

Tull, Delena. *Edible and Useful Plants of the Southwest: Texas, New Mexico, and Arizona.* Austin: University of Texas Press, revised 2013.

Index

About the Author

ABRIL CASTILLO

John Slattery is an avid forager of food and medicine in the Sonoran Desert. He is dedicated to the development of bioregional herbalism across the country, and founded Desert Tortoise Botanicals in 2005 to provide quality herbal remedies to the people of the Southwest and beyond. John has been invited to speak about the edible and medicinal flora of the Southwest at numerous venues throughout the region, offering experiential courses in the field and lectures on a wide variety of subjects. Since 2008, John has been leading foraging and plant-based cultural tours into Sonora, Mexico, where he has formed relationships with indigenous herbalists and wild-plant lovers of the Sonoran Desert region. John began offering the Sonoran Herbalist Apprenticeship Program in 2010 in Tucson, Arizona, helping participants develop a relationship with plants, and establishing the principles of vitalist healing philosophy, a holistic approach to healing. John writes for his blog at www.desertortoisebotanicals.com.